DUNMOW THROUGH THE AGES

Copy by David L. Lipson.

St. Mary's church, from an old engraving.

DUNMOW
Through the Ages

by
Dorothy C. Dowsett

Printed by
LETCHWORTH PRINTERS LTD.
NORTON WAY NORTH
LETCHWORTH
HERTS

962959
Printed by Letchworth Printers Ltd., Norton Way North, Letchworth, Herts

ACKNOWLEDGMENTS

My thanks are due to all those who have helped me in any way, by lending pictures, engravings or historical items, toward the compiling of this book. Also, to members of the staff of the Essex Record Office.

D. C. DOWSETT.

CONTENTS

ILLUSTRATIONS

King Edward VII's coronation celebrations, August 9, 1902.	Mr. Wm. Harris
The P.O. at Johnson's shop at Edward VII's coronation.	Mr. H. Johnson
Joe Hoy releasing the pigeons after walking the greasy pole, about 1908.	Mr. Wm. Harris
The pump and drinking trough at Braintree Road corner.	Mr. J. Harris
Election day—Col. Lockwood's victory.	Mrs. Roper
Rev. J. Evans and his choir.	Mr. A. Archer
Excelsior Band 1906.	Mrs. Cornell
The town band leads the horse-and-cart pararde 1904.	Mr. Wm. Harris
Lord Byng unveiling the town memorial, July 19, 1921.	Mr. Ashard
Dunmow Cricket Club shortly before World War I.	Mr. H. Johnson
Col. Tom Gibbons, D.S.O., who led the 1/5 Essex to victory	The Gibbons family
Composite : a look around the town at features of the past.	
Dunmow Football Club 1922-3.	Mrs. S. Spore
Dunmow Football Club 1913.	My own
Queen of Horticulture, August 2, 1948.	Mrs. S. Spore
The Misses Sewell and their O. and B. Light Infantry during World War I.	Mrs. Wright

FOREWORD

I FEEL it is now time to survey our town of Great Dunmow before it is "picked up and carried off" with the speed of the times. Therefore I trust you will read and digest its many centuries, and dwell upon them in passing. I do not think there will be a rapid change for many years to come, just a gradual creeping of the population. It is more a quiet place to return home to than an industrial town to work in. There must be some small towns left like that, before the world goes mad and cries out for peace. We hope one day in the distant future to have a by-pass, but the powers that be will not commit themselves. So, dear Dunmowites, read of the times your town has seen, and suffered, and rejoiced!

D. C. DOWSETT

CHAPTER I

Roman finds

IN writing this book on our town I find it impossible to start at its beginning, for that is obscured in the mists of time. We know that the Romans were here, because Dunmow stands on one of their roads—Stane Street—at a point where that "street" is joined by other Roman roads, north and south-west.

Many Roman remains have been turned up here from time to time, but no actual buildings have so far come to light. Several historians have thought Dunmow to be the Roman Cæsareamagnus, but this is almost certainly wrong. The position from London and from Colchester seems to contradict this. In 1760 nearly a dozen small urns were found at Merks Hill. They were in a layer of black earth, together with a few coins, among which were a Trajan and an Antoninus Pius, and some pieces of brass and iron. An amphora from Merks Hill was exhibited by the Essex Archæological Society in 1867. About the same time two or three first-century brasses of Commodus were found in a field near the church.

In 1935 six burial urns were found when building started at High Stile. Two of the urns were about ten inches high, another was about four inches. There were also a flat red bowl (Samian), part of a box tile and other fragments from the first and third centuries. These are now in the Colchester Museum.

A large gravel pit was dug in the New Street Garden Fields in 1862 (now built on and known as Springfields), and 100 years ago much pottery was found, including colour-coated and barbotined ware, amphoræ, bones, oyster shells, tiles, and a few coins, objects of bronze, pieces of iron and fragments of glass. These occurred at a depth of three to nine feet. In recent years, too, as the pits were being filled in for building, it has been of great interest to children to gather up broken fragments thrown about by the bulldozers.

Fragments of third-century pottery were found when digging the foundations of a house opposite Threaders Green in 1939. A gold coin of Horatius was found in the town about 1761, and in 1867 several local persons exhibited "finds." Mr. Cockayne showed coins, and Mr. Knight two vessels and fragments, part of a bronze vessel, and coins of silver and brass. Mr. Wade showed a collection of pottery in 1828, comprising two vases of red ware six inches high, two smaller ones, brown and red pateræ, a Samian basin, part of a bracelet, a hair-pin, a grass-green knob, two coins of Constantine, three of Valentinian and two Aurelians. Eleven Valuns were found in 1864. Mr. Stacey showed an iron spearhead, and Mr. Blyth coins. Several of these exhibits are now in Colchester Museum, as is also a Roman As of about 200 B.C. found in or near the town. This must have "seen its best days" before it landed in England.

Fragments of Samian ware, bronze hooks and other small objects are now in the British Museum. There has recently been Celtic pottery found, but it may have derived from Celtic employees of the Romans, probably in the first century.

Coming along to Saxon times, our town has a name. We do not know to what extent cultivation had advanced, but during the Saxon period it was a *tun* (town). About A.D. 951 it was Dunemowe, which could mean " hill meadows " or " meadows on the hill." The name soon changed to Dunauue or Dommawe. By " meadows " it does appear that some considerable amount of forest had been cleared. There was no doubt that cultivations proved worth while. That the soil was found to be productive one can be sure, as it still is London clay; therefore Dunmow became an agricultural area in early times.

By Edward the Confessor's day Dunmow had seven manors and around it were a number of small " vills." I estimate the population at the time as being 700-800, perhaps more, but let us have a look at the manors.

CHAPTER II

Manors of Dunmow

The manor of Dunmow

In Edward the Confessor's reign Wisgar held it, but at the time of the general survey part was held by Richard, son of Earl Gislebert, though claimed by a knight named Vitalis, and Hamo Dapifer with his under-tenant Serlo held the rest. This estate seems to have been centred in Hamo Dapifer, sewer to the Conqueror. Hamo left his heritage to Mabel, eldest daughter and co-heir of Robert Fitz-Hamon, his brother, who was married to Robert, Earl of Gloucester, natural son of Henry I, from whom by marriage it became incorporated into the Clare family, wherein it continued until the honours of Gloucester and Clare were united with the Duchy of Lancaster. A family surnamed Fitz-Richard held this manor under the Earls of Clare, for we find it recorded that Simon Fitz-Richard held twelve knights' fee and a quarter in Dunmow under Richard de Clare, Earl of Gloucester and Hertford, who died in 1262.

Gilbert Fitz-William was summoned at the court of pleas (or assizes) at Chelmsford in 1285 to show by what right he held a view of frank-pledge in Dunemawwe Magna, and Simon Fitz-Richard why he held a court in Dunmore. It was found that Nicolas Attenasse held a virgate of land in this manor, by the tenure of providing a pound for the king's bailiffs of this place, to impound cattle by the sheriff's precept and summons of the Exchequer, and the bailiffs received sixpence.

To break here may not be the thing to do, but the Rev. W. L. Scott (our vicar a century ago) says that there is (or was) a manuscript which settled the question of how our thirteenth-century church came to be built (not the present one): that Simon Fitz-Richard, whom we have seen as holding the manor under the Earls of Gloucester, gave a rood of land in Great Dunmow, together with the church there. One cannot understand how he could give away that which was his lord's. One is led to think that he took a lot upon himself without his lord's knowledge, but this was a big thing to get away with. It is one of those things which probably we shall never find out.

To get back to the Fitz-Richard family, Simon Fitz-Richard was impleaded in the King's Bench in 1298 for hunting in his own free warren in Dunmowe Magna. The tables had turned indeed. He held the same knight's fee as above, under Gilbert de Clare, who left his three sisters his co-heirs. Elizabeth, the youngest, married John de Burgh; William de Burgh, their son, left Elizabeth, his only daughter and heir. She married Lionel, Duke of Clarence, third son of Edward III. He died in 1368, leaving his only daughter, Philippa, his sole heir. She afterwards married Edmund Mortimer, who died in 1381, leaving his son Roger his heir. His son Edmund died in 1424 and was succeeded by his sister Anne, wife of Richard de Conisburgh, brother of Edmund, Duke of York, by whom she had Richard, Duke of York, father of Edward IV.

Henry VIII granted this lordship on June 10, 1509, by letters patent under the seal of the Duchy of Lancaster to his Queen, Catherine of Aragon, in satisfaction of dower. This was confirmed in that year by an Act of Parliament.

There belonged to this manor a park, which Edward VI granted on June 12, 1550, to William, Marquis of Northampton, by the name of the Park of Dunmow, and all lands, arable, meadow, pasture, wood and hereditaments, called by the name of Dannocke Park.

Sir Richard Weston, one of the justices of Common Pleas, was possessed of it at the time of his death on July 6, 1572, and his grandson William, Earl of Portland, who died on March 13, 1634, held Dunmow Park of the king, of his Duchy of Lancaster. Jerome his son inherited it after him, and it was undoubtedly granted by the Crown to that family. In the year 1634 William, first Lord Maynard, bought it in fee farm and through him it descended to his heirs until the last century.

The park, or the manor, of Dunmow—its house called The Lodge—is on the right side of the road leading to Braintree.

The manor of Bigods, or Alferestune, or Alfreston

In Saxon times Alfreston was a separate vill or hamlet. Some historians think there were two hamlets, Great and Little Alfreston, and distinct from Dunmow, but there is no certainty. In Edward the Confessor's time the manor belonged to Ansgar, and at the general survey to Geoffrey de Magnaville and his under-tenant, Martel. Hugh de Chatillon, Count de St. Paul, had this estate in 1201 and Thomas, Count de St. Paul is recorded to have held Alfrestone, Domemowe, about 1210-1. But much farther back Alfreston seems to have been dominated by some ancient possessor whose name is thought to be Alfred. Some time after it was escheated to the Crown and was granted to Reimund de Burgo about 1226, and afterwards to Bartholomew Bygod, who had a free warren here in his manor of Alfetstun, or Anferton. William de Bigod was enfeoffed of it in 1277, and the moiety of this manor came to Ralph Bigod, who died possessed of it in 1315, as did Sir Walter Bigod, on November 27, 1372, leaving Walter, his grandson by his son Thomas, his heir. He died on March 11, 1385, and was buried in the church. The last Sir Walter died in 1398, leaving William his son and heir.

It would seem that after William the line died out, for there is no information as to who owned it until the fifteenth century. In 1426 it was held by Isabella Doreward of the king, by the service of one knight's fee, and in 1434 it was divided into three parts. On April 20, 1529, Henry VIII granted to John Jenoure a pardon of intrusion into the manor of Alferston. This Jenoure family came from Aspall in Suffolk and this John was prothomotory of the Common Pleas. The family held this manor for 234 years. You will hear more about them during their long stay with us.

Newton Hall

In Edward the Confessor's time it was held by Ururic Cauna. At the time of the general survey it was held of Geoffrey de Magnaville and his under-tenant Hugh de Berners. Some new buildings here, distinct from the town of Dunmow, must have given this manor the name of "Nuie Tun," meaning new town. The descendants of Hugh de Berners held this estate almost to the end of the reign of Edward III. Marjory, wife of John de Gisors, who died in 1305, held a moiety of Newton Hall of Edmund by the service of an eighth part of a knight's fee, and thirty-five acres there of the king, as of the honour of Albemarle. John de Berners held this under Humfrey de Bohun, Earl of Essex and Hereford, who died in 1372. John de Goldington held it at the time of his decease in 1419. William Kynwelmarsh held this manor of Newton Hall of the master of Pleshey College, as of his manor of Bernston Hall.

Robert Gosnold had it in 1627, and sold it to Richard Deards, who died possessed of it in 1630. Next we find Sir John Swinnerton Dyer possessed of it. He died in 1701. The second wife of his son and heir was

Mary, sister of John Kempe, of Finchingfield. In 1741 he sold Newton Hall to the trustees of Sir Brownlow Sherrard, but that purchase did not go through and it was purchased by John Henniker, whose family lived there until the last century.

The manor of Merks

This manor took its name from Adelolp de Merc, who held it at the general survey under Eustace, Earl of Bologne, but in the Confessor's time it was held by Edmar, a freeman. Simon de Merc held it in 1210, and Ingelram de Merc in 1258. Robert was his son and heir and he died in 1305. Later on it came to another Robert de Merc, who sold the manor of Merks to Henry Ferrars, who died in 1343. It continued in this family till the death of William, Lord Ferrars of Groby, on May 23, 1439. Sir Thomas, second son and heir of the late William, granted a life estate in this manor to Sir John Bourchier and Elizabeth his wife. After several generations it was eventually bought by John Milborn. He married a daughter of —— Mead, of Great Easton, and died on May 17, 1594. This family of Melborn stayed at Merks, or Marks, for about 200 years, and you will be hearing more of them. Robert Melborne sold this estate, worth about £600 per annum, to Sir John Hallet, knight, who died on January 31, 1733, and is buried in Little Dunmow church with Mary his wife. Merks still belonged to his descendants till the last century.

The manor of Southall, or Suffehall

This manor seems to be made up of two parcels belonging in Saxon times to Ansgar, king of Mercia, and a freeman. At the general survey it was held by William de Warren and Sueve of Essex, and their under tenants Guilber and Edmar. About 1263 Jollan de Durmers held the manor of Suffehall in Dunmowe Magna of the king the honour of the Earl of St. Paul, by service of a pair of gilt spurs or 6d. He held also, of the fee of Ralph de Berners, half a virgate; and of the fee of John de Apeldersfield half a virgate; two acres and a half of the fee of Walter Fitz Robert. John was his son and heir, and was named in the Inquisition de Duresme. He also held eighty acres of land of John de Gisors, and of Warine Martel fourteen acres. Edmund was his son and heir. He held ten acres of this land of the prior and convent of Dunmawe Parva. It soon became invested in the above priory,

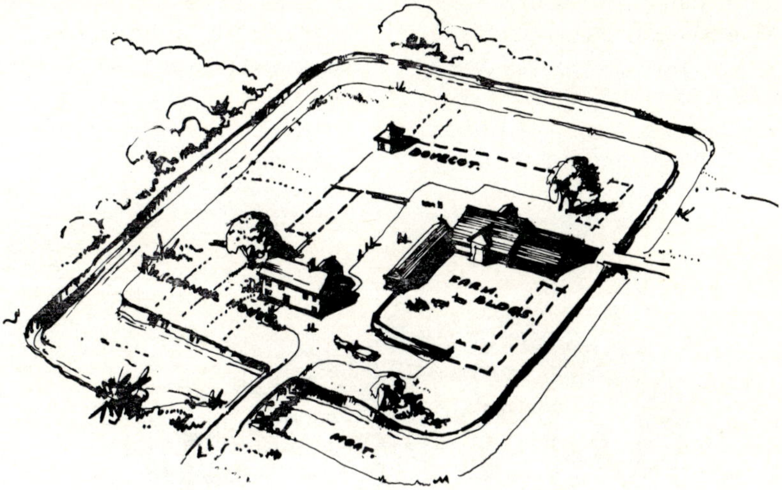

RECONSTRUCTION OF MARKS MANOR.

for Richard II in 1389 granted a licence to Robert Rikedon, Robert Knechbole, Thomas Houlet and John Eleyne, clerk, to give the manor of Southalle to the priory, holden of the king, but thirty acres were still holden of others.

Nothing plainly shows who held this estate after the dissolution, but it may be presumed that it was the noble family of Ratcliffe, Earls of Sussex. Clopton Hall was another name for this estate. The Lord Petre possessed it in 1634. In the eighteenth century it belonged to the Drapers' Company, purchased by the money of Mr. Bancroft, founder of the almshouses, Mile End, London.

The manor of Martels

This took the name of Martel from Geoffrey de Magnaville's tenant at Bigods and, as we see, the latter owned the greater part of the parish. This manor belonged in Edward the Confessor's reign to Ansgar, already mentioned. We do not find for a long time through whose hands this estate passed. In the church registers here, we find a William Long, tenant of Martels, buried in November 1593. In 1637 Robert Smith, gent, of Hatfield Broad Oak, held it. Later it was purchased by Michael Pepper, a rich merchant who also had Lower Hall. At the decease of Lady Pepper it passed to Lady Fitzgerald, later passing to her second son, Gerald Richard Fitzgerald.

Martels is on the road to High Easter and is two and a half miles from Great Dunmow church. The present owners of the house are Lord and Lady Plowden.

The manor of Shingle Hall, or Olives

Ansgar and a sochman of his held this manor in the Confessor's reign, but at the time of the general survey, of course, it was held by Geoffrey de Magnaville. William Glynes held it with Joan his wife till his death in 1361. I think it was a joint estate at some early date, because I find in Reaney's *Place-names* that it got its name of Olives from Hugh Olyve, whose family held this manor, or part of it, for some time, and William Olyve, who held Shingle Hall in 1361, the same date as William Glynes died. To carry on, quoting from Philip Morant, Shingle Hall was held by William de Bohun by the service of one knight's fee.

John Josslyn later purchased this manor, and dying in 1525 was succeeded by his son Thomas. Richard Jennings held it in 1627 and after him his son.

Manor of Minchons.

Just when Minchon became a manor is not clear. There is no mention of it at the Domesday survey, but half of it is about twelfth century and the rest about early sixteenth. We do not even know who lived there until the Glascocks. We are told that previous to

the dissolution Minchon formed part of the possession of the monastery of Clerkenwell. In a grant of 31 Henry VIII Minchons is distinctly described as a manor said to be worth £4/6/8 per annum.

It was granted in 1539 to one William Barnes or Berners. It also appears that this man of Thoby, in Essex, Walter Farr of London and William Glascock, also of London, had a grant in fee of the manor of Minchon. Later Berners and Farr alienated it to William Glascock, who made it his home. On April 5, 1540, he married at Great Canfield church Philippa, daughter of John Wiseman of that parish. In his will dated November 27, 1579, he mentions the house wherein he dwells called Mynchon and bequeaths this manor to his second son, Philip. The testator also left £20 to employ poor people of Dunmow in spinning. This was at a time when the Flemish were fleeing from the cruel Duke of Alva and many brought their trade to this country, " especially Essex and Suffolk." This £20 probably started up a few in Dunmow, till in a few years our population went up nearly forty per cent. Further legacies were left by William's sons Charles and Andrew. His son Philip, who succeeded to Mynchon on the death of his mother, married Ann, daughter of Andrew Jenour of Bigods. Philip died on September 1, 1640, and was buried at Dunmow church, as also were his parents. It is not certain if his sons lived at Mynchon, but his grandson John was rector of Little Canfield, and by his will left all his lands lying in Dunmow, including a capital messuage called Minchons, to John, the son by his first wife. This John resided there. His wife was buried at Dunmow on August 4, 1679. He died the next year and bequeathed Minchons to his half-brother, Francis, who left it to his sister Sarah, who was the last of the Glascocks of Minchon. It is not clear if she sold it in her lifetime, or to whom it went. We only know that it was bought later by the Beaumont family. Minchons was moated until recently. Internally the house bears evidence of having been altered and dismantled, although the staircase with its moulded and twisted balusters and its chamfered oak beams may still be seen.

DOMESDAY

We must see to what extent the land was cleared from the Confessor's time until the Conqueror made his great survey in 1087. Why was it called Domesday? Because nothing at all escaped it, not an ox, or a sheep, or even a hive of bees. A man might wish to go out and kill one of his herd of swine, but dare he? Nowhere was there an escape. Little wonder the people called it " Doomsday."

So we start off here with the

Manor of Dunmow

It was held in Edward's time for I manor

and for II hides and XXX acres. Always II teams in the demesne and II of the homogers and V villeins. Then IV borders, now VII, always IV in the demesne, then wood for 500 swine now CCC. XV acres of meadow, always I mill then and afterwards it was worth 7X shillings, now C.

Manor of Bigods or Alferstone

In Edward's time for I manor and for IV hides and X acres. Always III teams in the demesne, and II teams of the homagers. Then XV villeins, now VII, then XI bordars, now XXIV, then VI serfs, now IV. Wood then for CCCC swine, now for CCL. XXVI acres of meadow, always I mill. Then and afterwards it was worth VIII pounds, now X.

Manor of Newton Hall

In Edward's time for a manor and II hides and XXX acres. Always II teams in the demesne, now I and a half, and III teams of the homagers. Then CC swine. It was then worth IV pounds, now C shillings, and when he (William) received it the like sum.

Manor of Merks

In Edward's time for I manor and for II hides and XXX acres. Then III teams in the demesne and now II. Then I team of the homagers, now III. Then III villeins, now XIII. Now IX bordars. Then X serfs, now IV. Wood for CCC swine. XXXVI acres of meadow and I team could be re-established. XII beasts, I horse, IV hives of bees. It is worth VIII pounds.

Manor of Shingle Hall or Olives

In Dommauu Geofrey holds in demesne XXX acres which were held by Angar, and I soc-man. Always $\frac{1}{2}$ a team, then I bordar, now III wood for X swine, IV acres of meadow. It was then worth VII shillings, now X.

Manor of Southall

At the general survey for XXXVII acres and these VII acres were added to the estate by William de Warren. Then II bordars, now III. Always I serf. Wood for XXX swine, V acres of meadow, now I mill. It was then worth 73 shillings, now 100 shillings.

Manor of Martels

In Edward's time I manor and I hide and a half. Always II teams in the demesne, and II teams of the homagers. Then XIII villeins, now V. Then VII bordars, now VI. Then II serfs, now III. Wood for CC swine, XXVI acres of meadow. It was then worth C shillings, now VII pounds.

CHAPTER III

Dunmow's oldest churches

We know practically nothing of church life in Dunmow, but we know there was a church, because we find the people busy rebuilding it in the style (Decorated) that we have now. One reason by which we know there was a church here much earlier is that in 1045 we find that one Thurston willed half a hide of land and a toft to it. We do not know how long that church survived. It rather surprises me that if we had not a fairly substantial church the Normans would have built one. There was one here in 1197, for Geoffrey de Dunmow was rector. There were three mass chapels in Dunmow, one reckons, from Saxon times, as the town was divided into three quarters, Corporation, Bishop's Wood and Bigodswood, each having its own chapel.

At Bishopswood there is a field called Chapel Field. Some years ago while ploughing in this field a part of the foundation of the chapel was found. It was said to derive its name from Theodred, Bishop of London, who owned land in Dunmow and on his death left the lands to St. Paul's Cathedral. This field was sold in 1371 to Richard Hill and Robert Donne.

Two fields lying in front of Bigods Hall were until recently called Chapel Fields. There is no certainty when it was abolished. I would much like to know if it was still there in the early days of the Jenours. Of course, these chapels would have had to go at the Reformation.

The Corporation chapel remained until 1541, so therefore it went with the later religious places after the abbeys, priories, etc., had gone.

Pope Calixtus III in 1456 granted an indulgence to the parishioners who had erected and furnished a chapel of St. George the Martyr, to institute in it one or more priests to celebrate masses and other divine offices "whenever the weather was rough." How much this would be appreciated today! "Certain lands given by will and also put in feoffment to divers persons to find a priest for ever. The Priest to say divine service in the chapel' sett and buylde in Dunmow streat about which chapel is the chief part of the towne the number of 600 huslying people (communicants), and above which lands been worth by yere £9 19s. 3d. There is neither juell, ornament, goods or chattels appertaining to the chantries and free chapels within written."

The first of these show when and why this chapel was erected and the second shows it was in the chief part of the town and that its income made it independent of the parish church. After the chapel was closed it was bought by Dunmow Corporation and let to "Goodman Tailor." Its site was for a long time uncertain, but in 1899 two small houses were pulled down and shops now Brown (ironmonger) and Lea (draper) built in their place. The chapel of fine oak beams was found behind the little cottages. There is a steep fall-away at the back of these buildings and that is where the chapel lay. I think it a great shame that this was not preserved, but at that time there was no such thought as valuing that which was old.

CHAPTER IV

The stories the medieval rolls tell us

From the twelfth to the fifteenth centuries one does not get much idea of how our town is progressing except through the Courts, so it often seems as if we hear all the troubles and miss the good things. Folk often say that they wonder when Dunmow first became a town. That is something I do not know. That is an earlier story. I only know when it became a market town.

Liberate Rolls.

Westminster, July 3, 1239.

Liberate to Bertram le Gros, going to the Holy Land, 40 marks for his land in Dunmawe, of the Count of St. Paul, which he rendered to the King, which land he had in Dunmawe of the King's delivery.

Chester, September 14, 1257.

Liberate without delay Bartholamew de Bigod 10L of the King's gift to repair his buildings at Dunmawe, which were recently burnt by mis-chance while he was with the King of his service in Wales.

Dunmawe, August 31, 1271.

Walter de Essex, Sheriff, Delivered in the wardrobe to Peter de Wilton, keeper, on Wednesday, after the Decolleration of St. John £6.10. 6d. for 15 beevies bought by him when the King stayed at Havering, as testified by William de Wyntreshall, Steward of the Household.

Charter Rolls.

Farringdon, August 19, 1227. II Henry III.

Grant to Richard, son of Simon, and his heirs of a weekly Market on Saturday at his manor of Dunmawe and of a yearly fair there on the vigil of the feast and the morrow of the Decollation of St. John the Baptist.

CHARTER ROLL.

Now what went wrong? Did the Fitz-Richards follow it up or did they not? Because twenty-six years later—in 1253—Henry III granted the same (with the addition of another fair) to John de Berners. Whether or not it was started by Richard we cannot be sure, but it was started in 1253 for certain. Meanwhile Geoffrey de Dunmawe became the first rector in 1197, followed by Master Reginald in 1225, then by Simon Fitz-Simon. There is a " confirmation " by Pope Urban in 1225 of a settlement of about two-thirds of the tithe of the Count of St. Pol in Dunmow on October 23. The Bishop of London confirms this settlement. By Easter 1266 Simon agrees to pay for fifteen years' tithes in Dunmowe. Simon will pay 100/- for arrears, viz. four marks on August 1 at the New Temple and three and a half marks in the quendon at Easter next.

Apud Dommaune vjs viij.

Westminster, February 6, 1240. 24 Henry III.

Gift to Thomas de Dunholme, citizen of London and his heirs for his homage and service, and all the land of the Count of St. Pol in Dunmawe at Suthall [Southall] which

Bertram de Gros previously had of the Kings Bail, in exchange for 10L. To hold the land at Suthall by rendering yearly to the King at the exchequer at Michaelmas by his own hands a pair of gilt spurs, or 6d., until the King restore the lands to the rightful heirs of his free will, or by a peace.

CHARTER ROLL.

This settlement must remain with the king, but to us today the pair of gilt spurs appears a very small rent indeed.

Windsor, January 19, 1247. 31 Henry III.

Ingram de Merk has a charter for him and his heirs of free warren in all his demesne lands of his manor of Merks in Dunmawe.

CHARTER ROLL.

Westminster, June 2, 1252. 36 Henry III.

Grant to John de Berners and his heirs free warren in his demesne lands in Dunmawe, provided they are not within the King's forests.

CHARTER ROLL.

It would be interesting to know in which forest in Dunmow the king did hunt, but there was still so much forest left, although it was rapidly dwindling.

Canterbury, October 26, 1265. 49 Henry III.

Gift for his good service to William de Leyburn in Dunmawe and late of Robert de Merk, rebel and adherant of Simon de Montfordi, sometime Earl of Leicester. The said lands to be held by William and his heirs in the form aforesaid, provided that if the value increases, the surplus shall revert to the King.

CHARTER ROLLS.

I think that the Merks soon reverted back to the king after the death of their hero.

February 6, 1267. 51 Henry III.

Simple protection until Michaelmas for Simon son of Simon, parson of the church at Dunmawe, and Warren his son, on condition that if they have any offence against the King in the time of the disturbance in the realm, they should stand to the award of Kenilworth.

Apparently Rector Simon and his heirs are suspected of being followers of Simon de Montfort.

Westminster, April 20, 1270. 51 Henry III.

Confirmation of a Charter whereby Bartholomew de Bygod gave to Ralph his grandson, son of Ralph his son, deceased, all his land at Alfriston, with all the land which William Sinagun sometime held for life of the King's gift, with all appurtenances saving the land of Martin de Clayhangre and the land late of Ansgar but with the homage of Walter Sollarius of Dunmawe and all the land that the said Bartholomew gave to Robert his son, to be held by the said Ralph and the heirs of his body by performing the services due thence to the King, and if the said Ralph die without an heir of his body the said lands will revert to Robert, the son of the said Bartholomew and his heirs. Witnesses; Sir William Belet, Sir Nicholas de Strades, Sir Robert de Gaham, Sir Matthew de Luneroyn, Sir Simon, son of Richard, Sir Robert de Merk, Sir William called the Monk, William called the younger, Henry son of the Parson, Peter Richer, Walter Richer, Robert de la Dwone, and Waril Marcel, dated at Newburg, Friday after St. Gregory, 54 Henry III.

CHARTER ROLLS.

This was an extensive will of the Bygod family. The witnesses' names are mostly outside our story.

Westminster, November 24, 1286. 15 Edward I.

Gilbert, son of William de Dunmawe, acknowledges that he owes to Elisens de Luk 40/- to be levied in default of payment, of his lands and chattels in the county of Essex.

CLOSE ROLLS.

Newburgh, April 10, 1291. 20 Edward I.

Order to discharge by William (Sheriff of Essex) of 10L paid by him by the King's order to Ralph de Bigod, as Soloman de Roff and his fellows, justices, last eyre [year] in the County of Essex upon a presentment being made before them that Ralph held 10L yearly of land at Alfreston [Bigods] of the lands of the Normans pertaining to the King, took the land into the King's hands because Ralph had not a proper warrant, and Ralph afterwards showed to the King a Charter of Conformation that the King's father made to him of the said lands, whereupon the King ordered the Sheriff to restore the lands and the issues received thence to Ralph and William paid to him 10L by the King's order.

PATENT ROLLS.

How careful one had to be then, as now, to be sure of one's " receipt," as Ralph was at Alfreston many years ago.

Udimore, August 14, 1292. 25 Edward I.

Licence for Ralph Bigod who is going beyond the seas with the King, and on his service, in the company of Peter de Chaumpvent, to demise until 10 years after Michaelmas, his manor of Alfriston in Mutche Dunmawe, Co. Essex, to Ingram Belet and Bartholomew Bigod.

PATENT ROLLS.

We certainly hope they had a good trip in those ten years.

Carlisle, September 12, 1298. 27 Edward I.

Pardon to Simon le Tailleur of Dunmawe by reason of his service in Scotland, of a robbery committed some time ago in the town of Bracstede.

PATENT ROLLS.

Westminster, March 12, 1299. 27 Edward I.

Pardon to Ralph Fraunceys of Dunmawe, by reason of his service in Flanders, of robberies etc. before the King's transfratation into Flanders, and of his outlawry for the same.

One had only to serve in the forces to receive a royal pardon.

Westminster, November 6, 1302. 31 Edward I.

Order to release any restraint levied upon Gilbert, son of William de Dunmawe for his homage for the lands that he holds of the King in chief, reason of the lands that Humfrey de Bohun, Earl of Hereford and Essex lately rendered into the King's hands with the knight fees and all other appurtenances, as the King has taken his homage.

CLOSE ROLLS.

Westminster, March 5. 31 Edward I.

Licence in consideration of a fine made by him in the Chancery for Robert de Merk to enfeoff John Gamlyn of his manor in Dunmawe, held in chief as of the honour of Boulogne for the latter to re-enfeoff him and Jacomina his wife in fee tail with remainder to the heirs of Robert.

PATENT ROLLS.

The Merk land covered that part of Dunmow which includes the manor across to Merks Hill, to where until recently a footpath was retained.

Westminster, May 28, 1306. 34 Edward I.

Order to deliver to Jacomina, late wife of Robert de Merk of the Manor at Dunmawe, which has been taken into the King's hands by reason of Robert's death, and to deliver to her the issues received thence by the escheator that Robert and Jacomina were jointly enfeoffed by John Gamelyn of the said manor, which is held of the King in chief by the service of a moiety of one and one-sixth knights fee, as to the honour of Boulogne, which is on the King's hands, to hand to them and the heirs of their bodies that they continued their seisin thereof until Roberts death.

CLOSE ROLL.

Poor Jacomina's life was a hard one you will see as time goes on. Perhaps it was because she had come from France that she was so ill-treated.

PATENT ROLL.

Westminster, November 10, 1307.
I Edward II.

To John Buteturt and William Howard on the complaint of Robert de Merk, son of

Walter, that Adam de Waldingfield forcible broke open a box at his manor at Dunmawe, Co. Essex.

PATENT ROLLS.

I wonder what that box contained.

York, February 12, 1319. 12 Edward II.

Complaint by Jacomina de Merk that Gilbert de Bumpstead, Simon de Wolmongre, John le Storiers of Dunmawe, and 24 other men of the parishes around entered her manor at Lyndisele, broke her houses and gates, fished in her stews, carried away her tymbers as well as other goods including her charters and muniments and six horses, eight oxen, 116 sheep and two swans, of the price of 60L.

PATENT ROLLS.

York, May 30, same year.

Commission to John de Wengrave and John Gysors and John de Countibrigge to deliver to the gaol at Newgate of John Olyve and Simon de Wolmongre, and Johnson Olyve of Dunmawe, prisioners of divers felonies.

Westminster, May 26, 1324.

Thomas, son of Eustanes, acknowledges that he owes to Elizabeth de Burgo, and Master Richard de Clare priest of the church at Dunmawe 500s to be levied in default of payment or his lands and chattels in the Co. of Glos.

CLOSE ROLLS.

Westminster, July 27, 1337. II Edward III.

To the Sheriff of Essex. Order to deliver to Jacomina, late wife of Robert de Merk, Knight, who was a native of the Dominion of the King of France, his lands, goods, and chattels in Dunmawe and Lyndsele in the County of Essex, as she has shown the king that whereas her late husband was an Englishman and died in the allegiance of Edward I and was efeoffed jointly with her of the said lands by a fine levied before the justices of the bench of the King. Now for 40 years and more after his death, staying there continually, without ever leaving the realm, and that John de Marton took the said lands, goods and chattels into the king's hands and delivered them to the sheriff to be kept by virtue of the king's commission and that Jacomina came into chancery and found mainpernors for the king, to wit; Richard de Hatfield of Essex and Henry de Merk of Co's Hereford and Gloucester, to undertake that she will answer to the King for the said goods, chattels, and for the issues of the said lands if they ought to pertain to the King, and she has besought the King to order all her possessions to be restored to her by the aforesaid mainprise. John de Marton ordered to deliver the said land, goods, and chattels, to Jacomina without delay.

Poor Jacomina! She certainly had a hard life. Anyway, the escheator of Essex gets the second son to take over. His mother must be growing old, or perhaps is deceased.

The Tower, October 25, 1340. 14 Edward III.

To Robert de Clare, escheator of Essex, an order to cause Robert brother of Ingelram son of the late Robert and Jacomina his wife, to have seisin of the manor of Merks in the town of Dunmawe Magna, saving the relief of Robert due to the King in this respect, and as the king has learned by inquisition taken from the escheator that Jacomina held this manor at the time of her death by the grant of John Gamlyn to Robert and Herself and the heirs of their bodies by a fine levied in the Court of Edward I, as of the honour of Boulogne, by service of a knight's fee. Ingelram crossed to parts beyond the sea long before the death of his mother, and it is not known if he is alive or dead, and Robert is the next heir of full age, so that the King has taken Robert's fealty for the said manor and has given him respite for his homage until the Purification next.

Kennington, November 19, 1342.
16 Edward III.

To Henry Gernet, escheator of Essex and

Hertford. Order to receive security from Ada age 8, Elizabeth age 6, and Matilda age 5, daughters of Edmund de Duresme of rendering their reasonable relief at the exchequer and after making a legal partition of the tenement called "Suthalle" [Southall] in Dunmawe, Co. Essex, into three equal parts in the presence of the heirs and parceners, then, the children, of the late Edmund to have seisin of the purparties thereof touching them, informing the King of that partition in chancery, so that it may be enrolled, and not to intermeddle further with the lands which are held of other lords than the King, restoring the issues thereof, as the King has learned by inquisition, taken by the escheator, that Edmund at his death held the said tenement in his demesne as of fee in chief by the service of a pair of gilt spurs or 6d yearly by the hands of the Sheriff of Essex and Hertford that he held lands of other lords by divers services and that his said daughters are his next heirs. The King has taken the fealty of the children, for their purparties, and has rendered these to them.

PATENT ROLLS.

This young man did not live long to enjoy his manor.

Westminster, June 15, 1345. 19 Edward III

By letters patent dated 18th May 14 Edward III, the King granted to John Brocas the reversion of lands in Dunmawe, Co. Essex, late of Robert de Merk and Jacomina his wife, now deceased, expectant on the demise of Jacomina escheats to the forfeiture of Ingelram their son who was an adherant of Philipp de Velision, the King's enemy, to hold in fee in satisfaction of 10L 5S of an annuity of 50 marks previously granted to him at the exchequer until he should receive the same in land and rent and maintain his estate as a knight, and afterwards Robert, a son of Robert and Jacomina, born subsequently, asserting that his parents held the lands in tail, and that Jacomina was not attorned to John for the lands after the death of her husband, persuant to the grant aforesaid, entered after her death into the same a son and heir of Robert and Jacomina and efeoffed certain person of the land, of cunningly defrauding the King of what pertains to him of the forfeiture of Ingelram his elder brother and prevent John from having possession thereof. Wherefore the King, to give effect to his grant aforesaid, has again granted the lands which has caused to be taken into his hands for the cause aforesaid to John as above. Has also granted licence for him to enfeoff Isabella, late the wife of Henry de Ferarus, of the same, which are said to be held in chief, and as a further grace, as granted Isabella to charge the lands with 10L 5S yearly to be paid to John and his heirs into whosesoever hands the lands shall come.

PATENT ROLLS.

Reading, August 8, 1347. 21 Edward III.

To Richard de Helleshill, Robert de Teye and William de Lanerham on information of William le Somenour of Dunmawe.

William Knyvet, Rector of Dunmawe, John de Wardon, Abbot of Tilteye, Johanesser-nant de Bonlyton, parson of Eyston and about 16 others, broke into the park at Eyston, in the King's hands by reason of the nonage of the heir of John de Lonayne. tenant in chief. Hunted therein, fished in the stews and stanks, likewise in the King's hands on the same account and carried away fish and trees as well as deer from the park.

PATENT ROLLS.

(Those naughty clergy. They really were a disgrace.)

Westminster, May 1354. 28 Edward III.

On testimony of the King's Chaplain Edward de Bokenham, that John Proude of Dunmawe, Co. Essex, lately indicted of the death of Robert Hebcastel, and of a robbery in the rectory of Stapleford Abbots, killed the said Robert in self defence, and is indicted of the robbery whereof he is not guilty, maliciously. The King has pardoned the said John of the death and robbery and any consequent outlawries.

Westminster, February 19, 1358.
32 Edward III.

William de Faraus, knight, acknowledges that he owes to John Brocas, knight, 12L, to be levied in default of payment, of his lands and chattels in Dunmawe.

Enrolment of release by John Brocas, knight, to Sir William de Ferrars of all his right and claim in the manor of Dunmawe, Co. Essex. Memorandum. That the said John Brocas came into the chancery at Westminster on February 10 and acknowledged the preceding deed.

PATENT ROLLS.

Reading, December 20, 1359. 33 Edward III.

Enrolment of release by John de Lacy son and heir of Sir Henry de Lacy to Sir Thomas de Clapton, knight, and Ada his wife of all his right and claim that the manor of Dunmawe called Southalle, which lately belonged to Edmund de Duresme, knight. Memorandum. That John came into the chancery at Westminster on January 15 and acknowledged the preceding deed.

PATENT ROLLS.

Westminster, November 5, 1364,
38 Edward III.

Whereas Thomas Charman & Thomas Mountjoye are indicted of having, with others, broken the Stocks wherein a man called John Litherman, attached to Dunmawe fair, on suspicion of larceny had been put and taking him away against the peace, the King at the request of the Duke, has pardoned Thomas Mountjoye the suit of the peace for the breaking and taking away, whereof he was indicted and of any consequent outlawry. The like pardon to Thomas Charman.

CHARTER ROLLS.

(The market then was held in the street, and the stocks were near the town or guild hall, so the breaking of one from the stocks no doubt caused some amusement.)

Westminster, February 12, 1369.
43 Edward III.

Pardon to John Screveyn of Dunmawe Chepyng, Co. Essex, of his outlawry in the husting of London for non-appearance before the Justices of the Bench to answer Robert, son of Mareschal of Northwelde Co. Essex, touching a plea of debt of 8 marks; he having now surrendered to the Flete prison, as Robert de Thorpe, chief justice, has certified.

CHARTER ROLLS.

(This town was often called Dunmawe Chepyng, which means Dunmawe market.)

Westminster, February 13, 1370.
44 Edward III.

Pardon for 40s. paid to the King by Walter de Fitz Wanter to John Chareman of Riclyngg and Robert Kneehebole of Dunmow of their trespass in acquiring, in fee, from the said Walter, 45 acres of wood, in Dunmow Priory, held in chief, without the King's licence and licence for Walter to receive back the premises and hold them in fee.

CHARTER ROLLS.

Westminster, October 18, 1381. 5 Richard II.

To the Sheriff of Essex. Order upon petition of John Lependen of Dunmawe, if assured that he was unlawfully desecised of three cottages there by John Horro and Alice his wife, by aid of certain of his enemies who rose in the late insurrection, to give again seisin thereof; putting out the said John Horro and his wife, and telling them to sue according to the law if they think fit; as the King decrees, that things so done in time of that disturbance are of none effect. For ½ a mark in the hanaper.

(This was the Wat Tyler revolt, after which Richard II visited the counties. In Essex he found some resistance and 500 people were put to death.)

Westminster, July 18, 1389. 13 Richard II.

License for the alienation in mortmain by Richard Rikedon, Robert Kneechbole, Thomas Houlet. John Eleyne clerk of their manor of Southalle in Gt. Dunmawe, held by the Crown by the service of a pair of gilt spurs, or 6d. Certain parcels of the manor being held by other persons and by the Prior of the Convent of Lt. Dunmawe, for a fine of 40L.

PATENT ROLLS.

Westminster, June 4, 1394. 17 Richard II.

Commissioners of oyer and terminer to William Rikehill, William Hankeford, John Doreward and Robert Rykedon, on complaint by Walter atte Lee, constable and keeper of the Castle of Colchester Co. Essex, that William Holbeche, tailer and other evil doers, maliciously incited one John Redhede of Dunmawe, late receiver of the King's uncle Thomas Duke of Gloucester a prisoner committed to complainant's custody in Colchester Gaol until he paid the said Duke 400 marks, the arrears of account as found by the Auditors thereof, to break prison and escape, furnishing him with divers instruments and engines for the purpose, thereby obliging the petitioner to pay that sum to the said Duke.

PATENT ROLLS.

Westminster, August 16, 1401.
2 Henry IV.

Grant to Thomas, Earl of Worcester, steward, Thomas More, clerk, and Robert Brownfleet, knight, controller of the household, of all the goods late of Thomas Proudfote of Dunmawe Co. Essex, and forfeited to the King on account of a felony committed by him, for the expense of his household.

Lichfield, July 28, 1403. 4 Henry IV.

Pardon to John Proudfote, son of Thomas, one of the King's tenents in the town at Stebbyng Co. Essex, indicted of having on Tuesday St. Petrobilla 2 Henry IV, lain in ambush in a pasture called Rykemondesles, in the parish of Dunmawe and killed Robert, son of Robert Parker of Dunmawe.

The Tower, February 25, 1325. 18 Edward II.

To John le Porter, keeper of the Manor of Dunmawe, order to cause dower of the said manor to be assigned to Thomas de Hyndringham and Nichola his wife as the King learns by inquisition taken by John de Liston and Thomas de Reppers that Simon Fitz-Richard was seised of the manor in his demesne as of fee for a long time after he married the aforesaid Nichola so that he could dower her thereof and that he gave the manor to Humfrey de Bohun late Earl of Hereford and Essex by charter on Monday after St. Gregory in the 13th year of the King's reign, and that Simon died on the 4th of March in the 15th year of the King's reign and that the aforesaid Thomas de Hyndringham or Nichola never made quit claim or release of the Manor to the Earl after Simon's death and that the manor is in the King's hands solely by reason of the Earl's forefeiture and that it is held of the heirs of Gloucester as of the honour of Clare by knights service and by the service of rendering 40s yearly to the manor of Berdefeld and that it is worth yearly 30L .

CLOSE ROLLS.

This changed the authority in Dunmawe, particularly of the Church.

Dunmawe, August 3, 1325. 19 Edward II.

Writ of aid for one year for Hugh de Beauspaier, King's Seajeant, charged by the steward of the household and the keeper of the wardrobe to make pursevayances of hay, oats, beans, litter and other necessories and of some horses in their custody.

PATENT ROLLS.

I guess the local farmers were hard put to it to please the authorities.

Westminster, March 15, 1327. I Edward III.

Master Richard de Clare, parson of the Church of Donmowe, acknowledges that he owes to Anketynus de Gysors, citizen of London 100L, to be levied in default of payment, of his lands and chattels in County of Somerset.

CLOSE ROLLS.

These rectors, were they ever out of debt?

Oseney, July 10, 1330. 4 Edward III.

Licence to Edward de Duresme to efeoff John de Haye, parson of the church of Shellye, of twelve messuages, one of Dunmawe of 500 acres of land, 20 acres of pasture, 3 acres of wood and 8s rent in Gt.Dunmowe and for all the tresspasses held in chief and for the efeoffee to grant the same to the said Edmund and Joan his wife in fee tail, with remainder, if he die without issue to Joan, his sister, and to the rightful heirs of Edmund.

PATENT ROLLS.

Westminster, May 16, 1316. 9 Edward II.

Pardon to Richard de Clare parson of the church of Dunmow, on account of his great labour and expenses he sustained in the repulse of the Scots from Ireland, of 1000 marks out of the debts due from him at the exchequers of England and Ireland as well for himself as his ancestors. Grant also to him of a respite during pleasure from the payment of the residue.

PATENT ROLLS.

Continued May 17th Inspeximus of a letter percuratory under the seal of Gilbert, Bishop of London, May 13, 1316, notifying that Master Richard de Clare rector of the Church of Dunmawe and Sir John de Capel rector of Abresdon diocese of Lincoln, executors of the testament of Lady Margaret de Clare, appeared before him and appointed Master Richard de Brenchesle their proctor and attorney in all causes connected with her said will and testament.

PATENT ROLLS.

Most of these rectors were in debt. Perhaps Lady de Clare's will helped towards the residue.

Westminster, July 6, 1419. 7 Henry V.

Order to remove the King's hand and meddle no further with the manor of Newton Halle, 100 acres of land 20 acres of pasture and 4 acres of wood in Gt. Dunmawe delivering to Aris late the wife of John Goldyngton, the escheator, any issues thereof taken; as it is found by divers inquisition, taken before, the escheator.

That at his death John Goldyngton held the said manor and land in Gt. Dunmawe by gift of William Chasteseye and Thomas Kelhoe, clerks to them, their heirs and assigns, by name of their manor of Newton Halle and all their lands in Dunmowe by the name of John Goldyngton Esq., and Aris his wife and to the said John's heirs and that the same are not held of the King. Tested by John, Duke of Bedford, Guardian of England. To the same.

Order in Presence of the friends of Thomas Goldyngton son and heir of the late John Goldyngton, to assign to John Audeley and Arice who was wife of John Goldyngton dower of his lands taken into the King's hand by his death and by reason of his sons nonage. As for a fine paid in the hanaper, the King has pardoned the trespass of John Audeley for taking Aris to wife and her marrying him, without licence of the King.

CHARTER ROLLS.

Westminster, May 19, 1427. 5 Henry VI.

To the escheator of Essex. Order to take the fealty of Richard Fox and to give him seisin of a third part of the manor of Alfrestonhalle in Gt. Dunmow as it is found by inquisition that Isabel who was the wife of John Dorewarde, at her death held no lands in Essex.

Westminster, May 6, 1435. 13 Henry VI.

To the excheator of Essex. Order to take the fealty of Joan who was the wife of Richard Fox, to give her livery of a third part of Alfreston Halle in Gt. Dunmowe. That a third of the manor is held of knights fee and that by the death of Richard, the premises were taken into the King's hand and for a fine paid in the hanaper the King has pardoned the trespass, further granting that the said Joan shall have the premises again and hold them for her life without impeachment or disturbance by the King.

PATENT ROLLS.

Westminster, February 20, 1448. 27 Henry VI.

John Fulborne to Henry Filongley and John Ingowe.

Recoynisance for 100 marks, to be levied in Cambridgeshire. Condition that he and Agnes his wife, their feoffees and all who by them have an interest in the manor of Dunmowe, shall when required by fine with warranty to make a good estate, thereof in law to James Ormond, knight, or other nominees and to their heirs at his cost, and that if John Fulbourne shall be impleaded concerning the same, or any parcel thereof, he shall plead such pleas as shall by counsel of the said James or his heirs be ministered by him at their cost and in possession of the said manor he shall rule himself, as by them advised.

Westminster, 1470. 10 Edward IV.

Thomas Lyghtfote, son of John Lyghtfote (otherwise) Fuller to John Porter citizen and stokfisshmonger of London, Katherine his wife, Roger Gerneys and William Curteys, gent and John Freke yeoman, their executors, heirs and assigns. Gift with warranty of a messuage called " Watkyns " in Dunmowe, with well houses, 90 acres of arable land, 3 acres of meadow, 4 acres of wood, lying in Dunmowe parish, with 3s 11d rent, to be received of divers tenents i.e. 13d from John Carter for a croft called " Scottyscroft " 13d from John Lyghtfote the younger "scynener" for a croft called " Pessecroft " 4d from lands of the late William Glascock for a croft called " Londlond " 2d for a croft called " Markiscroft " 14d for the manor of Newton Hall and 1d from the farm of Bronds [Brands] for 3 crofts called " Tebawdescrofts " lying near " Mynchere " [Minchons]. A croft called " Waytescroft " wards, marriages and reliefs and escheats which lands the asaid Thomas recovered in the court of the Kings bench at Westminster against the said John Lyghtfote and Agnes his wife, mother of Thomas, by the King's hand to be held in capital demesne, as of fee.

Witnesses—Richard Rede, John Aleyn and John Nele—Dated Dunmowe July 14, 10 Edward IV.

Same as before—Demise with warranty of the land called Rothyngleye and 2 crofts called Chufferysland in Dunmowe, on either side of the Kings highway from the manor of Olynes to High Roothing which the granters held by enfeoffment of Roger, Prior of the conventual Church of St. Mary's Little Dunmow.

John Peke and Richard Rede to be held with hedges and ditches by the said John Porter in capital demesne as of fee.

Westminster, February 1, 1492.
7 Henry VII.

Letters patent, under the seal of the Duchy of Lancaster. Grant for life to Elizabeth, the queen consort. Grant to her of the lordships and manors of Gt. Waltham and Badowe, Masshebury, Dunmowe, Leighes and Farnham Co. Essex, parcel of the duchy, with the office of feodary and bailiff of the said lordships and manors.

Greenwich, February 16, 1556.
2 & 3 Philip & Mary.

Grant upon the petition of the inhabitants of the town and borough of Dunmowe Magna, parcel of the Duchy of Lancaster in Essex, that they be from henceforth a body corporate by the name of the Bailiff of and Burgesses of the borough of Dunmowe Magna and have a perpetual succession; able to pleas and be impleaded in all courts and places of the crown and in all actions, causes, etc.; as of other lieges are able and that they have a common seal. The bailiff and burgesses and inhabitants shall yearly on Tuesday after Michaelmas elect one of the burgesses to the office of bailiff for one year then ensuing; if the one so elected with six days after such decease or removal. The bailiff elect shall take to oath before the steward of the borough or his deputy for the faithful discharge of his office.

They shall yearly on the same date elect and appoint the constables and all other necessary ministers and officers of the borough.

The bailiff and burgesses from time to time as shall seem expedient have power to nominate, elect and appoint to the office of burgess any men, tenants and inhabitants within the borough who shall be necessary to its governance.

Thomas Edwycke to be the first and present bailiff and to continue in office until Tuesday after Michaelmas next or until another shall be elected and sworn to that office.

Thomas Moyne, John Clerk, John Joy, George Dearne, Robert Sawyer alias Draper, William Gager, John Vyntener, William Sawyer, alias Draper, Richard Cooke, Leonard Monke, Nicholas Moyne and John Savin, tenants and inhabitants of the borough, to be first and present burgesses during good behaviour.

Grant of a weekly market on Saturday and two yearly fairs, one on the feast, eve and morrow of St. Mark the Evangelist and the other on the feast, eve and morrow of SS. Simon and Jude, with court of pie powder during the said fairs, stallage, picage, tolls fines and all other profits belong to the like market and fairs and court, at a yearly rent of 10/- for the said fairs to the receiver of the lordship or manor of Dunmowe Magna.

July 21, 1558. 6 Philip & Mary.

Grant to Richard Weston, esq., solicitor general and Margaret his wife, a messuage and lands (40 acres) in Dunmow Magna, in the tenure of John Mott, arable lands (16 acres) next to a tenement called " Tanners " also in Mottes tenure, a messuage called Astes in the same parish, also arable lands (11 acres) usually leased with it, in the tenure of Richard Michell and a tenement late a chapel at Bishopswood in the tenure of Thomas Carder also in the parish of Dunmowe Magna.

January 6, 1559. 1 Elizabeth.

Presentament was made that Henry Gray married Agnes Livermere late of Gt. Dunmowe, Co. Essex, spynster and that William Penson also late of Gt. Dunmowe, taylour, who committed adultery with Agnes before and after her marriage, conspired with her at Stebbing Co. Essex, on June 3rd, 4th and 5th and July 2nd murdered Gray, asleep in bed with Agnes at Gray's dwelling house at Stebbing. Agnes abetting, Penson pleaded not guilty, but was found guilty and as he had no goods or lands he was condemned to death on July 18. He escaped, but was captured by the diligence of Thomas Pope, knight, John Swallowe of the exchequer and Nicholas Chapman under sheriff on July 28 and duly hanged.

May 23, 1560. 2 Elizabeth.

License for Thomas Wyseman of Gt. Waltham to alienate to William Glascock of Gt. Dunmowe as of his manors to his use for his lifetime with remainder to Stephen Wyseman intail, with remainder to his rightful heirs.

July 5, 1560. 2 Elizabeth.

Grant in fee simple to the Marquess of Northampton, Robert Kynge and Geffrey Scott of the tenure of Dunmow Park, once assigned to Catherine late queen of England, as jointure, afterwards of the Marquess and now annexed to the duchy of Lancaster.

(I have curtailed these rolls lest my readers find them irksome, but really they should not be, as they do show an early tendency to throw off the feudal yoke. The son and grandson of the rector Simon Fitz Simon were suspected of being followers of Simon de Montfort, also the de Merks, and it could be for this reason that Jacomina was so badly treated. Later on the Wat Tyler rising found favour here, as in all East Anglia and the South. How people longed for freedom.)

CHAPTER V

Great Dunmow Revels 1526–1547

The early churchwarden's account book describes the " revels " that were allowed on feast days. They were the only real holidays our forefathers knew, and those so soon to be debarred by the Reformation and later under the Commonwealth, when no amusements were allowed, particularly in connection with the Church.

Christmas revels

Manorial law from time out of mind had provided that for two weeks at Christmas the lord of the manor might require no cornee work from his serf-tenants. Of almost equal antiquity during these two weeks, a company of mummers, playing certain characters, was presided over by the " Lord of Misrule." For this performance the churchwardens sometimes provided the disguises, etc. " 1526 receyved off Nicolas Parcas of dansyng money 4s. 4d. payd for a blackk morres coott 12d. 1530 receyved of the lord of mysrewle, wych was gadred at Crystmas 51s. 8d. 1533 receyved of the Lord of mysrewle, money from Crystmas 40s. payd to Newton of Writtle for garments at Crystmas 20s. 1539 receyvd of the lord of mysserewell and for the plough fest 40s. payd to John Melborn in reward for playing the lord at Crystmas 2s. payd to John Parker in reward of playing the fool 12d. payd to Wyllyam Waskett for leverris 12d payd to the mynstrells for the Crystmas 20s. 1540 receyved of Skingle, the lord of myse-rule, that were gathered at Crystmas, clerk to the cherche 52s. 1d."

The Plough Feast

Soon after Christmas came the Plough Monday ceremony, which marked the resumption of field work. It was an old custom to keep certain lights perpetually burning in the church, by way of silent intercession for a blessing on the ploughs of the parish and their work. No one these days can have the least conception of what the hours of darkness meant to our ancestors before the time of any kind of illumination, such as rushlights or good candles, and the desire of all parishioners of those days that their church at least should have a light in the dark hours.

On the first Monday after the twelfth night, Epiphany, January 6, a group of rustics, disguised and beribboned, perhaps as an old woman of the traditional " merrie andrew," dragged a plough gaily decked with ribbons through the town, taking around with them a bag for collection and no doubt calling out " God speed the plough."

" In 1538 receyved to the ploughe fest 8s. receyved of Raffe Milbourne of the ploughe fest money of Bygwoods Quarter 9s."

May Day

The May Day festivities, with the morris dancers, Jack-in-the-green, maypole and other ancient observances, came at a much later date and only ended with World War I.

" 1528 receyved of May mony, the hole sum 28s. 4d. 1531 receyved of Lytell Salyng 48s. 4d. 1532 layed owght at the May at High Ester 8d. 1533 layed owght at myche Canfield Maye, to make the shott [to pay the bill in full] 20d. layed owgth at hie Eestre Maye 11d. 1538 receyved at the May fest 18s. 7½d. receyved for the sale of ale and bred sold at the May fest 10d." The churchwardens provided for the sale of bread and ale this year. It is the first recorded and previously it had been so only at Corpus Christi Day. " 1539 payd to Raymond the bocher for meate 15d. To John Saven for a calfe 2s. to the same John for a quarter of mutton 6d. To Thomas Wente for halfe a schepe 12d to John Toterych for halfe a calfe 11d. To John Carver the cooke 6d to John Agodshalfe and Agnes Morres for turning the spits 3d to mother Kobbe and Rafe at Dyclyng 2d to mother Bemyssh and John Byckener for spyce, salte and hony 7½d to Robert Melborn's wife for brewyng halfe a seme of malte 4d. To Med's wyff for brewyng 4d. To the mynstrells att that daye 6d. To Thomas Dyer for wood (for cooking the joints) 6d. 1540 chargis att the Maye—payd to Pomfrett for a calfe 3s. to Saven for a schepe 2s. 4d. to Robert Melbourne for a bussell of malte 7d for brewing and bakyng 6d. to hooks and hasteles (ostler) 10d. for a bushell of whete 7d."

Corpus Christi Day

The great day of the year was Corpus Christi Day. On this day, year by year, Great Dunmow presented to incomers from the surrounding villages a performance of a traditional mystery play. Unhappily, no text or description of this play has survived. A collection seems to have been made at the actual performance. The Dunmow players seem to have visited most of the villages around besides the village folk coming to see it in Dunmow. The latter years of the Corpus Christi plays appear to have been accompanied by athletic sports. There were archery competitions for men and boys and contests in running and leaping. After the Reformation the secular games seem to have ousted the more religious plays. " 1531 at Corpus Christi fest receyvd fyrst of Hyghe Ester 11s. 6d. of Hyghe Rodyng 3s. 6d. of Myche Canfyld 6s. 8d. of Little Dunmow 3s. 2d. of Stebbyng 9s. 11d. Lytell Canfield 4s. Lytell Eston 5s. 2d. Lyndesell 6s. 5d. of Much Eston 8s. 11d. of owyn towne 25s. of Barnstone 6s. 8d. Thereof, layde owght (as yt apered at the rekenyng made) at the same daye 49s. 5d. and remayneth to the churche clerely 40s."

The Corpus Christi feasts go on similarly each year, so I will pass on to

All Saints' and All Souls' Days

Many observances and superstitions centred around these days, November 1 and 2. As far as Great Dunmow is concerned there was a special collection in the church on the evening of November 1, with a special ringing of the bells and a collection for the ringers. " 1529 payd for ale att Halowmas for the tyngers 7d. 1530 gadred in the churche on Halowmas nyght at evynsong 4s. 1533 for drynke on All Sols evyn. 1534 seft clerely [saved clearly] of the mony that was gathard in the churche on Hallomase nyght 9d." Perhaps the weather was bad.

State occasions

In the later days, especially in Elizabeth's day, expenses were tightened up; for one thing, drink for the bellringers. This caused much controversy among them and in these days they would undoubtedly " go on strike." On *very* special occasions there were exceptions, such as " 1561 payd to the good wife Barker for ale for them that dyd rynge when the Queene's grace cam thorow the parysshe 8d." (Elizabeth left Great Leighs on August 24, 1561, to proceed to Gt. Hallingbury, then the seat of Lord Morley.) " 1573 to Dossiter for servinge as church clerk and drynke when the Queene cam through the towne 12d. 1582 for bell-roapes at the coronasion daye (anniversary) of our Queene 5s." Our revel players were reckoned to be some of the best in the county, with the possible exception of those at Maldon, to whom they sold their clothes when they finished here in 1547. Perhaps other churches did not have to go Presbyterian, like our own church. It is reckoned that few did outside East Anglia. I think our players brightened the town and the villages around, then finished up with a meal, and generally left about twelve and a half per cent to the church.

The Commonwealth was almost on their doorstep, and most forms of recreation became a sin. One was not allowed to play bowls on the Downs or skittles in the " Bowling Green," and the church must have become as an empty vault. We rarely hear much about these years, but, as in all civil wars, the pendulum swung too far in the opposite direction.

GREAT DUNMOW GILDS

A medieval gild was similar to a modern mutual benefit society. It was a voluntary association of individuals to make provision for its members against poverty incurred by sickness or old age. It governed its own affairs according to rules made by its members and through officers elected by its members, but its funds were frequently augmented by legacies. The medieval features of such a gild were partly religious and partly social. The gild chose for itself a patron saint, by whose name it was known. It had at least a mass sung especially for its own members in its own chapel, by a priest of its own choosing, using vestment and altar utensils belonging to the gild. It also had a gild dinner at least once a year, served up on its own pewter or plate. The humbler gild that had no hall of its own borrowed the gild-hall of the corporation. In the course of years, by benefactions of their former members, they came to own considerable property in trust for the relief of their sick and indigent members. Henry VIII in 1545 confiscated all this charitable property, as well as all the communion plate, pewter, or any articles of value belonging to the gilds. His officials who effected the seizure laid hold also on title deeds, rentals, books of accounts and all other records available. When the property of the gilds was subsequently sold by the Crown these records were all destroyed, with the result that it is extremely difficult to find information about them in any town.

Regarding Great Dunmow there is a little here about them in the churchwarden's book. This gives the names of two gilds, a list of the pewter vessels belonging to one of them, and an indication of the chapels built for them in the parish church. The list of pewter is written on the binding of that book.

St. John's and St. Saviour's gilds

" 1545 (?). That there is an olde vessell that belongs to Saynt John's gyld fyrst, of platars and dysshys xix & saltes vii—waynge xxvl et dim 25½ lbs. A grett panne wyth ii yeres=ears, & ii mete spyts, & ii cobarnes =spit-rests. Item for the lowance=allowance that the good man Bemysshe made for the waste of the forsayd vessells, and other things xvs, ixd and all these things remayne in the hands of Nicolas the joyner. 1539 receyved of the wardens of Seynt Savyers gyld towards thc making of the newe cherch doore—vis—[possibly a door giving access to the chapel of the gild, without passing through the church]." In 1533 fifty-three persons subscribed to the leading of the new gild chapel. 1527 payd for mendyne of lede over the newe chapell and over the yelde on the same syde iis; payd to Wylyam Blythe for mendynge of the glase wyndowes in the newe chapell, and other places of the cherche iis & iiiid. 1533 receyved to the reparasyons of the newe gyld, by dyvers persons viiis & viiid. 1533 payd to Thomas Turner for 9c of ledd iii quarters & xiii=19 cwt, 3 qtr, 11 lbs) pryce of every hundryth—cwt redy shott and layde viis sum of the hole iii Li—viiis xid; payd to the same Thomas for ii dayes and a halfe, and his son; for layng downe of the old ledd over the newe yelde xvs, vd payd to Rychard Scoryar for shotyng of the lyme and the sonde together xiid. payd for the lyme for battylment of the newe yelde xvs and xid; payd for bred and drynke and mete for the carters of the brykke xviiid payd to Robert Scott for VM=5000 brykk for the new battlymnt xxvs."

The gild-hall of the corporation

This occurs in a note of 1596 of money allowed towards " the provydyng of a clocke in Donmowe yeld hall."

GREAT DUNMOW BELLS 1526–51

From the time of its earliest records Great Dunmow has shown its pride in its ring of bells by laying out much money on the care of the bells themselves and on the building and maintenance of the belfry. Besides the ring of bells there were the sanctus bell, the four little bells that belonged to the Corpus Christi Day possession, and the bell on which the clock struck the hours. " 1526 payd to John Oltyng for mendynge of the clapers the yere afore thatt we cam on vis viiid; payd to Kynge for trussynge up the bell clappers id. payd to Marryon for mendyng the bells on All halows evyn viiid [to make them safe for the peal rung that night]. There was a collection for the belfry tower in 1526 and the names of the subscribers are given; 156 householders gave among them £13/1/8. The chief gifts were Thomas Savage, churchwarden £3/6/8; John Parcar, fletcher (arrow-maker), Mr. Kynwelmershe 18/-. Thomas Savage was a builder. His large gift probably represents the repayment of what he received for his work and advice regarding the church. Mr. Kynwelmershe's gift is the amount charged for timber bought from him. John Parker occurs several times as a wealthy and open-handed townsman. The church staff was represented by " Richard Sturton, sumtyme vycar 5s. mayster vycar thatt now ys 6s. 8d. Sur John Mylton 3s. Sur Wyllam Wroo 20d [these are two clergy connected with the church], Robard Sturton Cherche Clarke 8d, Richard Cokke (organist)12d."

Six poor parishioners gave 1d. each, one being " Jone Palgrave wedow."

In 1527 the bells were hung in the newly finished tower, but failed to give satisfaction. In 1528 an agreement was entered into with a London firm to have the bells recast. The collection for recasting the bells in 1529 is the most minutely recorded of the parish collections of the age, and a summary of it is interesting as showing the localities of Dunmow parish in 1529.

Locality	*Amount*			*Contributors*	*Refusals*
The hole towne	£3	0	4	15	2
The Hye strete ..		10	9	14	4
Rymell strete ..		4	6	18	2
Bulloke rowe ..		1	5	14	3
New strete......		6	4	8	3
Broke ende		6	2	11	2
Personage downs		1	10	8	1
Cherche ende ..		7	9	11	0
Byggodes quarter		8	1	8	0
Hywode quarter		6	5	8	0
Byshopwode quarter		9	7	14	3
Forthe ende			7	3	1

There is a record of expenditure on the recasting of the bells in 1529, on their carriage to and from London and on rehanging them. These were not a success and were still not in tune, and had to be returned to London, as some were too light. Therefore the bell-founder made a claim for " additional metal xxs." So henceforth the bells were insured.

The bells were apparently rung at first from the ground floor of the tower, but in 1533 steps seem to have been taken to provide a gallery or upper floor for the ringers.

In 1536 a public subscription for a new bell was started, but only about fifty householders responded. The sale of church plate in that year was possibly ordered to make up the amount required.

The next collection was for the great bell, which needed a new clapper.

The Curfew Bell 1541. Robert Dossyter was paid for a whole year's " ryngyng of the Curfew, vis & iiiid." (tips for the ringers). On All Saints' night (November 1) and on All Souls (November 2) there was a solemn ringing of the bells and an entertainment for the ringers. " 1550 payed for ryngyng on All Sowles viiid. 1551 payed to ryngers on All Seynts day at nyght iis."

CHAPTER VI

Great Dunmow church from 1526–1546

I would like to restrict this otherwise unpublished information as far as possible and let the records tell their own tale. So much happened in the Church in these years; our church was no exception.

The sanctus or sacring bell

The sanctus bell was a small bell rung to call the attention of the parish to the more solemn parts of the communion service, as when the words " Holy, holy, holy " were pronounced, or when the elements were lifted up after consecration. Usually the bell was in a small turret standing on the roof over the chancel arch and was rung by a cord from within the church. " 1526 payd for a sans-bell rope 11d. 1531 payd for viii vadam [fathom] lyne for the sanctus bell rope 11d. 1533 payd for nayles for the sannus bell and for the windowe into the re-vestyre 1d. 1534 payd to Robert Mason for mendyng of the sance bell whele vid. payd for lyne for the sakeryng-bell and for the chapel bell vd. 1542 payd to Robert Mason & Robert Dossiter for mendyng the whele of the sawnus-bell viiid. 1557 payd for making a new whele for the saunce-bell xiiiid. 1562 payd for lyne for the caunce bell xi fadem vd. 1568 payd for the sance-bell rope and a matt vid."

The corporas

The corporas, or corporas-case, was a cloth of fine linen laid upon the altar, on which the communion elements were placed during consecration and which was folded over them after consecration. " 1527 payd for ii ii [= 1lb.] and a halfe of whyght sope to washe the corpravis and receden of the church gere xd. 1543 payd to Mr. Vicar —— for the makyng off the cannape-clothe of velvet and of a corporas-case vii vid."

The pyx and canopies

The pyx was a small box of silver in which was placed the consecrated wafer, which was reserved for adoration in church or in readiness for such communion. The pyx was hung over the high altar by a cord and pulley to enable it to be raised or lowered at will. Over it was laid a cloth, called a canopy, sometimes a more elaborate canopy and probably painted with sacred emblems. " 1529 payd for a lyne for the Sacrament id. [for a cord to hang up the pyx] 1529 payd for clothynge of the canape and makynge the iryn warke and for payntynge of the same xivd. 1539 payd to Robert Dossyter, sexton for skoryng [scouring] the canapy vid. 1543 payd to Syr John for a canape clothe ivs."

At the end of Holy Week this canopy was draped in some particular way, which required many pins. " 1527 payd for pynnes and nayles for the canape iid. 1541 payd for the sepultar and the canype 11d."

The church lantern and handbell

For sick communion the pyx with the consecrated wafer was carried by the priest, wearing his surplice, from the altar to the sick person. To warn people on the street to prepare to meet it with due respect a clerk, or chorister, went in front with a handbell. In readiness for sick communion if required during the hours of darkness there was a lantern kept in the church. " 1541 payd for mendyng the lytle hand-bell viiid. 1551 payd for mendyng the hand-bell iiid. 1527 payd for hornyng of the church lantern viiid. 1534 payd for a lantorne to go with the sacrement viiid."

The sepulchre

This was a commemoration of the entombment from Good Friday evening till Easter morning. A wooden structure was set up against the north side of the chancel. On Good Friday the pyx containing the wafer consecrated on Maundy Thursday was taken from the high altar and ceremoniously placed in the sepulchre. Watchers remained by it till Easter morning, when it was replaced on the altar. These watchers were provided with a wax light and a fire of charcoal. In Edward VI's reign these boards were destroyed, and then at the coming of Mary they had to be replaced. Easter 1588 was the last time the sepulchre was set up at Dunmow. " 1529 payd for nayles for the sepoultre and pynnes for the canapy iiiid. 1534 payd for thred, pynnes and nayles for the sepulker iid. 1543 payd for pynns and nayles for the sepoultre id."

After 1551 and before 1558 " payd to Thomas Steward for iii crestes & vi transumes viii brases and viii or ix spars and ii postes for the sepulchre iiis payd out for nayles and staples for the same vid. Payd to Robert Parker, tyler, to sett in two staples into the wall iiiid. 1543 payd to William George to tendyng sepulcer lyght iiiid. Payd to John Bykener iiiis id. and half iis. iiid. 1545 payd Harry Tomson for ii bussell of coles to watche the sepulker at Ester iiiid. 1551 payd to George for wacchyng to sepulkyr iiiid."

The palm cross

Great Dunmow has a few notices concerning its palm cross, a church ornament but rather unusual. There was great use made of catkined willow branches to represent palm branches. The palm cross may have been a framework intended to be decorated in this way for Palm Sunday. It is not clear where it stood, but one might conjecture outside the church. It was discontinued under Edward and replaced under Mary. "1544. payd Mr. Kynwelmarsh for tymber for the palme crosse vid. Payd to John Scoryar for the mendyne of the sade crosse xiid, for the borde for the same with iii, nayles ixd. Payd to Hutt for spykes and for mendyng of the palme crosse yerns [irons] 1554 payd for making the palme crosse. To Buntyng for sawynge of flower spores [spars] iiid. To William Swetinge for 2 days and a half work and Barker one day iiis. To John Mayne for the converynge and the goblets and the bordes ivid to Nicholas Moyne for the tymber iis. vid."

The paschal

The paschal, generally spelt " pascall," was a wax candle of unusual length and thickness which was lit at Easter. It was placed on a wooden disc with a sharp spike and this disc was suspended by cords from the roof of the church in front of the high altar. Like most of these decorative accessories, it was done away with in Edward's time but was revived in Mary's. " 1541 payd for whipcorde for the pascall iid. 1553 payd for mendyne the pascall—to John Moyne for makynge a hede pece with a poolee [pulley] iiiid. To John Hawkins for makynge two strings with ii hookes and ii staples vd, for smale lyne xvi yards and a peece of great lyne xiiid; for iiii grete nayles for the pascall."

The processional canopy

On Corpus Christi Day the pyx was taken in solemn procession through the town. On this occasion the surpliced priest, who bore it, walked under a canopy, which was held up by four gilded staves and had a small bell at each corner to warn people of its approach. " 1526 payd for claperyng of iii letell bells for the canape id. 1541 payd to Harry Tomson for iiii staves for the canype xivd. and for paynctyng and gyldyng of the staves vid."

The lamp

A lamp was kept burning all night in the

chancel in front of the high altar. There are constant notices as to its oil-supply, its rush-wicks and sometimes a new glass funnel. " 1526 layde out for the cherche;—for iv galuns of oyle for the lampe vs.iiiid, for iii lampe glasses iiid; for mendyng of the furnes of the lampe to Skoryar iid. 1534 payd for oyle ii galons for the lampe iiis. iiiid; for roches [rushes] ½d. 1539 received Mr. Josselyn to kepe the lampe lyght vs. 1540 payd to Gilbert Cooke for two bottles of lampe oyle obulus. 1542 payd for a quarte of rape oyle for the lampe iiid."

The candlesticks

The light for the organist, choir and clergy was no doubt furnished by candles. There are several notices of latten (brass) candle-sticks, two very large ones and six smaller. These were " scored " (scoured) and polished once a year. " 1536 payd for shoryne off the cherche latyne xvid. 1539 received for a payer of candelstycks, sold to Rowland the pewterer vis, viiid; gathered in the cherche for the latten candelstycks (9s. 5d. from 73 sub-scribers, including iid. from ' Sir ' Thomas, the parysh priest and a i from ' Sir ' Nickolas). 1541 payd to mother West for skouryng the grete latten lecterne and chansel and standerds and small ones xxiid. 1543 payd to Johne West for oyle for [polishing] the small lecterne ½d. 1559 payd to Tylberies wife for scoringe the lecterne and candel-stycks xiiid."

Candles for Christmas

For a few years from 1546 the church-wardens provided candles for use on Christ-mas morning. " 1546 in the xxxviii yere of Henry the eyghthe; payd for iiii candells at crysmas iiiid. 1555 payd for candels at Christ-mas daye mornyng and for nayles for the canapie iid. 1559 payd for ii lbs of candels for Christmas morning vd."

The rood light

" 1526 payd to John Bykner for strykynge of iii. and ii off betyngs for the rood lyght iiid and to the sade John for strykynge the rood light xivd; for xxii ii [= two and twenty] lb of wax for the rood lyght xiis and [7d. a lb." This continues for many years, and one cannot quite understand what is meant by " betyngs." It could mean the gutterings of the old lights beaten off the candlesticks and scones.

In the same way a wax candle was burned before the image of the Virgin in the chancel in a " bason." This was more probably something like a nightlight and generally appears as a half-yearly charge. " 1529 payd for iii ii & iii quarter [3¾lb.] of wax for the lyght of oure laydy in the chansell and on the bason in the cherche with strykynge iis; payd to John Bykner for ii ii wax and the strykynge and for the bason afore oure lady in the cherche and afore oure lady in the chansell xiiid." This is repeated more or less every six months.

Burials

The church owned a bier. Wax torches were burned at funerals. These were provided by the church and a sum was paid on each occasion according to the time they were burned. Burials might take place in the floor of the church. For these a fee was charged, but the churchwardens had to pay for making the floor good. " 1531 payd to John Skorear for mendyng the bier and plancheryng the orgayn xiid and for nayles iid. 1543 payd to Masyn for mendyng the bier iid."

" 1531 payd to John Beckener for iiii torches xxs,xid. 1539 payd to John Beckener makyng iiii newe torches ivd. payd for quarter of wycke for the sede torches iiis. viiid. payd for xiii wax for the seyd torches xviis. iid. 1529 receyved of my laydy Gatyes for waste of the torchys xiid. 1542 receyved for the buryall of Mr. Jenour in the churche and for the torchys att his beryall xvis. iiiid."

Replacing of crosses, hangers and banners

" 1554 payd to Father Andrewes for a crosse of tymber xiid. 1554 payd for rings for the vayele and for the ii clothes in the qwyer [choir] and wyre for the same ii clothes iiiid and for a lyne for the vayele id 1554 payd to Wyllyam Joyner for shaninge the bannyer poles viiid to Thomas Hawkins for payntynge the bannyer staves ivd."

Rebuilding the fixed altars

" 1553 payd for the makyne the xis.iid. for carryyng the brycke xiis. to Hawkins for makynge ii yrons for the hange over curtains for the highe altar lld obolus [$=2\frac{1}{2}$d.] for whipcorde and rings to hange the blacke sykle clothe at the highe altar iid. 1553 to Want for xii foete [feet] of tymber for the gryer & of St. John altar xviiid."

Rebuilding the rood

The rood screen on which the rood rested, the rood-curtains and the apparatus (metal bowls) for the rood lights were also replaced. " 1554 payd in earneste for the roode to Burle vs. and to Andrews for his earneste vid. payd for the makynge of the rood, with the appurtances iii (i ix iiid); a staple and hooke for the rood, ii braised burthens to beare the curtein yrons long a yarde; for makyne ii stayes for ii images, John and Mary and for makynge xvi nayles xviid; halfe a dayes worke being with the smythe to tell him how to make the yron iiid; to John Moyse for ix foete of borde and joynynge vid; for xxii foete of borde for the same xiid; for making the skaffolds and other warke xvid, to nayle for the same iiid, for making the bordes meet for the standynge iid, payd to Andrewes iii tymes xixs, viiid; payd at another tyme xxviis & viiid for nayles iiid obolus [$3\frac{1}{2}$d.] to Dosseter [sexton] for his paynes xvid. for breade and ale at the settynge up of the rood vd; for father Andrewes bordyne for carrynge of the roode, for makyng ii yrons & iiii staples for the trimmer of the rood iid; for a keye for the roode-lofte door to Owtyng vid. Payd for sewing together of ii pieces of the churche lynnen and mendyng of them when they weare broken and the sewinge on of the rynges, to Barker's wife to kener the roode vd. [for the rood cloth] for xix ryngs of tyrone; xiii yards of ynckel, syx fadom of lyne ii pieces of whippcorde and to Bryce for a stable and for breade and drinke for them that dyd helpe to have upp the clothe xviid."

Reglazing the windows

During the Edwardian troubles much damage had been done to the windows, probably in the way of breaking panels with saints and mottoes on them. " 1554 to John Strachie for mendyne the glass wyndows throughout all the churche abd for the wyndowes over the chappell xxiiis. viiid. to John Turner for mendyne the wyndowe over Saint John's."

Replacing discarded utensils

" Payd for a payer of sensors [censers] viis for a crwett of tynne vid. to Wyllyam Strward for ii crwetts xxiid; for a holie breade pecke vid to John Neverd, church clerk, for a holie water poll iis."

Replacing and repairing vestments

" Payd for a skayne of redd thredd to mend the copes and for ii broade ynche for gyrdles for the ables id; and for ii gyadles of broade inkle iid."

Replacing and repairing service books

" Payd to John Neverd for a booke of parchment, conteyninge in yt a Venite booke an Ymnall and a booke for deriges and berialls vis. & xd. John Byckner for a antiphenar xxs and for byndynge the same. Payd for a lengent [legenda, a book of daily lessons] of the largest volume and for the carryage from London, xivs. & ivd."

Elizabeth's reign seems to have begun by a pawning of Church property. " 1559 payd to Mr. Glascock and to ' Goodman ' Melbourne for monye, they layed owte to redeme the latten lectern, the organes the iiii bell vs. & iiii hutches Is. [Wm. Glascock had been churchwarden in 1547.] Payd for ii ells of cavas which Mr. Josselen caused us to bye to put the churche goods in xvid. Receyved from Mr. Josselyn xxxvii ivd. Receyved for xxxis iid of latten [brass] of that which laye over the gravestones. ivs. viiid."

[The old brasses were no doubt torn off because they were inscribed with petitions, in Latin or French, craving mercy on the souls of the deceased.] "Receyved for a vestment and a booke of William Collen xiis. Receyved for ii chalyces sold wayenge xxxi ounces and a quarter at fower shyllings and fower pence the ownce, viii xvs. vd."

There followed, 1559-61, breaking of pictured windows, smashing of holy-water stoups in the porch, destruction of the rood, blotting out of murals and removal of the altars. " 1559 payd to Simon Blythe for mendynge of glass wyndowes in the churche and the greate wyndowe in the chancell; xvs iiiid; for vi bussells of lyme for the glasyer and for to fyll upp the holes in the churche [caused by taking down the rood screen] and the holy water stoups and for the whyghte lymyng ivs. spent at the burnynge of the roode-stode xiid. payd to John Keme for helpynge down the auter vid; for takynge downe of the ii auters and the pavynge iis.iid."

CHAPTER VII

Dunmow church through the Reformation

We are apt to think that the twelve years 1547-59 must have vividly impressed all parishioners of that time. During these years there occurred everywhere confiscation of parish property, suppression of ancient ceremonies, destruction of church furniture and the change of services into English. Mary's accession in 1553 brought back the antiquated usages and the discarded ornaments and furniture, but at her death these disappeared for good under Elizabeth. One would have thought that such drastic changes would have been well documented, but in fact contemporary records of these changes are very meagre indeed. They do not explain distinctly what was done, or give much idea of the stages by which the changes followed each other. The following is about all one can gather about Great Dunmow. I have looked up several other parishes and in each case it has been the same. People did not report much in those days—it was probably safer not to do so. Much of what is recorded is very confused and not easy to sort out. Wealthy testators often settled money on trustees to provide for them permanent commemorative services—if once a year on the anniversary of the founder's death it was called an obit, but if it was a daily commemoration the foundation was called a chantry. There does not seem to have been either at Great Dunmow, which is rather rare, but there were chantry and obit lands and one of the first acts of Edward VI was to confiscate these as being superstitious and illegal. The money from the sale of these lands was, of course, laid hold of by the king's exchequer. The only mention of this in Great Dunmow is very brief. Before1551: paid churchwardens' expenses " at Braintree before Commissioners of the chawntre and obyte lands 11s. VIIId."

Most churches had become possessed of a quantity of brass and silver vessels, richly embroidered vestments and curtains, candlesticks, crosses, lecterns, etc., given by many benefactors. In 1539: " payd Robert Dossyter [sexton and bellringer] for skoryng [polishing] the latten [brass] lectern and other latten in the church VIIId. Paid to Mr. John Kylwelmarsh for a paver [pair] of grett latten candylstycks XXVIs.VIIId. Paid to Mother Harte for shorying the grett candylstycks IIIId."

When hard pressed for money for church purposes the wardens often sold their plate. " 1529 payd for IIII casys for the chalyssys XVId. 1531 payd Syr George for a pyx of silver VIIs [Syr G. was probably the priest, who was generally called Syr]. 1534 payd for mendyng the sylver plate Xs. 1536 resayfyd for the cherche pllat solld by Robert May and Robert Howchyn and Richard Dykellyng [churchwardens] witnesses John Bycner and John Foster, the sum of XXXIIII ovnses CXIXS IId solde syne the laste accownte XV, ownesses of platt paxe sylver & II crewetts, for IIIs,VIIId a ownesse fower mark & xxd [=£2/15/-]. 1539 received of the wyffes of the parysh, whych they gathered in the

Church for to redeme the pax Vs. Payd to Robert Maye for the sylver pax XXIXs IIIId."

There were sets of vestments of different ecclesiastical colours and similar hangings of silk or velvet, often heavily worked with gold and silver thread. Vestments in the narrower sense meant chasuble, the sleeveless surplice worn at mass which the priest lifted up with his hands at each side. " 1529 payde for mendyng of the best sewte that father Dowe gave XXXIVs and VIIId the same coppys XV11d. 1532 payd to Ashebye for mending the rede cope XXd [the cope was a sleeveless, semi-circular shoulder-cape worn outside other vestments on occasions of special solemnity, and was richly embroidered]. 1536 payd for mendyng of 11 velvet coppys and 11 tunykylls andmaking of a cope and dying of festment [vestment] and for things that went to them [materials] wyth workemanshipe, XXIXs. Payd to Ashebye for mendyng the whyghte coppys XV1d. 1541 payd to Robert Ashebye for mendyng the blake cope XX11d. 1542 payd to Martyn for a vestment [or chasuble] and a tunycle of black velvet XXS. 1543 payd Ashebye for mendyng a cope of rede velvet and for mendyng the rede vestment of damaske X11d."

There were service books of all kinds for the use of the clergy and choir, written on parchment and originally acquired at great cost. The antiphoners, or books of music, were particularly costly both to acquire and to maintain. " 1535 payd for mendyng of the antiphoner XVs and for writing and collatyng 11 other antiphonaries, Payd for XIX days worke of 11 men V11d a daye each XX11s X1d; for a dayes worke of one man V11d. Payd for XX1 t 1 [one and twenty] dayes worke of 11 men V11d a daye each XX1Vs.V1d. Payd for the stuffe that went to the bokes X1Vs.V111d. 1541 payd, imprimis, to the stachenner [stationer] for V wekes worke correctyng and byndeyng of the antiphoner after, V111 daye XXs. Item for 11 burthens and 11 claspes for the sayd bokes 11d. Item to John Byckner for purchasyng the sayd boke [probably the parchment]. Item unto Thomas Bennyshe for a calves skynne [for bynding] VX1d. Item for a whyghte skynne and 11 rede X1111d. Item for the bowrdes for the sayd boke 11d. blake threde 1d. Item to John Neverd, church clerk for XX1111ti [four and twenty] dayes worke for to examen [collate] the sayd boke after 11d. the daye and also for ynke, both blake and rede IIIIs."

In 1551 an order was made by Edward VI's advisers that these church goods should be sold, partly as superstitious, partly superfluous. The intention was that the proceeds should go the same way as the money derived from the chantries, but the Dunmow churchwardens seem to have retained for their parish at least part of the plunder. They knew what was coming; they had been through the Reformation. So before 1551 we read that the churchwardens and others went to John Whales's to dinner to talk over the selling of the church plate. Whales knew what to expect; he had been churchwarden in 1537. One can just imagine that dinner at the local and their scheming how best to cheat the government of the time. Few people could write, and on all formal occasions a professional scribe was employed. " 1547 received for olde latten [brass] sold in London waying i C,iqtr. [1cwt. 1qtr. 18lb] XViii at XX11s cwt. which amounted in the hole to XXXis. Before 1551 " received for latten xxx1111s payd for carriage of latten to London iiis.iiiid." Before 1551 " received for church platt fyrst solde by Thomas Colfyld, Thomas Cooke and William Drapyr [churchwardens] viiilis.xd. Received for platt sold by Thomas Colfyld, John Melbourn, Alisander Sturton. Thomas Cooke and William Drapyr xlvli.viis,vid. Before 1551 " received for a cloth afore the crucifixe iis. Received of Launcet Maydson for bokes solde viiis."

The most striking features of medieval churches were the altars, great crucifixes and images. The altars were of stone or alabaster, fixed to the church wall, and each church in addition to the high altar had others in the aisles. Dunmow had two besides the high altar. " 1531 payd for dressyng the iii altars with alabaster iiis. 1536 payd for the burnys-scheyng of Seynt John's outer and seynt George auter iiis. & iiid."

Over the chancel screen stood the great wooden rood, with the figure of Christ in his passion and the traditional figures of St. Mary and St. John standing or kneeling at the foot of the cross. This screen was often gilded. It was furnished with a curtain, which was drawn over it on special occasions. A light was kept burning before it, especially on festival days. " 1532 payd to Thomas Turner for gyldyng the crosse vis. viiid. 1534 payd for goolde to gyld the crosse viis.vid and for v busshells of coles [charcoal, for the goldsmithe vd. for ii ounces of mercury for the sayd worke ivd. 1526 payd for xviii ryngs for the vavle & settyng on iiid payd for parte of the makyng of the closett for the roode iis. 1533 payd for a peys lyne for to draw up the rode clothe viid. 1541 payd for mendyng of the Rode loft clothe and for necessities that went thereto viid. 1542 payd to Byckner for sandwiche cord for the vayle id. 1545 payd to John Byckner for vilii mex and for strybyng the rode lyhgt at Ester ivs iid; payd to the same for Hallowmas iiis. vd. 1539 Recaynyd of the parysh and gathered in the churche to wards the buyng of the tabarnacle viis. and vid. Paid to Mr. Note for itt [the tabernacle] bought at Hatfield xxs."

In 1547 the king's ministers ordered a general visitation of all churches, to discover what changes were desirable. This resulted in orders in 1549 to remove all images and in 1550 to take down all fixed altars and replace them by one movable communion table of wood. Between 1549 and 50 " payd at the Kyngs visitation for the questes (sidesmen) and churchwardens att denner iiiis. and iiid. Payd to Yngram and Parker for takyng downe the altars and carrying aweye the rubbysh iiis; other expensys at the removyng thereof vid. Paid in 1550-1 for drynke at the pulling down of the rode, ivd. Received for a tabyll [the wooden back of the rood screen] iis. Received of Mr. Baker for the tabyrnakyll of Oure Lady of Petye vs. Received of George Raymond for gylt xvid." (Our Lady of Pity was an image of the Virgin supporting the dead body of Christ.)

In Henry VIII's time there had been a great whitewashing, to obliterate the more superstitious of the mural paintings. Edward VI's men completed the work. " 1543 payd to Thomas Bennysshe for a seme of lyme to whyte the churche wythe all xvid and to Thomas Cocke for ii busshells of lyme iiiid." The workmen were Rychard Hatche, who worked ten days and was paid " vs "; Peter, thirteen days, " vis. and vid "; and a labourer, Humphrey, eight days for " 11s. and viiid."

In 1539 the Great Bible (otherwise known as Cranmer's) appeared. The descriptive name was due to its size and the preface was written by Archbishop Thomas Cranmer. It had been expressly printed to be chained at a desk in churches by royal command so as to be accessible to all who could read. The cost of this Bible and the fixing of it was to be defrayed half by the vicar and half by the parish. At Michaelmas 1550 the out-going churchwardens retained the sum of " viiis wych was toward the byng of the byble."

In 1549 the parish had to provide the new service books in English, and also to contri-bute half costs towards a public copy of the " Paraphrase of Erasmus upon the Newe Testament." 1549-50 " payd for the com-munyon books iis for iii Saltyrs books vis. payd for half of the paraphrasye vs."

Great lamentation was made over the absence of charity. The confiscation of the chantries and the suppression of the masses had done away with parish subsidies and offerings which formerly had been available for relief of the poor. To meet this difficulty the king's advisers ordered that every church should have an alms-box. " 1549 payd John

Hutt for stapylls and claspys for the almes box iid."

When Mary came to the throne the Privy Council sent out officials to see that the ancient ornaments and furniture were replaced. " 1553 payd the pryvie sercher for thinges wanting in the churche. Receyved of Mr. Kynwelmarsh for the beryall of his daughter in the church xxd; payd to Richard Parcar for pavyng of the grave in the churche of the same vid [possibly an infant, to judge by the fees]. 1543 payd to Richard Barker for laying the stone over master Jenour's grave xiiid. Payd for quartern of pament [pavement] tyle for the same grave viiid. February 8, 1546/7, receyvd of Robert Parker and Nycolas Parker, for the buriall of olde Parker in the churche vis and viiid."

Incense

Incense was used freely in the services, but no charge appears for it, so it was probably given privately by members of the congregation. " 1541 payd for a frye-panne to fctche in coles to sense vd."

Church furniture

The font is mentioned in connection with " holes over it," possibly caused by the font-cover suspended from the roof. The font-cover seems to have been secured by a lock. Perhaps it had something to do with the superstition concerning evil spirits. There were two hutches or chests. " Stools " occur more than once, but not as stools has anything of the sort come down to our day. A pew is mentioned, apparently as being removed because it was made without leave. " 1526 payd to Richard Scoryar for pavynge the cherche and for mendyne of a hole over the funtt xd. 1553 [after the Edwardian destruction]. Payd to Bryce for makyng 2 sqware staples and ii lesser, and a bolte for the fonte iiid, and for hewyage the holes in the stone and for settynge in of the said staples and a locke vd. 1553 payd to John Carvar for swepyng of the Churche and for scowryng of the lecterne vid. 1526 to John Skoryar for mendyng of the hotchys and of the stoles viid for his bord the same tyme iiid. and ii planks for the same hotchys vid to Wyllem Hott for nayles yerne [iron] warke xd and for other small nales for the same iid; and for ii dayes warke of Thomas Savage in the same tyme viiid. 1532 payd for sowdreng a hold in the lead over Master Kynwelmarsh stool iiid."

The Kynwelmarsh family, of Newton Hall, were important. Towards the new organ in 1531 this family subscribed " vis. viiid " and masters John Richard and Edmond " xxs. vid vis viiid " as their own offering. " 1543 payd to Clement the joyner for xi dayes warke of his man to joyne the stolys vis vid. 1557 payd to the joyner for takynge upp Mrs. Bakers pewe iiid."

Church linen and vestments

The more important references to vestments have been dealt with elsewhere. However, the leading notices of the surplice, the proper dress of officiating clergy during service, except mass, were much the same as today. " 1529 gatherde of the wynes for the makynge of the surplys seys iiis and iiid. Payd for 13 ells of hollan clothe at viid an ell and xvi ells of whytyd normundy at vid an ell—the pryce of the hole xxs with the whyted clothes we made iii surplysses and vi rochalls payd for the same iiis and iiiid. 1531 payd for mendyng of ' Sir John's ' syrplas iid [John Melton, vicar]. 1543 payd for xvi yerds of locram for making surplyeses viis and id. 1556 payd for x ells of licram for makynge the same into iiii playne surplysses and for mendynge of viii old ones xis and vid."

Then comes the alb, the special robe worn at mass under the vestment or chasuble. It was a narrow linen gown, sleeved and often richly embroidered at the lower border. It was confined at the waist by a girdle. " 1526 payd for sleuyng [sleeving] of an al b with new clothe vid. 1531 payd to Perse for mendyng ii gowyns iiiid. 1541 payd for mendyng of an alb and for clothe that went there to iiiid."

Queen Elizabeth's commissioners issued

injunctions on October 10, 1561, to the effect that although the rood was to be taken down the screen could remain if it had not already been destroyed. I can only suppose that it had been burnt with the rood, for I find no trace of a screen since that time. " 1559 payd for a communion book [now lost] in the fyrst years of the reigne of Elizabeth oure Queene ivs; for the booke of Holilyes xd. 1561 payd for the Ten Commandments at Hatfield xvid; for the lockes for the Regester cofer and for the poor man's hutche [alms] bos xiid. 1562 payd for a Register book from London xxd."

CHAPTER VIII

Feet of fines

25 Edward I. Easter Term 1297.

Jollan de Dunoln and Ada his wife plaintiff. Richard Loveday of Berardeshey and Basilia his wife imp. 16 acres of land in Gt. Dumore. Pleas of warranty of charter. Plaintiff and the heirs of Jollan to hold of the chief lords. Consideration 10L.

34 Edward I. Hilary Term 1306.

Ralph Bigot of Gt. Dunmawe plaintiff. Reyner Fitz Reyner of Gt. Dunmawe and Sabina his wife defendants. One messuage 60 acres of land 3 acres of meadow and 10 acres of pasture in Gt. Dunmawe. Plea of covenant. Reyner acknowledged the premises to be the right of plaintiff, as those which he has of his gift, and for this plea granted the same to the defendant and the heirs of the body of Sabina, they rendering 1 rose at the Nat of St. J.B. and doing to the chief lords all other services with reversion to plaintiff and his heirs.

3 Edward II. Michaelmas 1310.

John Olyne and Margery his wife plaintiff. Hugh Olyne def. One messuage, 28 acres of land and 5s. 4d. of rent in Gt. Dunmawe. Plaintiff and the heirs of John to hold of the chief lords consideration 20L.

7 Edward II. Michaelmas 1314.

Wm. Saward the Elder plaintiff. Stephen de Lorimer and Mabel his wife defendants. 2 acres and a moiety of 1 rood of land at Gt. Dunmawe. Plaintiff and his heirs to hold of the chief lords.

8 Edward II. Trinity 1315.

Wm. le Drapere and Maud his wife, plaintiff. Richard rector of Gt. Dunmawe defendant. 1 messuage in Gt. Dunmawe. William acknowledged the messuage to be the right of defendant as that which defendant has of his gift, and for this defendant granted it to plaintiff and the heirs of their bodies to hold of the chief lords, with remainder to the right heirs of William.

10 Edward II. Michaelmas 1317.

Warin Martel and Margaret his wife, plaintiff. Richard, vicar of Gt. Dunmawe defendant. 3 messuages, 130 acres of land, 4 acres of meadow, 2 acres of pasture, 8 acres of wood and 26s. 8d. rent in Gt. Dunmawe. Warin acknowledged the tenements to be the right of defendant, as those which defendant had of his gift, and for this defendant granted them to plantiff to hold for their life of the chief lords with successive remainders to John son of Warin and William and Ralph his brothers, and the heirs of their bodies, and the right heirs of Warin.

11 Edward II. Hilary 1318.

Richard son of Brownessone, plaintiff. Warin son of William le Draper and Margery his wife, defendants. Messuage in Gt. Dunmawe plaintiff and his heirs to hold of the chief lords, consideration 100s of silver.

13 Edward II. Michaelmas 1300.

Agnes Perrles plaintiff. Nicholas le Meleward of Gt. Donmawe and Alice his wife defendants. 1 messuage in Gt. Dunmawe.

Defendants quitclaimed from themselves and the heirs of Nicholas to plaintiff and her heirs. Consideration 100s silver.

19 Edward II. Trinity 1326.

Edmund Pygown plaintiff. Henry Frawceys and Gunnora his wife defendants. 1 messuage and 7 acres of land in Gt. Dunmawe. Plaintiff and his heirs to hold of the chief lords. Consideration 10 marks of silver.

II Edward I. Easter 1283.

William son of Robert de Bumpstede, and Maud his wife plaintiff. Richard de la Vache defendant. Manor of Rocoltehall. Plea of covenant. Plaintiff and heirs of the body of William to hold of defendant by the yearly rent of ½ a knights fee for all service and exaction. If William die without issue, the manor to revert after death of Maud to defendant. For this agreement William granted to defendant I messuage, 1 carucate of land, 12 acres of wood, 6 acres of meadow, and 18s rent in Bumpstede, to hold to defendant and his heirs of the chief lords of that fee. Also the reversion (after the death of Geoffrey, son of Matthew de Bumpstede who held for the term of his life) of 1 messuage, 1 acre of land, 8 acres of wood, 7 acres of wood in Dunmawe; to hold, together with the first said premises, of the chief lords of that fee. This agreement was made in the presence of the said Geoffrey, who acknowledged he had no claim in the said premises save for term of his life, and did fealty to defendant in court.

21 Edward I. Trinity 1293.

Robert Fitz Walter and Walter his son plaintiffs. Robert Pech and Agnes his wife impedients. Plea of warranty of charter. Plaintiff and heirs of Walter to hold of the chief lords. And for this the same Robert Fitz Walter granted to the impedients the manor of Dunmawe to hold for their lives, rendering 1d yearly at the Nat of J.B. and doing to the chief lords all other services, with reversion to Robert Fitz Walter and his heirs.

31 Edward I. Trinity 1301.

John Gamelm plaintiff by John Dyen. Robert de Merk defendant by Thomas Scharp. The manor of Dunmawe. Plea of Covenant. Defendant acknowledged the manor to be the right of plaintiff as that which he had of his gift and for this plaintiff granted the same to defendant and to Jackomina his wife and the heir of defendant of her body, with remainder to the right heirs of defendant, This agreement was made precept of the King.

48 Edward III. Michaelmas 1375.

John de Haryngworth of Barton and his wife Agnes plaintiff, by Henry Banastre in her place. Richard Bakere of Gt. Dunmawe and Ismania his wife. 1 messuage in Dunmawe, defendant quitclaimed to plaintiff and the heirs of John. Consideration 100 marks.

4 Edward III. Michaelmas 1330.

John Olyne and Avice his wife, and Hugh Olyne plaintiff by John de Dependen keeper of Hugh. Luke Primerole defendant. 1 messuage 42½ acres of land and 1½ acres of meadow in Gt. Dunmawe. Plaintiff of the heirs of the bodies of John and Avice to hold of the chief lords, with remainder to the right heirs of John. Endorsed John son of John Olyne puts in his claim.

19 Edward III. October 1345.

Stephen de Cantebrigg and Avice his wife plaintiffs. Henry Gernet and John his wife defendants. 3 acres of meadow in Gt. Dunmawe plaintiffs and the heirs of Stephen to hold of the chief lords. Consideration 100s.

20 Edward III. Trinity 1346.

Adam de Lynford plaintiff Hugh de Portesmuth and Alice his wife defendant, 4 messuages, 15 acres of land, and 1 acre of meadow in Great Dunmawe, plaintiff and his heirs to hold 2 messuages and the land and meadow of the chief lords, and also the reversion of 2 messuages which John Uggle and Denise his wife hold for her life. Consideration 20 marks.

21 Edward III. Trinity 1347.

Gilbert le Smith of Gt. Dunmowe and Margaret his wife, plaintiff by Richard de Fifhide in her place. Walter Denemed of Gt. Dunmowe and Christina his wife defendants. 9 acres of land in Gt. Dunmow. Plaintiff and the heirs of Gilbert to hold six acres of the chief lords, and Gilbert and his heirs to hold 3 of the chief lords. Consideration 100s.

22 Edward III. Trinity and Michaelmas 1348.

John Peneral and Lucy his wife plaintiff. John atte Landbrok and Isabel his wife. 1 messuage in Dunmowe. Plaintiff and the heirs of John to hold of the chief lords. Consideration 100s.

25 Edward III. October of Hilary 1351.

John atte House the elder and Joan his wife, plaintiff. John de Sabrichesworth defendant. 90 acres of land, 5 acres of meadow, 2 acres of wood and 8s. rent in High Estre, Bernston and Gt. Dunmowe. Plaintiff and the heirs male of their bodies to hold of the chief Lords, with remainder to the right heirs of John.

26 Edward III. Michaelmas 1352.

Robert Crowe of Gt. Eystanes, plaintiff. John Buntyng of London (goldsmyth) and Joan his wife, defendant. 1 messuage 33 acres land 2 acres of meadow $1\frac{1}{2}$ acres of wood and 2s. rent in Gt. Dunmowe and Gt. Canefield. Defendant quitclaimed to plaintiff and his heirs. Consideration 20 marks.

30 Edward III. Easter 1357.

John Arnold of Gt. Dunmowe plaintiff. John Walram, knight and Eleaner his wife, defendant. I messuage, 1 shop, 140 acres of land, 4 acres of meadow, 4 acres of wood, 7 acres of pasture, and 8sd. rent in Gt. Dunmow. Plaintiff and his heirs to hold of the chief lords. Consideration 20 marks.

32 and 33 Edward III. Easter and Michaelmas 1359.

John Lucas of Plesseys and Margaret his wife plaintiff, by John Dars in her place. Walter Yonge of Gt. Dunmowe defendant. 1 messuage, 100 acres of land, 8 acres of meadow, 4 acres of pasture, $2\frac{1}{2}$ acres of wood, and 24s. rent in Gt. Dunmowe which Alice Heisele holds for life. Plaintiff and the heirs male of their bodies to hold the remainder of the chief lords, with remainder to the right heirs of John. Consideration 100 marks. This agreement was made in the presence of Alice, and she did fealty.

34 Edward III. Quin of Hilary 1360.

Roger Hergast, plaintiff. John atte Pole of Gt. Dunmowe and Margery his wife, defendant. 3 messuages, 10 acres of land and 3 roods of meadow in Gt. Dunmow. Plaintiff and his heirs to hold of the chief lords. Consideration 20 marks.

48 Edward III. Michaelmas 1374.

Simon Smith of Gt. Dunmowe and Margaret his wife, and John his son, plaintiff, by John Dunmowe in place of Margaret and as guardian of John. Richard Straunge of Great Dunmow and Joan quitclaimed to plaintiff and the heirs of John.

50 Edward III. Easter 1376.

Roger Loveday draper of Gt. Dunmowe, plaintiff. John Parker of Rouhey and Agnes his wife, defendant. $7\frac{1}{2}$ acres of land in Great Dunmow defendant quitclaimed to plaintiff and his heirs. Consideration 10 marks.

6 Richard II. Michaelmas 1383.

John Spicer, clerk, John Barton, John Skynnere of Gt. Dunmowe and William Saward the elder, plaintiff by Thomas May in place of the last three. John Northwode of Gt. Dunmowe and Margery his wife defendant. 3 messuages in Gt. Dunmowe. Plaintiff and the heirs of John Spicer to hold of the chief lords. Consideration 100 marks.

QUARTER SESSIONS

September 25, 1562

Indictment of Christian Stret of Barnston, yeoman, and Robert Kynwelmarshe, of Newton Hall, Gent, and Thomas Mason, tailor, both of Great Dunmow, for unlawful entry into a water-mill at Dunmow Priory, the premises of William Benet. Each fined 5/-.

Thursday after Epiphany A.D. 1564. Sessions of the peace held at Braintree. A bridge in Great Dunmow called Park Bridge was usually made by the Queen's Magtie, when the park was in her hands, and not the said Park as in Mr. Justin Weston's hands.

We find another bridge broke and gone, between Moche Donmawe and Rayne call Stebbeyng Ford Bryge, but who shall make them, we do not know. Master Wisemans land on the one side, Vuckes on the other.

The [jury] presenteth that there ys a hye-way from Moche Dunmawe parish to Braintre that is so noysesome that no man can pass without jepardy of horse and man that the parsyshe of Moche Donmowe outht to make it, and it is ordered by the Justices that they shall amend it next yerre, and bestowe all their days works there.

Also we present that at Churche Ende, Dunmore, there is a bridge whiche is daungerous, and so evill that neither horse, nor cart may well pass without danger, neither can men convenientlie parse therebi being the Church path without great annoyaunce. The whiche bridge is to be repaired by the landeholders of the Parsonage. Also the bridge commonlie called Langeholders bridge in the afforesaid parish of Dunmow is likewyse out of repair which must be re-dressed by the landowner thereof being Mr. Jennings and William Longe, both of Dunmore.

Great Dunmow September 19, 14 Elizabeth (A.D. *1572*)

Petty Sessions held before Thomas Aylett and William Collen High Constables, and Thomas Franke and Keneln Throkmorton Justices. John Longe, John Sewell, William Steward and William Bickner, sub-constables, also Henry Barker and Robert Vintner, true and lawful men of Great Dunmow, present William Clark labourer, Hugh Tomson, petty chapman, Robert Hutt, Smith, William Savyn, butcher, to be unlicenced tipplers in Great Dunmow.

September 20, 1573

Anthony Isgore of Great Dunmow husbandman, keeps a common alehouse at the same without licence, and sells beer and ale there contrary to the statute of 5 Edward VI.

July 4, 1573

John Deane of Great Dunmow, Woolen draper, kept play in his house at cards, Richard Cook of Great Dunmow, Tanner, did bowle upon Dunmow Downe the same day. John Sare of Great Dunmow was one month without his furniture of Artillery. William Sweeting and John Johnsone, joiner, were one month the same without their furnyture of Artillery.

That Embres mill leading from Dunmow to Easton parva is very noisome and that Mr. Andrew Jenour and Mr. John Coffell of Embredge mill ought to repair this.

Presentation of the Duchy of Lancaster. That a bridge at Dunmow Park (called Park bridge) is very noisome and ought to be repaired by the Queen.

September 16, 1574

John Sweeting of Great Dunmow, Cloth-worker for entering unlawfully into the free tenement, and possession of Sir Robert Rich, knight, in his manor at Felsted, and catching partridges there with nets, snares, and other engines, contrary to the Act of 11 Henry II. Bound over.

April 14, 1575

Robert Foxe of Great Dunmow, Yeoman, and William Turner of the same Husband-man, to keep the peace towards John Playle of Barnston, husbandman.

D/D

December 29, 1575

William Johnson of Great Dunmow, joiner, for entering the house and close of William Pakeman of the same, and forcibly keeping him out of his own premises, contrary to the statute of 8 Henry VI.

General sessions held April 18, 1577

James Aylett has retained Stephen —— for one year for 41s. Edward Plancke to serve John Moyne for one year for £3 6s. 8d. Evered Gurton, smith to serve Richard Brownyng for one year from Saturday, "cum sennyghte next" and his wages to be 40s. and a shirt 3d. and a pair of hose 7s. and meat and drink. Robert Tamner has retained for one year John Bradshaw, singleman, and his wages are 46s. 8d. and meat and drink. William Phillype, shoe-maker, is retained with Nicholas Aylett for one year and his wages are 50s. with meat and drink.

April 6, 1580

Richard Melbourne of Great Dunmow " hath encroched of the quenes hey waye by estemeacyon iiii rods be yt more or less in length, and in bredth one rod, be it more or les."

April 11, 1580

Phillip Sare of Great Dunmow is bound to his uncle for 1 year and a half, taking by the year 26s. 8d. and for the half year 13s. 4d. Richard Belchampe is bound to Robert Vale of Great Dunmow for one year beginning May 1st next at 40s. for the year.

July 12, 1583

John Pomfrett of Great Dunmow, Butcher, Edward Moynes and William Watson husbandmen, for the said John to keep the peace towards John Collett of Stebbing.

Recoynizances November 24, 1583

William Bickner of Great Dunmow, taverner and John Bickner yeoman, for the said William to appear before Robert, Lord Riche. William Barker of Great Dunmow, butcher, and Henry Barker, yeoman, for the said William to appear. William Lyllye of Great Dunmow, husbandman, Ralph Edwicke and Henry Doughtye to appear and abstain from all unlawful games.

March 18, 1584

William Chamberlayn of Great Dunmow, gentleman, Richard Jennings, yeoman, for the said William to keep the peace towards Geoffrey Luckin of the same, husbandman.

June 9, 1585

Order given at Leez [Great Leighs] by Robert, Lord Riche to the keepers of the gaol at Colchester to receive John Sewell of Great Dunmow, and keep him there until he shall be delivered according to order and form of law, for that he refuses to find sufficient sureties for his good behaviour and for his appearance at the next General Sessions to answer such matters as shall be objected against him. John Sewell's libel against Virgin's wife of Great Dunmow in the next Sessions. Examination taken before Robert, Lord Riche of Faith Virgin, wife of Thomas Virgin of Great Dunmow, mason. She says that John Sewell, for about three years last, before she married her husband, did manye tymes assulte and allure her to committe filthynes with him and to have the use of her body, and also since she had married he had continued to pursue her to that purpose.

October 10, 1585

Peter Jenkynson, of Stebbing, butcher, Thomas Cr—— tailer, John Dunmow, labourer, and John Taylor, locksmith, all of the same. George Dygbye of Great Dunmow, husbandman and Robert Pechye, labourer, for playing unlawful games called "the bowles" on Sunday at Little Dunmow.

Jury list for John Sewell

William Yonge of Thaxted, William Westlye, Henry Westlye and Christopher Kentt alias Reynolds, all of the same. Simular writ to summon a special Jury from the neighbourhood of Dunmow to try John

Sewell the younger, yeoman, at the said sessions. John pleads " not guilty."

Duchy of Lancaster

We do present William Turner, Vittuler, of the perrisshe of Moche Dunmow who doth keep a " Boullinge alle, and other ill rewelle " for one month.

Indictment of July 2, 1589

Thomas Ramsey of Great Dunmow, tailer, for breaking into the close of John Cooke and cutting down his hedge lately erected there.

April 30, 1590

Indictment of Thomas Shoreland of High Ongar, tailor and John Estland of Braintree Fletcher. For making composition and receiving money from divers of the Queen's subjects at Great Dunmow under pretext of offences against divers penal statutes, without the order and consent of any Court of the Lady the Queen at Westminster, to wit, from John Moyne 5s. from John Bridge Miller 10s. from Richard Vaughan, Vicar 10s. Query for Thomas Shoreland of High Ongar, tailor for receiving money upon information without license; has judgement to stand upon the Pillory in the market of Great Dunmow.

October 25, 1590

Bartholomew Hamond of Great Dunmow, tinker, for breaking into the close of Edward Moyne and stealing a shirt, a smock and a napkin 2s. Puts himself guilty to the value of 10½d. petty larceny.

January 8 and 9, 1595-6

We present Mr. Cranish of Great Dunmow and Robert his son, and his wife, and Mistress Jennyngs and Mistress Chamberlaine and the wife of —— Threder and Mr. Clarke, for not coming to our parish Church of Dunmow for the space of one year and have not received the sacrament.

September 30, 1596

We find that in Great Dunmow there was bloudeshed betwene Robert Raymond and Robert Wallis and the bloude was drawen from Raymond.

Essex sessions roll January 13, 14 and 15, 1596

On December 16, 1596, John Vintener of Great Dunmow, butcher, for breaking in to the close of Thomas Cooke and assaulting and beating him so that he despaired of his life.

October 1, 1597

Petty Sessions held at Great Dunmow, before Henry Collen and Thomas Gooch gentlemen, and chief constables. Present that Joan Payne, Joan Gamlyn, Joan Parker, Susan Randoll, Thomas Underwood, George Davis and Richard Barker have not worked as they ought to do this year. (Did not appear).

Same dates under the Duchy of Lancaster

First of matters concerning the crown and dignity, we present Thomas Clarke, Mrs. Chamberlain and her son William and her daughter Isabel, also Mrs. Gininges also the wife of Robert Cranish the younger, Robert Cranish the elder, the wife of Smarte the wife of Roger Threder, Silvester Denes and his wife and Joan Godfre all of Much Dunmow, for not coming to Church. Henry Topper of Braintree, tailor, for stealing a gelding worth 40s. belonging to John Aylett of Great Dunmow. Not Guilty.

October 13, 1660

Henry Fowler of Great Dunmow husbandman, for stealing a horse colour sorrell worth £3. belonging to John Clarke, at Wethersfield. Guilty to be hanged.

Essex sessions roll January 7—9, 1660

We present Thomas Maunde of Great Dunmow and John Tayler for keeping their alehouses unlicensed, having lawful warning of the Bailiff, for the same, by the space of 6 months. Ralph Ravens D.D. Vicar presents, besides those which are before presented by the Churchwardens and sidesmen, Robert Smith a weaver and Winifred his wife, William Rawlyn age 20 and John Thredder age 17 both bound to the said Robert Smith, also a sojourner, the wife of Mr. Thorne who is a parson at Leading Roding, Gregory Cooke; the brother of Wm. Cooke, Mary Wiseman and George Jenour brother of Andrew Jenour Gent. that do not attend Divine Service.

Quarter sessions roll July 4 and 5, 1605

Richard Fletcher handed in bail to Henry Branham of Waltham Holy Cross, yeoman, and Thomas Garroll of Great Dunmow, to appear, unless meanwhile Sir Nicolas Coote certifies the Clerk of the Peace that he is not the father of the child, in question. Discharged. Item that Thomas Jones and Thomas Lytherman of Great Dunmow keep alehouses without license, for 3 months or more.

October 1, 1607

John Gamlin of Great Dunmow Victualler for much misdemeanour in his house for keeping unlawful games in his tippling house and entertaining mens servents and mens sons, both in the time of Divine Service, suppressed.

January 8, 1609

Richard Aylett, Roger Jonson and William Kinge, all of Great Dunmow, for keeping their alehouses without license.

January 11

We present —— Parsons of Great Dunmow, shoemaker, for abusing the Constables viz: John Robarson and John Fleming and striking up one of the constable's heels. We present Roger Jonson and Richard Aylett, musicians for fiddling in the town without license.

October 28

William Gurnard of Great Dunmow, baker, for baking and selling in the open market there, spiced cakes and black bread called " groat loaves " for 4d. not having the measure appointed by law for baking bread, also for baking the white bread called " penye white loaves for ½d., lacking 3½ ounces troy in weight and black bread called " a twoe penye household loaf for 2d., lacking 15 ounces Troy in weight. True bill. Witnesses William Willington, Walter Fuller and Robert Draper.

Michaelmas 1611

Steven Chaundler against William Fuller of Great Dunmow Jun. butcher, that between May 1 and October 1 1611 at Little Dunmow he engrossed and obtained into his hands by purchase from Ralph Eve, 8 acres of Oats worth 40s. an acre, then growing in the fields there, with the intention of reselling the same in lots against the statute; by which information there should accrue to the King £16. being the value of the grain so engrossed, whereof Chaundler sues for one half. Widow Poulter and Richard Aylett of Great Dunmow for keeping alehouses of great disorder and evil rule and Aylett for many threatening speeches against the constable, for that he hath found fault with the said disorders. William Church Great Dunmow, husbandman, November 1, 1610, built a cottage at Hatfield Broad Oak without assigning 4 acres thereto and maintained the same until October 1 following.

Epiphany sessions 1612

Wm. Dennis of Dunmow to scour his ditches against the highway from High Roding to Dunmow belonging to a farm called Brands about 40 rod of it.

Midsummer 1612

Jas. Prior, labourer and Richard Poulter labourer, both of Great Dunmow, June 29th assaulted John German at Stebbing, wounding and ill-treating him and they feloniously took and carried away a hat worth 8d, and " *unum colare* anglice band " worth 2d. for the battery, belonging to German Fined 6d. Poulter confessed Ignoramus for the felony.

W. Barnard of Great Dunmow yeoman carried away about 40 cartloads of soil out of the highway there and took it to his own ground, whereby the highway is very dangerous. John Robinson of Great Dunmow, Farrier being a common Victualler on June 2 lodged " rogues & Tinkers " in his house there and interfered with Thom. Bushe, one of the constables of the Town in the execution of his office.

January 1602-3. 45 Elizabeth I

We present that Howe Lane in Great Dunmow is overhanged with great loppes by the lande owners of the feame called " Pittockes" in the occupation of Christopher Beard and also it has becom full of slowes so that travelers cannot pass, but in grett danger, by the reson of fower dytches wych oughte to be made by land holders of the manor of Southalle whch lye agenste the sayd lane, now in the tenure of Thomas Beeson, gent. Christopher Beard fined 6d. We present that Mell Lane in Great Dunmow " leadynge from Brodgrooes to a Myll called Poole myll " slowes so that passengers cannot pass without great danger and it is to be amended by the parishioners of Great Dunmow. We present that a horse bridge called Langools [or Lampholes] in Great Dunmow is in decay, so that passengers cannot pass and is to be made by Nicolas Longe of Langoles [Langleys].

Epiphany 1668/9 quarter sessions

The churchwardens of Muche Dubnmowe for pulling down the 12 almshouses on Parsonage Downs belonging to the poor and leaving open the fence next adjoining a tenement in the occupation of Geo. Mason, which time out of mind, used to be fenced in by a pale, to the said Mason's annoyance.

CHAPTER IX

The corporation of Dunmow—the charters

A Saturday market was granted to Much Donnawe by Henry III to John de Berners in 1253. Here two fairs were held annually—on May 6 and November 8. These were finally discontinued in the nineteenth century. Also in that century the market was changed from Saturday to Tuesday.

The next Dunmow charter was granted on February 16 in the second and third years of the reign of Philip and Mary (1555) and confirmed by letters patent in the thirty-second year of Queen Elizabeth I (1590). These granted a bailiff and burgesses of the borough of Great Dunmow, from which a bailiff was annually elected.

One important effect of the charter was to give Dunmow, on payment of 10/- annually, the privilege of holding two fairs yearly— one " on the day of St. Mark and on the vigil and morrow of the same day " and the other " on the feast of Sts. Simon and Jude and on the vigil and morrow of the same feast "—and at the same time bestowed upon the town all the " stallage, picage, tolls, fines, amercements and all other profits, commodities, privileges, advantages, revenues and emoluments" arising therefrom. The court of piepowder granted to Dunmow was the usual court held in most fairs under the direction of the steward of the town for the immediate settlement of all commercial disputes. Concerning this court a statute of Edward IV says " In which court it hath been all times accustomed, that every person coming to the fairs, should have lawful remedy of all manner of contracts, trespasses, covenants, debts and other deeds made or done within any of the same fair and within jurisdiction of the same, and to be tried by merchants of the same fair."

By-laws of the corporation

It may be of interest to quote a few by-laws from the corporation minute books. These are for the year 1571. The corporation to meet quarterly. The secrets of the corporation to be preserved. The burgesses to attend every meeting; non-attendance fined unless a reasonable excuse is given. The burgesses to treat the Bayliff with reverence. The inhabitants shall show themselves obediently and reverently towards the Bayliff and Burgesses. No alehouse shall be resorted to on Sunday or Holy Day. Every artificer not living in the town for seven years before the making of these by-laws to pay for his freedom. Every householder to keep the street clean in front of his door. No burgesses to speak unseeming words to and against his brother. Every artificer or householder shall bring his servants, journeymen and apprentices to pay their quarterages. Every apprentice to have his name enrolled in the corporation books. No man shall take in a lodger or let his house without first acquainting the corporation. Every person to pay a fine before being allowed to dwell in the town. If any person " deryd, scorne, mocke, rayle at " the Bailiff or burgesses he shall be fined 6/8d. No person to go before a justice to complain of any wrong without he first acquaint the corporation. No apprentice, servant or journeyman to be out after 9 o'clock, neither in an alehouse, tippling house or inn after that time, nor playing dice, cards, or any unlawful game. Everyone to pay the rates levied by the corporation or forfeit double, and if any man resist the officer executing a lawful warrant he shall suffer imprisonment for one month.

No inhabitant to take in any stranger from a town infected by the plague. All butchers to take their offal to a convenient place outside the town. Stubborn apprentices to be brought before the bailiff and burgesses. All unmarried persons " not having an honest vocation " to be brought before a justice. All alehouses to be licensed by the corporation. The constable to search frequently the alehouses for disorderly persons and players of unlawful games.

All these rules and regulations were enforced by fines which, if exacted, must have greatly added to the funds of the corporation.

We will leave the Dunmow corporation for a century and return in 1671. The by-laws now show considerable advance in town management. The burgesses shall assemble on the Tuesday after the feast of St. Michael the Archangel and elect the bailiff for the year. The bailiff to be sworn in after his election. Every bailiff after the expiration of the term of office shall deliver up all books and records and give a true and just account of the money received and expended by him. Bailiff and burgesses to assemble within six days after the death or removal of any burgess and elect his successor.

The corporation to meet monthly and the Sergeant " shall warne to this Court all the Constables, Surveyors of the Streetes and Highwayes, and viewer of the markett, The Serchers and Sealers of Leather fflesh and ffish, Aletasters, and Breadweighers whoe shall then and there present all offences and misdemeaners relateinge to their small offices." Any Bailiff, burgess, freeman or inhabitant using any " approbrious or uncivill language " in the Town Hall, or in any other place within the said borough, to be fined. Secrets of the council chamber not to be divulged. Every inhabitant of the town to appear at the Town Hall when required. No person allowed to utter any protest against acts of laws of the corporation except

Richard Roper, the last bailiff of Dunmow Corporation, 1885.

to one of the burgesses, or openly in the Town Hall.

All letters, patents and evidences to be sealed with the seal of the town. Freedom of town to be bought. Any burgess may in his lifetime make any one of his sons a freeman, but after his death the eldest son can claim freedom on paying 3/4. All indentures of apprentices to be enrolled and every apprentice after seven years service can claim his freedom. Every person made free to swear that " hee shall well and duely keep and observe the Ordinances and Constitution of the Burrow." No person shall " buy upp any butter, cheese, fflesh, ffish or any other Victuals coming to the markett to be sold within the said Burrough, nor shall buy any such Victualls within the said Burrow and sell the same there againe to a greater price."

The Churchwardens and Overseers to see that no " fforeign poore people," likely to be a charge to the inhabitants, are allowed to settle in the town. No cottage to be erected, or buildings converted into cottages, unless well built, with chimneys of brick. No person to receive any inmate, or more families than one in a house. Every butcher before sunrise or after sunset shall carry away " the entrailes and draff of Beasts and bury the same." No person " shall suffer any dead doggs, soyle, dunge or carryon in the streets to bye fower to the annoyance of ye inhabitants." The Bailiff to order the streets to be kept and the dirt against an inhabitant's house to be shovelled up. No one to suffer his sink to run in the street. The market place to be swept after every market or fair. Two inhabitants to be chosen every year to see that there are no annoyances or encroachments in the Borough.

No " Highers, Loaders, Kidders or Carriers " to buy any victuals on market day without a licence and none to buy before the market bell rings, nor in any man's house privately, but in open market. No person to sell corn in any private shop, or any other place, save only in the open market. No butcher to expose to sale any " Blowen Veale, or Lambe, or any putrified or unwholesome meate." Every freeman and inhabitant, upon request, to assist the bailiff, burgesses, constables and sergeant, and other officers. Every freeman to pay quanterages. By-laws to be read once a quarter openly in the Town Hall. Sergeant to collect all fines and dues, and to levy distress of the goods and chattels of offenders in case of nonpayment. Obedience to these by-laws was enforced by very large fines, which went into the corporation coffers.

One can see from the foregoing that Dunmow must not only have been a fairly prosperous little town, not only through the bay and say trade—which I would say at the time of these later by-laws was just coming up to its height of prosperity—but also by the powers granted to it by its charter.

The corporation of Dunmow survived 330 years, but in 1885 the then Radical Government passed an Act abolishing all corporations with a population of less than 5,000; therefore Dunmow lost her charter and bailiff and burgesses ceased to be. All we have left are the Town Hall, three old minute books and the original charters now on the north wall of the parish church.

CHAPTER X

Bay and say industry

About 1570 a number of Flemish refugees fled to England to escape the persecution of the Duke of Alva and settled in Colchester, where they introduced the manufacture of bay and say and other kinds of material. This industry soon became such a commercial success that it spread to neighbouring towns, of which Dunmow was one.

During its heyday this trade brought to the town at least £500 a year, and probably an increase of up to forty per cent of the population, around the early seventeenth century.

Bays was a coarse woollen cloth with a long nap raised by teasels, much grown in Essex for that purpose. Say was a fine thin cloth more like serge and used for linings, shirts and even outer garments. The people could weave these materials in their own homes, and one can imagine how happy the poor people were to be able to earn a little more money, especially those who were not able to go into the fields to work.

These materials were afterwards taken by the fullers to the tenterfields to be washed, dyed and dried. Note here a reference to this industry in an estate in Dunmow—Tenterfields. In the eighteenth century this industry began to decline owing to more mechanized methods in the north and foreign competition. By the end of the eighteenth century it had almost faded out here, much to the distress of the local inhabitants, as it brought about a dreadful state of pauperism mentioned in another chapter.

I might mention here that in 1669 Thomas Burr produced a halfpenny, bearing on one side a woolpack and packing staff and on the other " of Dunmow in Essex, his halfpenny." Robert Draper produced a similar coin. He had a retail shop in the town and no doubt became short of small change.

It is quite certain that in days gone by Dunmow possessed very extensive tan works. This industry began to decline owing to factory-produced leather products and foreign competition. Pleasant Terrace was built on an old tannery. When these houses were built the old pits were discovered and quantities of horns, hoofs and hides were dug up. Likewise when the bacon factory was built it was on an old tanyard, and again a lot of remains of animals' hides, etc., were unearthed. Here the tanner's house remained for some time and was occupied by the foreman of the woodcarving works of Mr. T. Gibbons (father of the colonel). Other tanneries were on the left side of the causeway going towards the Clock House and another was in Mill Lane somewhere at the back of the gasworks.

CHAPTER XI

Dunmow martyrs

During the Reformation it was not just " a tooth for a tooth " but a life for a life. Catholics and Protestants alike were willing to die for their faith.

On June 6, 1556, ten persons, all Essex folk, appeared before Derbyshire, Bonner's chancellor. One was Thomas Bowyer of Great Dunmow, a weaver, aged 36, committed because he would not go to church under the re-established papist religion of Mary. First Bowyer was brought before Master Wiseman, of Felsted, who sent him to Colchester castle, and from there to Bonner, Bishop of London, who condemned him. He was burnt at Stratford-le-Bow towards the end of June, together with ten other men and two women. The men were tied to the stakes, but the women were left loose in the fire. The number burnt that day was the most on any occasion throughout the country, chiefly labourers and artisans. On the martyrs' memorial, near St. John's church, Stratford, Bowyer's name is recorded, together with many others. I feel we should know more about him. It does not seem as if anyone troubled. I suppose they dare not take sides. Was he a married man with a young family? Why was the bridge near Little Easton named after him? We will never know.

Our other martyr was of opposite persuasion. She was arrested at Clock House for harbouring priests. Ann Line was a widowed gentlewoman and a native of Dunmow. She was in very ill health, but her soul was strong and vigorous and ever tended by spiritual exercise to Christian perfection. On Candlemas Day, February 2, 1601, the spies and priest hunters having had a hint that Mrs. Line was housing a priest, invaded her house at the very moment that mass was about to be celebrated. Father Page escaped, but Mrs. Line and her friend Mrs. Gage were arrested, although the latter was later set free.

Mrs. Line was brought up for trial at the Old Bailey before Lord Chief Justice Popham. She was borne to her trial in a chair, being at that time too ill and weary to be able to walk. The Lord Chief Justice needed little proof to arrive at his verdict of guilt and pronounced the death penalty by hanging. Mrs. Line was taken back to Newgate to prepare for her execution. When she was taken on her journey to Tyburn she was " unmoved and of calm countenance." At Tyburn when she was ready to die she declared in a loud voice " I am sentenced to die for harbouring a Catholic priest, and as far as I am from repenting I wish with all my soul I could have entertained a thousand."

She suffered before two priests. Father Barworth, who came next after her, embraced her dead body while it was still hanging, saying " O blessed Mrs. Line, who hast now happily received thy reward, thou hast gone before us, but we shall quickly follow thee to bliss, if it pleases the Almighty."

The Duchess of Arundel was at Ann's execution, and when her body was cut down the duchess sent her servants to recover it from among the felons and evil-doers, that she might have her decently buried. Ann Line was the daughter of William Heigham, of

Dunmow, a strict Calvinist. When his son went to college he met a young man who had lately been converted to the Roman faith. These two soon became great friends, and it was not long before young William was also in the net and coming home and bringing his friend, who on meeting Miss Ann fell deeply in love, and they were later married. Both the Heighams were disinherited, and also young Line, whose father had large estates. Very shortly after their marriages the two men were thrown into prison. Lines escaped to Ghent, but died there in 1594. Brother William must have also escaped and became a lay brother in Spain, for we find him still carrying on the good work there in 1609.

In 1590 when he, William, was young and carefree he and five other gentlemen's sons, having hosted at " att Bemshes in Donmowe," rode to Easton Park. " Later, led by one Christopher Hatton who was apparelled in black sylke and had a gylte rapier at his syde, they broke into the parke and killed one male deere. After they had killed and horsed the deere, they went altogether towards Bishops Stortford." Boys will be boys, and little did William Heigham know of the kind of life that lay ahead of him.

JOHN BIRD, D.D., 1554-8

THE Rev. Langston Scott found in a fragment of a Foxe manuscript in the British Museum an interesting account of the visit of Bishop Bonner to Dunmow church when Dr. Bird was vicar and Suffragan Bishop of Colchester. Foxe tells a story of Dr. Bird for which he quotes as his authority " the voyce of the parish." His description of the reception of Bonner in Dunmow is here in modern spelling (Foxe's would be in Latin). Dr. Bird had been Bishop of Chester and thereof deprived on March 16, 1554, with the coming of Mary Tudor, when it became known that he had married during the reign of Edward VI. But being the turncoat that he was, he declared he had been forced into the marriage. He made out that he was very repentant, and thereupon repudiated his lawful wife, and was again invested and made vicar of Dunmow and suffragan. At this time Dr. Bird was well stricken in years, and had lost one eye. He preached this day before Bonner from the text " Thou Peter on this rock will I build my church," intending to prove the stability of Peter and so successively of the pope's seat, but he wandered away so completely that the congregation and the bishop became hot and agitated. The bishop looked toward Bird, giving such signs as were almost speaking, to proceed to the full event of the cause in hand. Dr. Bird died one month before Queen Mary, which was as well for him.

It appears that Dr. Bird was a Carmelite friar, made provincial of that order in England in 1516, was a D.D. of Oxford and was one of the persons sent by Henry VII to Catherine of Aragon to advise her to forbear the title of queen. He preached before the king in 1537 against the pope's supremacy. He was then Bishop of Bangor and then of Chester.

Before Bonner was Bishop of London in Edward VI's reign Master Ridley was the Bishop of London. He visited Dunmow church and advised what was to be taken down and done away with. By the time of the above article Bonner had long since sent Ridley to the stake at Oxford.

CHAPTER XII

Dunmow's seventeenth-century doctor

The day-book of a country practitioner kept during the civil war makes us wonder if it is worse to be drugged to death or to suffer Dr. William Swallow's " mysterious potions."

Our Dunmow doctor was William Swallow. " Gulielmus " (Latin for William) Swallow.

His practice extended many miles around Dunmow and the notes of patients are full of local interest. Lady Jenoure, the second wife of Andrew Jenoure, of Great Dunmow, sometimes employed this doctor. There are prescriptions for pills for Mrs. Elizabeth Wale, or child of Mr. Woodroofe, the Leez Priory chaplain, Johannes Creed of Felsted, Richard Marshall of Lindsell, John Milbank of Aythorpe Roding, and Nicholas Humfrey and Edward Chinnery of Stebbing, where the doctor had many patients, including one " Materfamilias Levitt." Domina Wiseman was another patient; she was evidently a profitable " case " to our doctor and was probably a widowed dowager of the old family of Wiseman of Great Canfield Park.

There are some prescriptions " Pro wxure mea," but they seem simple enough, and we will not suspect the doctor of trying experiments at home.

The last prescription in the book (or written on the cover) is for " my daughter Francis." Another relation is " my cousin Pilcher " and there is one for " my littel boy." Lady Maynard of " Easten Parna att ye Lodge " was one who sought the doctor's ministrations, and there are special notes of another patient at Easton Lodge called Parnella Patteridge or Partridge, who suffered from paroxysms of epilepsy. Many visits were paid to this patient in October 1645 (by this time it was " spuria epilepsia," which necessitated many more of the doctor's bedside visits). His book is closely filled with recipes for the cure or alleviation of every ill that mortal flesh (in the seventeenth century) was known to be heir to.

The changes were rung merrily around the clock of complaints—consumption, the flux, fistula, hystericke, discnterie, green wound, fitts, goute, ricketts. The recipes seemed to be considered possessed of additional efficacy if they had received royal or noble usage. Thus " the Kinge of ffrance, his Balsame " could be a never-failing remedy. My Lady Bannister's faith in " 4 glisters [blisters] day and night " is truly pathetic. This famous doctor's apothecarie tells me that he " bled the Earl of Lester's daughter after the small pox was out, when she had above 40 comed out uppon her face and elsewhere and I did it and she did well." Other distinguished patients were Sir Andrew Jenour of Bigods and Mr. James Milborne of Merks, and they did well.

Doctor Swallow's account shows that treatment often went on after visits had finished: " Mr. Wales pills that he used to take in the Spring, especially noted to be ready for when needed." Then there were " Mr. Sowells fitts." Mr. Sowell was evidently bailiff to my Lord Maynard. These attacks were apparently cured by applying pigeons to his feet, plasters to the insides of his arms and glisters when he was a little better. This remedy was a favourite one, as we find many instances of it.

No doubt our modern dentists would not forbear a smile at our Dr. Swallow's infallible remedy for toothache: " Mix 4 peppercorns, rosemarie and oyster shells powdered, mixed with honey and vinegar and apply with a fine ragge."

Our Dunmow physician seems to have wrought marvellous cures with very simple means. Oil of aniseed, balsam, aloes and rhubarb are still used today, but " Snayle Milk " or, to put it " professionally," " Lac Linacium " was a choice drug not found in the pharmacopæia. The next one is not too bad: a gentlewoman who could not " digest her meate and could not drink wine, or strong beere " was " wisht to take a littel Cinamon water in a draught of small beere after her meate or meals," and this did her much good.

A gentleman was told to swallow, once or twice a day, five or six olive stones, " an excellent thing for ye stone." There were "the intrales of a hare " for the heart. " Ye liver and ye lunges, dried and beaten to powder, did cure one of convulsion fitts, that had laboured for a long time and had tried divers medicines, but in vain." Occasionally among these wonders of hearsay we light on a passage of ethics and philosophy that emanates from the *Religio Medici*, or the *Pseudodoxia Epidemica* of that great master of minds and eminent physician Sir Thomas Browne. But the country practitioner has often no time to soar to such heights and is more interested in boiling " the blacke tops of Crabbs clawes, with white amber and the bone that is found in the heart of a ffarle [hawk]."

In other ways Dr. Swallow seems to have acted normally. He was one of the men who chose Samuel Gentrie to be registrar at the parish church when it had to become Presbyterian during the Commonwealth.

He was elected one of the three elders through this difficult time.

CHAPTER XIII

The civil war

Dunmow stood 100 per cent against Charles. The political struggle between king and Parliament was thus embittered by the poison of theological controversy, and by 1642, marked in the Dunmow registers "the Year of ye Rebellion," it was clear that the issue could only be decided by civil war.

On June 10 of that year a meeting of the Trained Bands and volunteer companies was held at Dunmow and the following resolution was received with universal approbation," by holding up of hands, throwing of hattes and exclamations professing that they held them unworthy to live, that should

A document from Fairfax giving the Jenours of Bigods a safe passage through the lines near Colchester at the time of the siege.

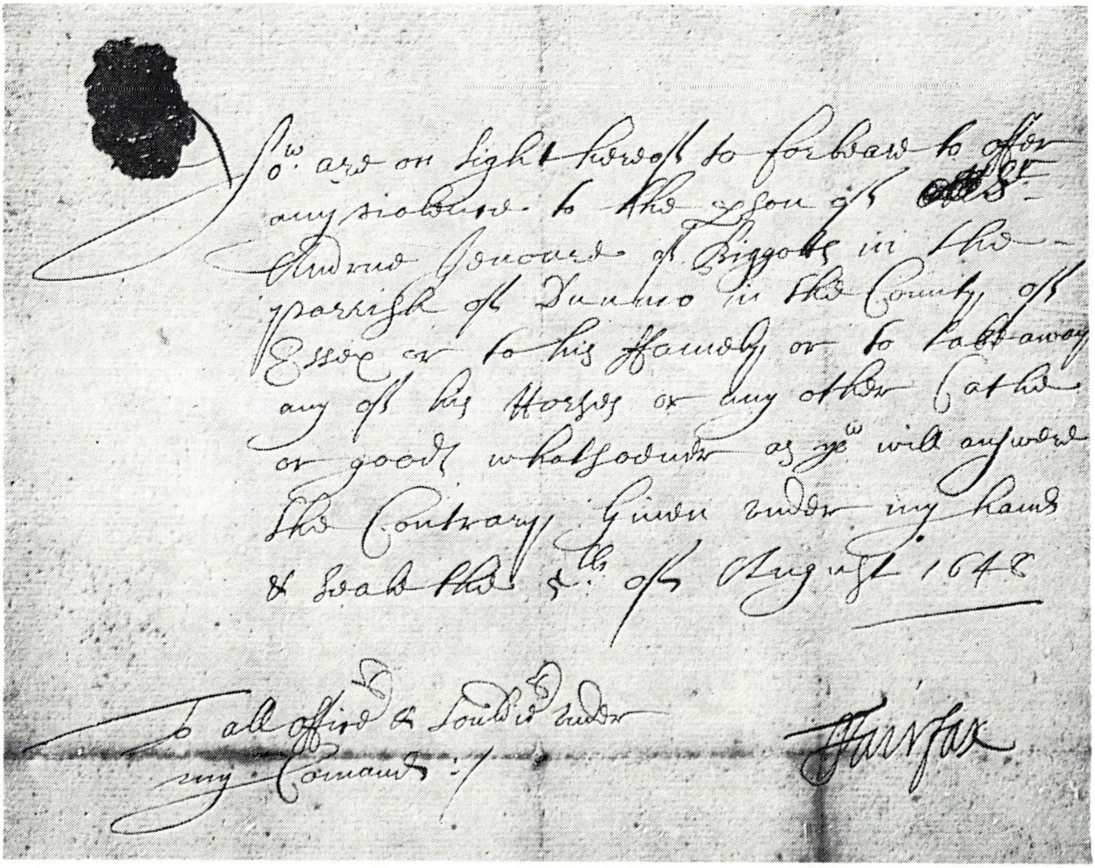
Yo: are on sight hereof to forbear to offer any violence to the person of Andrew Jenoure of Biggotts in the parrish of Dunmo in the County of Essex or to his Family or to take away any of his Horses or any other Cattle or goods whatsoever as yo: will answer the Contrary Given under my hand & Seale the 5th of August 1648

To all officers & Souldiers under my Comand

Fairfax

Reproduced by kind permission of the Essex Archæological Society.

dislike it." The resolution was signed "by ten thousand hands" and within three days presented to Parliament in the form of a petition.

Printed on a broadsheet by order of the House of Commons on June 17, 1642, it is too long to quote here, but one or two of its ringing sentences will give its main purport: "We, understanding not by misinformation of flying report, but by the late votes of both your honourable Houses, that his Majestie, served by wicked counsell intends to make war against the Parliament that so to doe is a breach of the trust reposed in him by his people, contrary to his oath, and that Whosoever shall serve or assist him in his warres are trayters to the fundamental laws of the kingdom. . . . With our hands upon our swords, we stand ready at your command . . . to spend our dearest blood in defence of the lives and liberties of our countrymen, the lawes which are the life of our liberty and peace, and religion more precious than both." Three days later this very loyal declaration was sent to Parliament on a broadsheet. There is nothing to show that any reply was received. I feel it would be the same today. I would like to have seen that meeting, probably held on the downs or in the square! One person not there would be the vicar, the Rev. Joseph Crowther, as he was a strong supporter of the king and shortly after this time was ejected from the living.

CHAPTER XIV

Sales and bargains, etc.

4th December 14, 18 January, 1620. Bargain and sale. Cons. £260.

Richard Jennyn of Great Dunmow Esq., to Ambrose Vintner (Tanner) Messuage curtlage and croft of land adjoining together commonly known as the Swanne in the occupation of John Cornell and Thom. Moyne, known as Pollards in Great Dunmow, but messuage and tenement late of John Aylett, and now of A. Ambrose in the occupation of Silvester Barker, and the late William Fuller, now in the occupation of John Cooke. One head abutting on the highway leading from the Market of Dunmow towards Chelmsford, and the other upon the crop of pasture of Richard Barnard, now in the occ: of John Cornell. Also a field called Mellfield [10 acres] in two parcels [divided] one in occ: of J. Cornell at Ford End in Great Dunmow between the meadow of Robt. Milborne, gent in occ: —— Overall on one part and the land called Dedmans Lane on the other, one head abutting on the highway leading from the Market at Dunmow, towards Braintree, and the other a parcel of pasture of Nicholas Blincoe, gent in occ: of Robt. Beardon of Braintree, recites that Richard Jennyns purchased the " Swan " of Thom. Pavett in 1571 and Millfield of Wm. Lilly and John Aylett by deeds dated June 23 Elizabeth. Recites demense of lease of said premises dated 1st Sept 7 James 1st to Grissell Dyllie widow, whereupon the annual rent of £15-1s.-9d and one of capons, Richard's wife Elizabeth.

This is a copy made on May 22, 1649, of the original deed in the hands of John Vintner, son and heir of John Vintner, and he was brother and heir of Ambrose Vintner.

March 29, 1667. Charles II. Cons. £200.

Jeffrey Draper of Great Dunmow, clothier, to Thom. Porter, Jun. of Great Dunmow yeoman. Capital messuage—an Inn called " The Swan " and a cottage or tenement in occ. of Hannabell Eastaugh, widow.

Recites lease by Jeffrey D unto say Easthaugh (at an annual rent of £12) signed Jeffrey Draper. Witnesses Jac. Calthorp, Robert Hasler, Thom. Wheeler, Thom. Burgis, Danl. Watts, and John Surridge.

December 27, 1705

James Stokes of Great Dunmow, maltster —to his wife Mary, tenement or cottage in Great Dunmow in occ: of Richard Felsted and then to testator's daughter Mary Sawen, widow, for life, and then to testator's grandson James Sawen son of Mary. To my daughter Mary, the tenement wherein I now dwell, called " The Swann " with all the outhouses, barns, stables, malthouses, kylnhouse, and appurtances and one close or orchard adjoining for the life of his widow, to whom the said Mary shall pay a yearly rent of £10, then to grandson James, who is to pay his mother £2. 10s. 0d. for life. To daughter Mary all my goods and household stuff and £10. To grandson James S. my clock and my watch, and the rest of my personal estate to my daughter Mary my executrix.

Agreement of purchase

December 14, 1771

Wm. Paine did agree to sell to Lional

Lukin all that freehold messuage or tenements in Great Dunmow and the millhouse, malthouse, barns, stables, oasthouses, yard, gardns and appurtanances therunto belonging contrary to three roods all in occ: of the said Wm. Paine or £30 [Lukin to have possession on March 25]. Wm. Paine to have use of malthouse until May 1, purchase money is to be paid by May 31. Cons of conveyance to be equally shared. And it is agreed that the Lead Cistern of the Malting and Wash couch boards and the Beaufet in the parlour of the said messuage and all the locks, bolts and keys of the doors shall be the property of the said Lional Lukin and also the horse malt mill, in the millhouse, with the utensils thereof. Witness Thom. Clubbe, Lional Lukin, William Payne.

WEIGHTS AND MEASURES SURVEY LADY DAY 1756

When this measure was first introduced it was looked upon with the greatest suspicion. The surveyor was often thrown out or locked out, or treated in some other rough way.

Here we have a list of those who, even if they were not for it, acted as the law demanded:

Sarah Colman, " The Bell "
James Wilson, " The Harp "
Thos. Jonas, tanner
Ann German, " King's Head "
Robt. Sorvell, miller
Margaret Guy, " The Bowling Green "
Eyekial Stone, wind miller
Thos. Reynolds, " The Three Tuns "
Daniel Thorn, " The Chequers "
Roger Hoskin, tallow chandler
William Barker, flour shop
In. Noon, butcher
In. Waistcoat, grocer
Geo. Pansy, flower [flour] shop
Thos. Shepherd, " The Star "
Matthams Tims, grocer
Simon Goslings at " Prines "
Henry Rolph, " Saracen's Head "
Rodger Hodgins, grocer
William Born, baker
Robt. Felsted, " The White Horse "
Geo. Cox, grocer
Robt. Taillor, baker
William Wallem, grocer
Thos. Thorn, butcher
In. Rowell, " The Royal Oak "
William Tayler, baker
Mary Taylor, grocer and flour shop
Daniel Monk, grocer
William Pans, " The White Hart "
In. Bridge, flower [flour] shop
William Griggs, flower [flour] shop

All examined and found correct—William Dines.

NAMES OF FARMS, STREETS AND LANDS

Horsted in 1254, Lovedays Horsted in 1547, Pydlers Horsted in 1577. A muddy hork, stede, or horseplace. This was the name of a considerable district from which Horstedafort, now Stebbingford Bridge, was named. If you look right at the top of the second hill you will still see a farm called Horsted.

Stratford or Stratfordfelde, or Stratford Brigg (extra Dunmawe) 1285. This is the ford where Stane Street crossed the Chelmer. The Ford Farm was then called St. John's.

Langleys was Langwells in 1768.

Barley Hall was Barleycroft in 1370.

Ford Farm and Roffey were probably the homes of Arnulf de Flaxine and John de la Ford (thirteenth century) and Ralph de Rowney. Roughey Parkehend 1353, Rowhey Frith end 1384-92 (a rough enclosure).

Dunmow Park was Matche Dunmawe Park in 1561. Church End was ye Churcheyend in 1549.

Mynehonys 1504—the prioress of Clerkenwell held a virgate here in 1199.

Highwood Crossa 1546, Heghwode 1336.

Park Corner was Perklonde (park land) in 1488.

Philpot End (Thomas Fylgate) 1544-7 or Filbert 1777.

Tanners Farm, Richard Tanner, 1364.

Proverbs Green (John Prophete) 1363, Prophets Green 1805.

Little Doves (John Dove) 1538.

Puttocks Farm, Puddox 1777.

The Bedfords since 1541, from John Bedeford 1381.

Birds Farm, from Alan de Brid 1327.

Brands Farm, from Stephen Brond 1381.

Coopers Farm, from John Compere 1381.

Cox Hall, Colkesmore 1422-1510. These farms have now disappeared or been swallowed up by Mountains Farm and Roughy, together with Gages Farm, more recently Cages (John Gauges) 1366.

Little Garnett (Robert Gernet) 1235.

Bumpsted Hill Farm (Johanne de Bumpstead) 1254. Bunpstedehalle 1368. The ruins of a farmhouse remained until fifty years ago, an orchard for scrumping and a garden for picking flowers.

Toolies. To(o)lyes (croft) Wm. Toly 1274, One of our oldest farms still in production.

FRAGMENTS OF THE SEVENTEENTH CENTURY

Bailiff and burgesses appointed for the ensuing year October 29, 1630: Edmund Tillingham, bailiff; Robert Donnell, John Gyvor, John Remington (surgeon), William Skinner, John Ffraygan, Richard Barnard, Ffrancis Raymond (tanner), Richard Calthorp (attorney).

Uncommon wild plants found in and around Dunmow by John Gerard, the famous herbalist 1545-1611/2. He paid many visits to Dunmow as a friend of Mr. Threights, of Dunmow, " a learned gentleman excellently well seen in the knowledge of plants." Friesland and Liege lady traces, the yellow kind, were shown him by his friend in Muche Dunmow.

" Tway Blade or Herbe Bifoils groweth in the woods by Dunmow. Saracens Consound groweth on a wood on the north side of Muche Dunmow. The wild White Hellebore bee found in dankish and shadowie place in the woods there. Finger Hartstongue I found in the garden of Master Cranish, surgeon, who gave me a plant for my garden. Teasels are found all around that district, Licourice Hatchet Vetch is found in many places there, the Milke Vetches grow there also."

Interesting documents of 1647 and 1691 throw some light on Angel Lane, or Shoppers Rowe. A Thomas Drake had a smithy there adjoining the Angel inn. It belonged to Sir James Milborne of Merks. He sold it to Wm. Fuller and John Neole. Later in 1691 these premises were bought by Wm. Raymond, tanner, and Thomas Wheeler, attorney. Robert Roker and his wife, Amy, bought this property later. In each of the deeds the Drakes, first Thomas and then Joseph, had an assurance of protection against being turned out of their smithy.

Dunmow tokens

Through several reigns there had been a shortage of small coins. All I can find issued by Dunmow tradesmen is one of Charles I and one of Charles II: "John Draper, Woolen Draper, Dunmawe," the reverse side " his halfpeny 1633."

Thomas Bvrges 1669 a woolpack and packing, reverse " of Dunmow in Essex—his half-peny."

A farthing of Edward Keatchener, crossed keys, and reverse " of Dunmow Loksmith." A monogram.

An odd bequest

Thomas Cecil, rector of Great Easton, in his will left a volume in Greek and Latin to Kenelm Jenour of Bigods and the " great map of the world hanging in the palour " to Robert Milborne of Marks.

COACHES AND CARRIERS, ETC.

In studying our town through the centuries it would seem to me that the seventeenth century was a prosperous time in which Dunmow was " up and with it." The bay and say trade was at its height, the tanneries were going strong, the corporation by-laws were very quick on the heels of any offender, and carriers were taking and bringing goods and people to and from London. I am saying this latter was good, but it may have been the means which brought us three bouts of plague. The registers tell us that in 1603 forty-eight persons here died from the dread visitation, in 1625 twenty-three and in 1665 thirty-eight. Where or how they were buried we do not know, but it may be presumed that it was a " mass " burial. It is doubtful if all of them died in the pest house. I rather think it might have either been built at the first plague or first used in this way at that time. There is no doubt whatsoever that it was Deadmans Lane from that time on. At a sale of property in 1620 it was cited as "Dedmans Lane." By the number of persons who died there, not only from the plague but from smallpox, until less than 100 years ago its name stuck. The present name of St. Edmunds is so very much healthier, whether he passed that way or not.

To get back to the carriers and wagoners of the seventeenth century, we read " The Carriers from Dunmow in Essex doe lodge at the Saracen's Head in Gracious Strete [Gracechurch]. They do come and goe on Thursdaies & Fridaies. The Wagons from Dunmow doe come on Wednesdaies to the Crown at Algate Street without."

CHAPTER XV

Tithes due from ye Inhabitants of Great Dunmow and paid to the Vicar this year of our Lord 1661. Dr. Will Parsons, Vicar

CORPORATION

	£	s.	d.
Thomas Burges for park land 11 acres, 3 rod Pasture	1	10	0
Tawbutt Loahs 3 acres, 2 rod Pasture		10	0
Antony Jennings land 12 acres plowed		2	0
W. A. Wiseman 1 acre, 1 rod Hopp Ground (Pennymont). .		12	0
Church Land Pasture 2/- per annum		2	0
3 Acres plowed land. He gave me a Barrel of Colchester Oysters brought to my home for my Soup		16	0
John Houchin for 10 acres of plowed land being part of Mr. Raggs land		1	8
Thos. Houchin for Park Land, 32 acres pasture	2	10	0
Edward Aylett for his Orchard and land by his house		5	0
for New Barn ground meadow		14	0
for Cateshead Mill Farm		1	10
received in lot		19	10
Robert Seex for Mr. Raggs land for which he paid 9/- per annum		18	0
for Mr. Smiths land for which he paid 6/- per annum		6	0
for Caloan acres of Hopp land a pound of Hopps paid in kind		5	0
John Pettit for Orchard and land which he sold		18	4
for 3 acres of pasture formerly sold by Ed. Bell		5	8
John Barker for ground and household (shopkeeper)		4	4
John Barker for house and Orchard (carpenter) for tithe Goslings		6	0
Edmund Harris for Cockebrooke Mead and for hay he bought of Simon Smith's ground for which he paid..............		30	0
Henry Seex for the tithe of ye ground he sold		7	0
Richard Sherley for Great Dunmow Watermill		16	0
and for his Windmill........		1	0
Francis Watts Gallop Hill, part of Olives 14s. annum 2 rood of Hopp Ground	2	3	0
John Barnard for all his tithes paid till May 26, 1662	1	6	0
Wm. Yinyour, where Dr. Swallow dwelt, and for his house. .		1	0
James Edwicke one small orchard			2
Robert Calthorp jun, Land of my Lord Maynard which was his grant, but sold to Thos. Baker		5	0
The field behind his house 3 acres plowed and 3 of pasture......		6	0
for his Orchard and the house in which he dwells		1	0

for Mr. Remington's field 7 acres arable 1 0

John Gyvor for his tithe 6

John Heath for Swanfield 9 acres plowed 1 6

Dan Fuller Fords field 2 acres plowed 6

Say Easthough for the land he sold 8 0

Henry Saywill for his Orchard and 2 acres of plowed land .. 1 0

Wm. Brampton Park land 2 roods plowed 1 6

4 acres 2 roods 4s. 11d. Hopp ground 1 acre 2 roods 4 11

for his Orchard formerly 2/- now 1 6

Jeffrey Draper Jun. for 2 acres and 1 rood with mowing grounds 5 0

John Taylor for Richard Cowland sold in this year, see Bishopswood Qtr.

John Angar for his Orchard, which is very good 1 6

Isaac Page Hurthill My Lord Maynard's land ....
John Stones at Rayne 4 acres 2 rood ....
1 acre, 2 roods pasture, 3 acres plowed ....
Brands Farm, Bissopswood Qtr. Customary Eggs paid for the Eggs 7d. 1 13 4

Thos. Younglove holds 4 acres of James Vales land in Bissopswood Qtr, it lyes on Highwood Green, plowed .. 8

Thos. Creed for his house 1 0

Thos. Baker beyond New Street, Mr. Calthorp paid his tithes this year ....

George Starr 1 acre, 1 rood pasture.................... 8

Biggots Quarter 1661

Sir Andrew Jenour In Mr. Colnold's, ye Vicar's book, he paid 12th panne now it is 10 0 0

paid me in Numbrod. Out of his respect and love he sent my wife and so he did to Mr. John Smith ye Minister 2 0 0

Mr. James Milborne formerly Robert his uncle, paid £9 4. 6. Mr. James Milborne now paid £8 and for Poole field 10/-

The Parsonage formerly paid yearly to the Vicar £6 13. 4d. and the Vicar enjoyed the field, and the little meadow on the North side of ye Churchyard for which the Vicar payd out of ye £6 13. 4. .... 3 0 0

but this year the money was relain by Mr. Robert Calthorp, tenent of ye Parsonage, payd 9 0 0

John Lockwood Kitchen Mead 2 acres. Crouchfarm land 5 acres plowed, Mill field, 9 acres 1 10 0

Customary Eggs 15 paid for the Eggs 4d.

Thos. Barker payd this year for his tithes, Customary Eggs payd in kind 5 .... 5 0

Andrew Rodes payd for his tithes this year 5 0

Thos. Church formerly sold by Wm. Little, he payd 13 0

Customary Eggs payd in kind 5

Mrs. Tillingham widow payd her tithe 10 0

John Stoaks for his tithes he payed customary eggs 20 to 6
pay for Nether Hall 12 0

Henry Handly payd all his tithes customary eggs payd in kind 18 0

Thos. Milborne payd all his tithes this year 2 15 6

John Tyler he sold part of Mr. Milborne 8 0

Customary eggs 7 payd in kind

John Burr of the Priory. He sold Mr. May's land payd in money. He payd me also 1 acre 1 rood out of Bumsted Mead 1 15 0

Langnels Farm customary eggs 10 payd in kind 1 8 0

Ralph Milborne for Sir Andrew Jenour's land £20 per annum, Mr. Reynold's land £7 per annum 1 1 0

his own land £10 per annum customary eggs 14

Wm. Mills Pan Mead is payd among Mr. Milborne's tithes

Toolies Farm. He payd his tithes this year 1 9 0

Dan Barnard Homerly farm. He payd his petty tithes this year 5 0

Mrs. Aylett for an acre and 2 rood of Hopp ground and 18 0
pasture. 1 6

Rebecca Bridge ye Ford farm, widow, She payd 1 acre and a half 2 0

Anne and Elizabeth Pruine, widows, for their Orchard payd fruit in kind

Adam Enel for rent land of Elizabeth Marshall 10 acres of pasture. 1 0 0

Parsonage Downs

Newton Hall by Mr. Colenets book ye payd £3 10s. 0d. for Newton and Hulstocks. For Hulstocks 18/- its now sold to Francis Inniger who farms it for £20, the Church for which he pays for rent £24 6s. 0d. Part of Olines, 6 acres of meadow land, for all to be payd to ye Vicar. Customary from Newton Hall and Hulstocks 10 eggs.

Mrs. Wiseman for her Hopp ground (Corporation) she was of Brick House. Now Clock House, to pay two quarters to Mr. Thos. Cullam. Payd up to May 1662 £2 0s. 0d.

Bishopswood Quarter 1661

£ s. d.

Mr. Charles Jennings Olives and Mrs. Jennings widow { Luke Church payd his year customary eggs } 1 16 0

Rich. Chapman payd for Clopton Hall and payd part of Olives Lay 4 0 0

Customary Eggs from Clopton Hall 10 . . . . 8 0

John Bright "Puttox" Blowed ground only to pay 6 0

Wm. Barnard "Trutons" for Trutons and part of Minchons 2 0 0

Moutons Farm Samuel Wybert { alias Woods left 2 acres of pasture 2 acres of arable 25 acres of blowed land } 15 0

Customary Eggs 7.

John Bright "Samners" payd this year 13 4

Roger Bright "Fishers" payd this year 2 4

Rich. Clarke pasture and arable land 3 cows, 20 sheep and lambs 8 4

Customary Eggs 18 payd in kind

Thos. Playle for High Lutts . . 10 0

Thos. Smith "Gladyns" Farm sold 40 to 50 acres 8 0

Customary Eggs 3

Rich. Havers payd. 5 10

Dionyions Spooner for "Tanners" Farm 8 0

James White Warelesse farm plowed land and pasture 4 0

Henry Sweeting "Cages" farm 5 acres arable, pasture 1 acre 3 0

"Baws" farm . . . . 2 rood 0 6

Edward Bell "Broadgroves" (formerly Thos. Rust) Customary eggs 5 0

Henry Sweeting "Hulls" farm for all his petty tithes 14 9 0

Sarah Choppin widow. Church land, some plowed some pasture 3 0

John Redhede, New House Farm and for Cox and Larks pasture 4 4

Widow Philpot and Peter Philpot for pasture	1	0
John Philpot for a small strip of pasture, and 4 acres of plowed	1	3
Francis Miller for plowed land and some green	2	0
Thos. Warner plowed land	3	0
Mr. Thaires plowed land	3	0
Mr. Archer " Lower Roffie " ..	4	0
Sam Bright " Pinchways " for the farm formerly of Thos. Wood	3	0
Benjeman Newell, his Orchard he sold 2 acres of land, 1 acre 2 roods pasture, 18 acres 2 roods plowed, Customary Eggs 6	5	0
Rich. Stowell his rent £9 per annum of Church 10 acres pasture	12	0

Thos. Heywood " Martels " for the farm, and Mr. Jenning's meadow called Olynes Mead Customary Eggs 30	2	17	6
Henry Porter " Housegrounds " formerly Edward Brewex		12	0
Isaac Paye, " Brands farm " of ye Corporation Robt. Rowley to pay Customary Eggs 3			
Wm. Burr his own land 5 per annum 1 acre 2 roods pasture 5 acres blowed ground, 1 acre Hopp ground		10	0
Rich. Gamely for Churches alias Broadfields. His rent 14s. 10d. per annum whereof 10 acres plowed. Customary Eggs payd in kind		7	0
John Skinner for " Cauels farm" Customary Eggs		15	0

CHAPTER XVI

Officers Chosen by ye Minister and Parishioners on Easter Monday each year from 1679–1715. Vicar, Thomas Beaumont

	Churchwardens	*Overseers for the poor*	*Surveyors of the highways*	*Sidesmen*
1679	Thos. White	Wm. Dier, Corpn.	Wm. Taylor, Webster Corp.	Newman Mead
		James White sen., Bigods Quarter	Nicholas Wright, Bigods	Geo. Parry
		James Norris, Bishopswood	Weston Pavely, Bishops.	John Barnard
1680	Newman Mead	Thos. Smith, Clothier, Corp.	Wm. Taylor, Webster Corp.	Robt. Gyvor
		Joseph Stokes, Corp.	Nicholas Wright, Bigods	James Chopping
		Robt. Remington, Bigods	Weston Pavely, Bishops.	Geo. Parry
		John Stokes, Bishops.		
1681	Robt. Gysor	James Luckin	Thos. Wheeler	Thos. Ball
		Peter Spicer	Wm. Beaumont, Esq.	Jer. Perry
		Samuel Porter	John Stokes	James Chopping
		Richard Clerk		
1682	Thos. Ball	Geo. Ripley	Thos. Wheeler	Thos. Barker
		David Watts	Wm. Beaumont, Esq.	Rich. Havos
		Thos. Shovey	John Stokes	Jer. Perry
		John Bright		
1683	Thos. Barker	Richard Longe	Thos. Wheeler	John Sandford
		John Brewett	Wm. Beaumont, Esq.	John White
		Wm. Raymond	John Stokes	Rich. Havos
		Edward Surridge		
1684	John Sandford	Michael Wilsher	Henry Baxter	Abra. Bulling
		Wm. Seex	Wm. German jun.	John White
		Francis Skinner	John Brown	Nich. Branch
		John Mills		

Robert Wright, Constable for Bigods Quarter, in place of Geo. Perry.

1685	Abra. Bulling	Thos. White	Henry Baxter	John Taylor
		Thos. Fuller	Wm. German jun.	Nick Branch
		John Turnidge	John Brown	Andrew Rhodes
		Samuel Fitch		

	Churchwardens	Overseers for the poor	Surveyors of the highways	Sidesmen
1686	John Taylor	Thos. Wheeler	John Barrington, Esq.	Wm. Wallace
		Wm. Tailer, Clothier	Wm. Beaumont, Esq.	Andrew Rhodes
		Wm. Mills	John Stokes	John Saltmarsh
		John Sweeting		
1687	Wm. Wallace	John Barker, Carpenter	John Barrington, Esq.	Wm. Fuller, Tailor
		John Tailor, Clothier	Wm. Beaumont, Esq.	Richard Low
		Thos. Milborne	Henry Montford	John Saltmarsh
		George Lea		
1688	Henry Gilder	Henry Seex	Surveyors as previous year	Wm. Fuller, Tailor
		James Stokes		Rich. Long
		Peter Burles		John Reynolds
		Daniel Rolph		
1689	Wm. Fuller	Wm. Marriage	Sir John Dier, Bart.	John Young
		John Torman	Joseph Stokes	Ralph Sandford
		James Suckling	Francis Barnard	John Reynolds
		John Living		
1690	Wm. Sandford	John Leader	Surveyors as previous year	Simon White
		James Norris		John German
		John Mawn		John Philpot
		Richard Clerk		
1691	Simon White	Peter Spicer	Thos. Reynolds	Phillip Barker
		John Brown	Joseph Suckling	John German
		Wm. Raymond	Daniel Tharies	John Philopt
		Thos. Waskett		
1692	Philip Barker	Mark Warren	Daniel Wattes	Thos. Hisper
		John Burre	Samuel Fyche	John Turnidge
		Andrew Rodes	John Mills	Daniel White
		James Ruffle		
1693	Thos. Hisper	Joseph Drake	John Taylor sen.	Richard Long
		Wm. Seex	Wm. German	John Turnidge
		Wm. Mills	Samuel Bright	Daniel White
		Richard Havos		
1694	Thos. Hisper	Thos. White	John Collin	No change
		John Taylor jun.	Samuel Bright	
		John Burles	Thomas Shovey	
		Wm. Stileman		
1695	Richard Long	Thos. Rowley	John Wyatt	Henry Baxter
		Thos. Fuller	Thos. Shovey	John Turnidge
		James Suckling	Samuel Bright	Daniel White
		Henry Barnard		
1696	Richard Long	Thos. Reynolds	John Wyatt	Henry Baxter
		James Stokes	Edward Clerk	Richard Stockbridge
		Robt. Hanley	Samuel Bright	Daniel White
		John Stokes		

	Churchwardens	*Overseers for the poor*	*Surveyors of the highways*	*Sidesmen*
1697	Richard Long	Henry Seex	Henry Gilder	Henry Baxter
		Thomas Ball	John Mason	John Turnidge
		Andrew Rodes	Josias Warner	Daniel White
		Daniel Guvor		
1698	Henry Baxter	Samuel Porter	Henry Gilder	Wm. Barker
		Samuel Thurgood	James Suckling	Joseph Suckling
		Wm. Mills	Josias Warner jun.	Thos. Mead
		Thos. Smith		
1699	Henry Baxter	Wm. Marriage	John Sweeting	
	Wm. Barker	Josias Portway	Thos. Fuller	
	Joseph Suckling	Thos. Waskett		
	Thos. Mead	Geo. Fyche		
1700	Wm. Barker	Peter Spicer	John Gin	
	John Wyatt	John Warner	Thos. Rowley	
	Joseph Suckling	John Purchas	Edward Surridge	
	Peter Philpot	Robt. Lea		
1701	Wm. Barker	Thos. Cramphorn	Wm. Raymond	
	Wm. Wyatt	Robt. Taylor	John Taylour	
	Wm. Radley	John Little	James Ruffle	
	Peter Philpot			
1702	John Wyatt	John Leader	Wm. Beaumont, Esq.	
	Wm. Seex	John Fordham	George Cole, gent.	
	Wm. Radley	James Alliston	George Fitche	
	John Rolph	John Skinner		
1703	Wm.Wyatt	John Burr	Wm. Raymond	
	Wm. Seex	Henry Gilder	John Taylour	
	George Downs	Thos. Gyver	James Ruffle	
	John Rolph	Daniel Rolph		
1704	John Wyatt	John Torman	Thos. Shovey	
	Wm. Seex	Josias Taylor	Thos. Reynolds	
	George Downs	Thos. Rodes	Daniel White	
	John Reynolds	Daniel Smith		
1705	Wm. Seex	Joseph Drake	Humphrey Dixon	
	Robt. Waskett	Thos. Porter	John Wright	
	Jos. Alliston	Joseph Suckling	Daniel White	
	John Philpot	Samuel Bright		
1706	Wm. Seex	Thos. White	Wm. Wallis, Corp.	
	Rob. Waskett	Joseph Sandford	Robt. Tiler, Bigods	
	Joseph Alliston	John Purchas	Josias Warner, Bishops.	
	Thos. Mead	Thos. Knight		
1707	Wm. Seex	Henry Seex	Wm. Wallis	
	Robt. Waskett	Wm. Barker	Robt. Tiler	
	Joseph Alliston	Edward Surridge	Josias Warner	
	Thos. Mead jun.			
1708	Robt. Waskett	Thos. Fuller sen.	Wm. Wallis	
	Josias Portway	James Stokes	Thos. Paiment	
	Thom. Everard	Samuel Philborn	Daniel Sweeting	
	Thos. Mead jun.	Thos. Gyvor		

	Churchwardens	*Overseers for the poor*	*Surveyors of the highways*	*Sidesmen*
1709	Presume no vestry meeting held for 1709; writing is very bad.			
1710	Robt. Waskett	Joseph Wyatt	No surveyors mentioned	
	Josias Portway	Samuel Porter		
	Thom. Everard	Robt. Marriage	Robt. Falconer, vicar	
	Thos. Mead jun.	Daniel Sweeting		
1711	Robt. Falconer, vicar, being away there is no mention of churchwardens.			
		John Wyatt		
		Wm. Smith	Joseph Smith	
		Geo. Fitch	Joseph Alliston	
		Henry Baxter	Samuel Bright	
1712	Thos. Cramphorn	John Wyatt	Josias Smith	
	Thos. Everard	John Warner	Joseph Alliston	
	Thos. Mead	Robt. Lea	Samuel Bright	
1713	No change	John Burre	Rich. Reynolds	
		John Baines	John Mills	
		Thos. Rhodes		
		Daniel Rolph	John White as sidesman	
1714	No change	Peter Spicer	Geo. Cole, surveyor	
		Robt. Taylor	John White	
		Thos. Gryvor	2 for Bigods quarter	
		Henry Judd		
1715	John Wright	John Wyatt	Thos. Porter	
	Henry Gilder jun.	Thos. Low	John Wright	
	Thos. Mead	Edward Knight		
		John Skinner	Simon Jocelyn, sidesman	

CHAPTER XVII

Churchwardens' account book

This is a volume of ninety-seven folios measuring sixteen inches by ten inches. It contains the yearly accounts of the churchwardens from 1526, continuing more or less until 1584, and from there till 1621 only balances are given once a year. Then follow some resolutions at vestry meetings. From folio eighty to the end are the names of the churchwardens, sidesmen, overseers of the poor, and surveyors of the highways 1679-1761, part of which I have given you.

The binding of this book is a specimen of leather work. The outer leather binding is decorated by lines scored across it, and by fillets, cusped ormanents, and Gothic letters stamped on it by dies from the back, and so showing in relief outside. The inscription on the front is " JHESUS AND MARIA " in two panels in two-inch letters.

The following is badly formed, either by a false stroke or by the dye running. I take these to be a continuation of " JHESUS hix NASARENUS BENEDIC ILLIS," this being " Jesus of Nazareth bless them." It had undoubtedly been a service book before it came to the churchwardens.

In 1526 there is a restoration of the " steeple," by which they mean the tower. Why it should need repairing or rebuilding so soon is a query, as it was only built between 1400 and 1450. Maybe the weight of the tower was pulling away from the church because the balance was wrong. This extra expense does not sound much to us today, but it meant a lot then. There was a collection made around the parish. Robert Sturtin Sumtyme Vicar of a late tyme gave 5/- Mayster Vicar that now is gave 6s. 8d. The Church Clerk 8d. Thomas Savage gave £3 6s. 8d. John Kyng haberdasher, Rychard Parcey Fletcher, William Thyler glover. Twice a messenger was sent to Thaxted, where one by the name of Buttol was an expert in scaffold building, but without success. Robarde Kelynge was paid xjs for making the staging. The stone was quarried in the midlands and brought down in barges to Ditton, near Cambridge, thence by road to Dunmow. The lime came from Hadham and from Shelford, near Cambridge. The nails came from Takeley and the bricks (4/8 for 1,200) from Easton. Mr. Kynwelmarsh was paid 18/- for " okys and hardell " rods. The trees were cut down and used in a green state. A labourer was paid 4d. a day and a journeyman 6d. The rebuilding cost in all £18/15/9. When we look at this same tower today we must think it is the biggest bargain we have. It gives an idea of costs now compared with 450 years ago.

Particulars of the leases, indentures, bonds and securities to the inhabitants of Great Dunmow, and the writings are this present day 23rd of December 1673, delivered into the Vestry of Great Dunmow aforesaid to be there on behalf of the said parish, as follows:

1. Imprimis One lease of plowed land belonging to the Church, to James Choppin for the duration of 21 years beginning at Michaelmas, for a rent of £2 per annnm.
2. A bond from the inhabitants of Little Easton of the wish of Francis Pigaram. Dated January 22, 1669.
3. Hannah Constable's Indenture of

apprenticeship to John Parsley for 7 years dated October 6, 1710.

4. Articles from the inhabitants of Little Easton to the officers of this parish the wish of Isaac Page his wife and family dated 20th April, 1669.

5. A bond for the performance of the same Articles of the same date.

6. An Indenture of Apprenticeship from Matthias Elliott to John Allen of Chelmsford.

7. An Indenture of Apprenticeship from Matthew Till to William Kirkham of Great Easton, shoemaker, for seven years, dated June 10, 1667.

8. A bagg of evidence concerning the house bought of the widdow Hammond for the use of the poore at Great Dunmow.

Church accounts 1700-01

These are very fragmentary. There are only snatches one can pick out. William Barker is evidently the churchwarden. On June 17, 1702, he pays in rates £20/4/6 but asks that £3 may be deducted for communion wine.

	£	s.	d.
From Mr. Barker for rates ..	17	4	6
for rates ..	5	6	10
Received of Joseph Luckin....	5	6	9
Cooper Phillpott..	18	7	0
William Radley ..	6	0	0
William Taylor of Trutons	3	0	0
John Loader where the Windmill now stands	3	0	0
William Witham..		17	0
William Prior	1	7	6
John Wyatt	1	10	0

Thos. Beaumont, Vicar
William Barker
William Dyer
Neil Seers
Robert Loker
Jas. Cramphome

	£	s.	d.
1727-8 for 2 years burial of the poor, wafhing the linen, checking the clock	4	0	0
1730 Pr Mark Selby for overlooking and balancing the carpentry work done in the church		5	6
Daniel Root's Bill, as balanced by Mark Selby	20	4	0

Vicar—Samuel Burges

	£	s.	d.
1732 Vicar Samuel Burges ..			
Paid Josiah Portway's bill for 5 Tyles for the Church House ..		12	6
Paid Samuel Dennis's bill for work done at the Pest House		10	0
Paid Mr. John Bances bill for a splint to ye Church House....		11	8
Paid Mr. Pettitts bill for 52 faggotts for the Pest House ..		8	8

Churchwardens' accounts 1773. Vicar, John Mangey

	£	s.	d.
For 5 days ringing	2	10	0
John Fordham's bill for mending the clock		3	6
Robert Poulton's 2 bills for Ironwork			
Mr. Burgess and Geo. Burton's bill for burying the poor, washing the linen and looking to the clock................	2	0	0
Paid Robert Benson's bill for 2 qrs. of Lyme		16	0
Paid Henry Perry's bill for Glazing and Plumbing			
Paid John Coleman's bill for Beer to the Bricklayers and carpenters		9	2
Paid Mr. Wood's bill for beer and materials	2	16	4
Paid Mr. Vincent's bill for Communion Wine		18	8
Gave a traveller		1	6
Paid for 2 foxes		2	0

Paid for 7 days work in pulling down the old Vestry and removing the rubbish	7	0
Paid at the Spiritual Court	7	0
Paid for killing a fox..........	3	4

This is to certify that we, the Vicar and Churchwardens of Great Dunmow, did give permission to Mr. John Tolleday who had no pew to his farm called " Langwells " to build one for that farm joining to that pew that belongs to " Merks " near the Church.

Likewise, we gave leave to Richard Wyatt to build a pew joining to it for the Follie Farm, and that it was built at his own cost.

Also, we gave leave to Mr. Vincent who lives by the " Star " and to Mr. Daniel Root, a carpenter, to build two pews themselves, and their families, at their own cost, and on ye place which belonged to ye Leaders who are all gone.

Witness our hand
Samuel Burges, Vicar
Jno. Wright, Churchwarden.

Churchwardens' accounts

Paid Mark Selby for cleaning the Clock 1741.

Paid Samuel Pilbrow and Daniel Root for " palen " painting the Church House maken the Clock strike on ye little Bell May 1741.

It was agreed at the Parish Meeting to have a rate of 4d. in the £.

	£	s.	d.
Paid for ye cleaning ye Church with Pamment and Brush 1746		3	6
Paid Wm. Sweeting for thatching ye Church House 1746 ..			
Paid John Archer for looking after the Church 1748		4	0
Paid Andrew Dowsett for 3 Foxes 1761		10	0
Paid for cleaning the Vault May 1798		3	0
Paid for emptying the Vault April 1799		4	0

Churchwardens' accounts

Churchwardens - Edward Swinborne Philbrick
Isaac Malster

Vicar - - - Rev. H. L. Majendie

Disbursements Vestry—Easter 1844

	£	s.	d.
Holgate and Jarvis expenses at Visitation		5	0
Thomas Bradshaw for candles		2	11½
Joseph Ginn—Cleaning the Churchyard................		3	0
Visitation Fees and Espense	1	18	0
Joseph Parmaine for ringing (chiming)		18	0
John Coates ditto		18	0
Timothy Cock ditto		18	0
Joseph Ginn cleaning the Churchyard		5	0
Joseph Paremane ringing		18	0
Joseph Ginn cleaning the Churchyard................		5	0
Visitation Fees and expenses ..	1	1	6
Chimers 1 year to Lady-day ..	1	4	0
James Drance, Blacksmith		8	2
Dansie Carter Almanack etc.		5	2
Charles Knight, attending Clock	2	0	0
Joseph Sewell's Bill	2	3	7
Ben Cheek's Bill, sexton	6	5	6
Joseph Ginn cleaning the Churchyard................		5	0
Copying Registers of Births and Deaths	2	0	0

T. Bradshaw, Bill for Candles ..		4	6
Ann Holgate's Carpenters Bill ..	3	2	9½

Rates to be collected

April 25, 1845. H. H. Majendie, Chairman.
William Johnson
William Randell
Francis Cates
Dansie Carter
John Perry Gunn

Robt. Falconer, vicar 1710—1729

This is to certify whom it may concern that according to the Register of Baptisms of the Parish of Great Dunmow in the County of Essex, Mary Smith, once a Quaker, was born September 19, 1682 and Baptized July 5, 1707—Robt. Falconer, Vicar of Dunmow.

The Parents' names are not mentioned in the Register which is always done when the children are born in the Parish. We cannot find that any such person as the Father of Mary Smith lived in this Parish at the time of her birth—Robert Falconer, Vicar.

Whereas of complaint hath been made by you unto us two of his Magisties Justices of the poore touching the coming of Mary Smith, singlewoman (a person very infirmt) into your Parish and endeavouring to settle there, contrary to Law. And upon the examination of the said Mary Smith, duly taken upon Oath before us it does appear to us that the place of her settlement is Braintree. We do therefore adjudge ye same to and that the said Mary Smith be removed thereto and there to deliver her to ye Churchwardens or overseers of ye poore (together with a copy of this order) to be by them received and provided for according to the Law. Given under our own hands ye 29th Oct. 1702.

Mark Selby, Dunmow.

CHAPTER XVIII

Sales, bonds, leases, probates, etc.

Sale.	Robt. Calthorpe of Great Dunmow, gent. Thos. Wragg, of Ingley, gent., Christopher Wragg of Little Waltham, clerk, and Alice his wife. John Yardley of Brentwood, D.D., and Alice his wife.	Eleanor Deane of Great Dunmow and Thos. Wheeler of Great Dunmow, gent.	3 messuages lying together, in Dunmow part lately erected on lands called " Boyers " by highway from Market Cross to Church End April 25th, 1675
Sale	Greeneough Carter of Exning Suff., clerk	Samuel Bordman of Dalham, Suff., gent.	Fields, etc., called " Great Browning" 8ac " Lower Trowton" 7ac "Upper Trowton" 12ac "Angurs Field " 4ac " Lowfalls " 8ac " Sixacres" & Doe 8ac " Oldbury " 12ac " Church Lye" 6ac " Shipborden " 4ac " Westfield Meadow " 4ac " Coweyard " 2ac " Broad Meadow" 7ac abutting in par on the river running from Dunmow to Chelmsford May 1st, 1675
	Dernise George Clapham of Felsted, tanner	Elizabeth Clapham of Felsted, spinster	A messuage with orchard yards in North End Hamlet, abutting on a lane called Craddoct St., & on the highway from the Market Cross to Braintree. Aug. 24th 1681

Sale	Henry Wood of Gt. Dunmow, shoemaker	Thomas White of Gt. Dunmow, shoemaker	A mess. & cutylage with part of a house on the land of the curtilage between the tenement of the late John Bryceney, gent., now of Jas. Edwick. The tenement late of John Vintners & the Town House or Guildhall. Nov. 9th, 1685
Bond	Robt. Wright sen. of Gt. Dunmow	William Raymond of Gt. Dunmow, tanner	£31 Mar. 14th, 1700
Sale	Robt. Wright sen. of Great Dunmow, husband, and Mary his wife and Robert Wright of Gt. Easton, tailor, his eldest son	William Raymond of Gt. Dunmow, tanner	Messuage, once 2 cottages formerly in the occupation of Robert Mumford 14th March, 1700
Lease for a year	Wm. Radley of Gt. Easton, husbandman, son and heir of Wm. Radley, late of Gt. Dunmow, and grandson of Geo. Radley of Gt. Hallingbury, yeoman, decd.	Sir John Jenour, bart., of Gt. Dunmow, Sir Swinnerton Dyer, bart., of Gt. Dunmow, Wm. Beaumont, Esq., of Gt. Dunmow, and Jas. Raymond of S. Walden	Messuage in Church End adjoining the Vicarage 17th Sept. 1724
Sale	Arnold Elsall of Gt. Dunmow, perukemaker, and Sarah his wife	William Barrik of Lt. Coggeshall, yeoman	Messuage abutting on the tenement called the "White Horse" in the highway towards the Market Cross 23rd Sept., 1729
Sale	Alexander Youle of Gt. Dunmow, shopkeeper	John Wallis of Lt. Hallingbury, yeoman	A messuage in "Tanners Lane"
Sale	Joseph Banes of Gt. Dunmow, maltster, brother and heir of John Banes of the same, wheelwright, decd.	William Wallis of Gt. Dunmow, wheelwright	A messuage once 2 tenements abutting on the tenement called the "Horse Shoes" on the way from the Market Cross to Chelmsford 13th March, 1739

	Charles Sweeting surrenders by the hand of James Callthorpe, gent. to	Simon White	Messuage and tenement with gardens and orchards, etc. 30th March, 1758
Lease	Robert Clerke, Baron of the Exchequer, and Marie his daughter	Henry Longe, sen. of Gt. Dunmow, gent.	" Pound Mead " & " Kitchen Mead" and other pieces of meadows
Copy of Court Roll manor of Markes belonging to Robt. Melbourne, Esq.	Thos. Barker and Eleanor his wife	Admitted to	A tenement of 16 acres called " Cotwolders " formerly of Alexander Ingram, of whom Eleanor Barker is the nearest heir 17th Oct., 1625
Sale	Richard Crabb of Gt. Dunmow, weaver, and his wife Margaret	George Chapman of Leaden Roding, thatcher	Moiety of the Mill House
Will	John Saward of Gt. Dunmow, baker	To his wife, Winifred, the house at Gt. Dunmow in which Wm. Judd lives, until his daughters Philippa and Annis become of age. To Sarah and Grace Feedome, daughters of his dau. Winifred Freedome 20s. To his wife the house in which they dwell and after her death to his other daughters, Elizabeth, Margaret and Martha. 13th Feb., 1638	
Sale	Thos. Brand of Gt. Dunmow, weaver and Mary his wife	William Saward of Gt. Dunmow, husbandman	Messuage called the " Mill House " with garden etc., in Windmill Street, one end abutting on the way from the Market to Stortford S, tenement and garden of Wm. Purley after of John Younglove, W and messuage once of John Parkes, now of Henry Cavell 20th Oct., 1666

Copy of manorial roll Manor of Gt. Dunmow of Wm. Lord Maynard	Charles Sweeting	Admitted to	Messuage etc., of William Sweeting his brother
Quit-claim	Mary Burr, widow of John Burr of Lt. Dunmow, yeoman, and Edward Burr of Lt. Dunmow, yeoman, executors of last will of John Burr	William Barnard of Gt. Dunmow, yeoman	Crofts of land and pasture with the moor adjoining called " Hobbekyns " 10 acres. Nov. 20th, 1662
	Notification Charles, Earl of Warwick	That Thos. Luckin and Mr. Edwd. Minyorin commissary Court of the Bishop of London appointed Joan Terry as guardian of Mary, infant daughter of John Terry	27th May, 1668
Fine	William Brampton and Thos. Porter, pll.	William Brampton jun. and Mary his wife, John King, John Preene and Sarah his wife, Rich. Crabbe and Margaret his wife	2 messuages, 2 cottages, gardens, etc., and the moiety of 2 messuages and one orchard, Martinmas in 15 days 1664
Copy of will	William Sandford of Gt. Dunmow, bricklayer	To his wife his freehold messuage etc., proved in the court of the Archdeacon of Middx. 23rd Feb. 1703	
Sale	William Raymond of Earls Colne, tanner	Robert Seex of Gt. Dunmow, butcher	3 messuages in Mill St. abutting on the George E and " Windmill " Street N 16th July, 1680
Copy of Court Roll Manor of Bannister Maynard	Hannabal Constable surrenders to	Henry Baxter	Piece of land 46ft. x 75ft. abutting on tenement of Jos. Stokes, N. Tanners Lane E 4th October 1690

Sale	John Barnard of Good Easter, yeoman, son of Wm. Barnard late of Gt. Dunmow, yeoman	Henry Seex Gt. Dunmow, butcher	2 crofts called Hobkyns with a pasture called " The Moor " (10 ac) & a close on which a barn has been built 15th November, 1693
Sale	Thos. Champhorne of Gt. Dunmow, plummer	Jeffrey Staines, Esq. of Hatfield Regis, Richard Raymolds of Gt. Dunmow, innholder	Lands as above 15th Sept., 1718 " The Bull " in Windmill Street
Release	Mary Broomhead, Hatfield Regis, widow, her son Wm. Broomhead of St. Botolph's, Bishopsgate, carpenter, and Mary his wife	Richard Reynolds of Great Dunmow. Innholder.	Messuage called " The Bull " in Windmill Street.
Sale	Elizabeth Cramphorne, widow of Thos. Cramphorne of Gt. Dunmow, glazier	James Goney jun. & Richard Goney his brother, Gt. Dunmow, websters	Messuage in Windmill St. abutting on the highway to Stortford & tenement heretofore a common Inn called " The Green Man " March 27th, 1723
Copy of Court Roll Manor of Gt. Dunmow	Henry Baxter of Bethnal Green Middx, mariner, surrender to	Henry Baxter sen. of Gt. Dunmow	Messuage near " Tanners Lane " 4th May, 1730
Sale	James Govey of High Easter, son of James Govey jun. of Gt. Dunmow, and Richard Govey his uncle of Bocking, webster	Roger Hodglain of Gt. Dunmow, glover	Messuage in " Windmill Street " with a piece of land added 25th June, 1739
Release	Simon White of Gt. Dunmow, tailor	Mark Selby of Gt. Dunmow, joiner	Messuage in Windmill Street 7th June, 1747
Lease (paper)	Edmund Moore of Gt. Dunmow, tailor	Wm. Hocklie of Thaxted, currier	Tenement with gardens 7th July, 1682
Lease (on paper)	George Chapman, thatcher, and Elizabeth his wife	Thomas Porter of Gt. Dunmow, innkeeper	Messuage called " The Mill House " 28th Oct., 1661

Lease for a year	Alice Stokes of Gt. Dunmow, widow of Joseph Stokes, clothier	Josias Taylor of Gt. Dunmow, clothier	Messuage, etc., & a croft, called Talberds Lease 1st Oct., 1705
Probate of Will	Mary Millbank	To her daughter Ann, wife of William Thorn, To her grandsons William and Abraham Thorn £5 each To her granddaughters Mary Yalden & Mary Wood the same	A croft called " Paled Piece " 9th March, 1750
Lease	Daniel Philpott of Gt. Dunmow, sone and heir of Dan Philpott	Rebecka Philpott of Gt. Dunmow	Messuage in Gt. Dunmow 28th Nov., 1771
Lease	Ezekiel Nichols of Dunmow, miller	William Woodham & Thos. Bird, both of Bps. Stortford, brewers	Public House called " The Royal Oak " 30th Oct., 1790
Sale by Recovery	Robert Baxter & George Scullard of Boswell Court St. Clement Danes & Hester Wade his wife	Stafford Squire, gent.	Messuage with garden, 50 acres of land, 10 of meadows, and 10 of pasture in Gt. Dunmow and High Easter
Sale	Gregory Lythe of Ashdon, husbandman	Clement Rawlinson, of Gt. Dunmow, yeoman	5 acres at upper end of Sparrows land with buildings etc., between way to Church End and the wood of Robert Melbourne called Marks manor. 9 acres in great field of " Sparrows Land " a barn standing on " Codcopps "
Sale	Thomas Playle of Gt. Dunmow, husbandman	James Calthorpe of Gt. Sampford, gent.	Messuage called " Martells," & a close of 6 acres & another field of 8 acres 7th May, 1677

Sale	John Everard of Stisted, tailor, & Susan, his wife	John Taylor of Gt. Dunmow, cooper	Messuage with curtilage, between the messuage late of Will Cherke, gent., and the tenement of Job Guiver & orchard of Rose Moyne, abutting at one end on the way to the market cross and on the other end " Tabotts " or " Taberds Lease " 1st July, 1630
Release and Quitclaim	John Vintner of Gt. Dunmow, butcher, son & heir of John Vintner & Richard Vintner his younger brother	Robert Calthorpe of Gt. Dunmow, gent.	Messuage by highway from Dunmow market to Chelmsford called " Causie Croft " 3rd May, 1650
Bond assurer title	Thos. Barnard of Lt. Canfield, yeoman, Wm. Barnard of Lt. Canfield, yeoman	Sir Andrew Jenour of Gt. Dunmow, bart.	£40 Messuage in Gt. Dunmow, in occupation of Richard Lea 1st May, 1650
Sale	Theodore Haak of City of London, Esq. & Elizabeth his wife	Nicholas Ashton, cit. merchant tailor, of London, & John Kendall of Bassingbourne Hall	" Cowlease " " Broke Mead " & Little Wood Field in Gt. Dunmow 13th Feb., 1667
Assignment of lease	John Yardley, of Bps. Stortford, Dr. of Physic, & Thos. Creed of Gt. Dunmow	Sarah Balls of Gt. Dunmow, widow	Messuage between tenement late in occupation of Eleanor Deane, widow, & tenement late of Thos Balls and now in occupation of his widow Sarah Balls
Sale	James Lerett of Kelvedon, yeoman	Thomas Beaumont Vicar, Gt. Dunmow	Messuage in " Church End " between way from Dunmow market & Gt. Bardfield by the river 13th Dec., 1681

Sale	Joan Smith, widow of Thomas Smith late of Gt. Dunmow, clothier	Thomas Smith eldest son of the late Thos.	Messuage between mess. sometime of Thos. Creed now of Josias Portway & mess. of James Edwick abutting on way from Dunmow Market to Thaxted 17th June, 1691
Lease	Isaac Dawes of Hatfield Regis, yeoman, and Hannah his wife. Francis Bowsell of the same, cordwainer and Mary his wife	Wm. Seex of Gt. Dunmow, butcher	Messuage with 12 acres abutting on highway from Dunmow to Chelmsford and called Katys-at-Mill 2nd June, 1701
Sale	Henry Leader of Gt. Easton, gent., bro. and heir of John Leader of Gt. Easton, gent.	Robert Taylor of Great Dunmow, webster	Messuage at Rude End between those of John Rouse and Thos. Cramphos and abutting on the way to Stortford 7th May, 1719
Sale	William Seex of Coggeshall, tanner, Thos. Abraham, yeoman	Mary Seex of Great Dunmow	Messuage called "Yardleys" at a place called "Park" Corner by way from the Market Cross to Chelmsford 13th Oct., 1730
Lease	John Vintner of Dunmow, butcher	Edward Vessey of Great Dunmow, yeoman	Messuage on the highway from Dunmow Market to Chelmsford, also Causie Croft (5 acres) 7th Nov., 1646
Grant	Richard Vintner of Great Dunmow	John Vintner of Great Dunmow, yeoman, and his brother	Messuage sometime two tenements called Barbois which John Vintner's father purchased of Wm. Cooke, gent, and Margery his wife in 1609 19th July 1646

Assignment	Robert Calthorne jun. of Dunmow, gent., executor of Edward Vessey of Gt. Easton, yeoman	Thos. Stokes of Little Easton, gent.	Mesuage called "Causie Croft"
Sale	John Sorrell of Stebbing, gent., John Barnard of Gt. Dunmow, gent., and Margary his wife (for the poor of Dunmow)	Rt. Hon. Sir Andrew Jenour, bart., of Gt. Dunmow, and Robert Calthorpe jun, of Gt. Dunmow, gent.	Messuage called "Dame Agnus" and Dame Agnas Field in Thaxted and "Wiston Croft" at Cutlars Green 1st June, 1652
Sale	Richard Jennyns of St. Georges in the Borough of Southwark, grandson of Anthony Jennyns and Priscilla his wife	Robert Calthorpe jun. Gt. Dunmow, gent.	3 closes called "Whites Crofts," abutting on "Porters" on way to High Roding 3rd April, 1663
Sale	Elizabeth Cramphorne widow of Thos. Cramphorne of Gt.	James Govey of Gt. Dunmow, jun., webster	Messuage in "Windmill Street" once used as an inn called "The Green Man" abutting in the highway from the Market to Stortford 23rd March, 1723
Lease	Rt. Worshipful Robert Clerke, Baron of the exchequer, & Mary Clerke one of his daughters	Henry Longe of Gt. Dunmow, gent.	"Kitchen Mead" planted with hops 6 acres, "Pounds" Mead 7 acres, Hopground called "Quattages" 3 acres, "Great Maundfield" 13 acres and "Little Maudfield" 4 acres 13th Nov., 1596
	Robert Smythe of Woking, Surrey, gent.	George Skarpe, servant of John Mallowes, of the Inner Temple, gent.	To take seisin of the above lands from Robert & Mary Clerke 12th May, 1597

Sale	William Pollard of Barnston, gent., and Thos. Bridge of Gt. Dunmow, gent.	Thos. Rhodes of Gt. Dunmow, yeoman	Messuage with a close of meadow called " Onyons " and a pightle, containing in all 2 acres abutting on way to Merks Hill lands holden of Bigods and Ingrams Mead 4th Oct., 1736
Copy of Court Roll as above Lord Maynard	Death of Mary Warner, widow	Admission of Jane Frisby, glover	Messuage in " Rood End " 13th Oct., 1759
	Ezekiel Nicholls of Gt. Dunmow, miller	George Wade of Gt. Dunmow, gent.	A stable in Gt. Dunmow, as per schedule 17th Feb., 1794
Sale	Ann Raymond of Ipswich, widow of Rich. Raymond, clerk	Henry Wood of Gt. Dunmow, cordwainer	Messuage the Chapel or Townhouse 13th July, 1659
Agreement	John Enever of Islington, apothecary	Geoffrey Stanes of Ryes Hatfield Broad Oak	Land and tenements in Gt. Dunmow Feb. 28th, 1717
Lease	Thomas Drake of Gt. Dunmow, blacksmith	Robert Remington of the same, surgeon	Messuage and Smithy adjoining " The Angel Inn, " Shop Row Aug. 13th, 1672
Deed to lead use of fine	John Judd of Lt. Canfield, yeoman, & Dorothy his wife	Wm. Leader of Broxted, surgeon, and Rbt. Seex of Gt. Dunmow, butcher	Messuage next to the " Saracen's Head " Feb. 2nd, 1677
Sale	William Fuller of Fyfield, tailor	William Seex of Dunmow, butcher	Shop in " Bullocks Row " 25th June, 1685
Lease	Sir Andrew Jennour, bart., Robt. Melbourne, Thomas Pomphrett of Buttsbury, with Samuel Wiberd and James Raymond, churchwardens	William Barnard of Gt. Dunmow	" Church Acre " Sept. 30th, 1654

Bond	John Bernard of Gt. Dunmow, gent.	Sir Andrew Jenour and Robt. Calthorpe jun., gent.	£460 June 1st, 1652
Copy of Court roll Clapton Hall or South Hall Anne Petre	Death of Thomas Pomphrett, gent.	Admission of Edward Franklin	Messuage called "Heynotts" and land called "Lyons" 20 acres June 4th, 1667
Fine	Edmund Baker, gent., Thomas Myborne, pl.	Edward Eldred and Dorothy his wife. James Reynold and Margaret his wife. William Stocke & Helen his wife, dec.	A messuage, 2 barns, garden, orchard 200 acres of land, 20 of pasture and 20 of wood in Dunmow and Stebbing 1599
Sale	William Raymond of Earls Colne, tanner	Thos. Sewell of Lt. Easton & Edwin Morrell of Thaxted	2 messuages and a loft in Windmill Street
Fine	Richard Weston, Esq.	Kenelm Throkmorton	8 acres of pasture called Dunmow Park Octave of St. Mich. 1561
Sale	John Aylett late of High Roding, yeoman	Anne Courtman, widow of Will Courtman of "Dagnams," Hornchurch, and Thomas Postumas Legatt of Dagnams, eldest son of the said Anne	Lands at Gt. Dunmow known as "Rothingelye" or "Gt. Dunmow Field," Lt. Dunmow Field "Cliffords Mead," in all 80 acres 1st Nov., 1627
Sale	Gregory Little of Ashdon, husbandman	Wm. Fuller of Gt. Dunmow, butcher	Croft of $2\frac{1}{2}$ acres called Sedcopps with a barn built on it, by the lane from Gt. Dunmow church to the Ford. 22nd Nov., 1628

Sale	John Vyntner of Gt. Dunmow, butcher, brother and heir of Ambrose Vyntner of Gt. Dunmow, tanner, decd.	Robert Melbourne of Gt. Dunmow, gent.	Close of pasture between Milbournes houses and land and a chase leading from the way from Dunmow Market to Braintree to a parcel of the demesne lands of Robt. Melbourne Sept. 24th, 1628
Sale	Gregory Little of Ashdon, husbandman	Clement Dawlinson of Gt. Dunmow	Two closes of pasture called "Sparrows Land" by the highway from Dunmow Market to Church End 11th July, 1629
Sale	John Whitinge alias Androwes of Gt. Dunmow	Ambrose Vintner of Gt. Dunmow, tanner	Close of pasture called "Causey croft" between "Land meade" and highway to Chelmsford and abutting on a lane leading from the highway to the meadow of the manor of Clopton Hall March 8th, 1622
Sale	John Pampelyn of Maldon, son and heir of John Pampelyn late of Gt. Dunmow, also John Pampelyn of Gt. Dunmow, son of the above	John Babbe of Gt. Dunmow, butcher	A curtilage and garden called "Sprangers" by the croft of pasture, late of George Melbourne 10th March, 1632
Sale	John Lord of White Roding, yeoman	John Mowland of Lt. Canfield & John of Guyner Tilty, yeoman	Mess. called "Broadgores close" of 3 acres called Claypitt field and parcel of land and meadow cont. 2 acres called "Blackacres" Feb. 20th, 1635
Bond	John Vintner of Gt. Dunmow, butcher	Edward Vessey of Gt. Dunmow, yeoman	£200 Nov. 7th, 1646

Sale	William Barnard of Gt. Dunmow, yeoman	Samuel Boardman of Denham, Suff., gent.	Field called " Lesalls " cont. 4 acres 4th Oct., 1662
Receipt	Theo. Haak, Esq., of London	Nicholas Ashton, cit. merchant tailor of London	£445, in discharge of a mortgage on lands in Dunmow, the redemption of which was conveyed in trust to Nich. Ashton by Eliz. Mordaunt, widow of Chas. Jenys, Sir Wm. Wiseman, bart., George Stradling, D.D., and William Twinour, gent., in persuance of the will of Chas. Jenys Feb. 14th, 1666
Sale	George Radley of Gt. Hallingbury, yeoman	William Wright, son of George Radley	Mess. & curtilage at Church End abutting on way from Market Place to the Church Oct. 20th, 1668
Sale	Dionis Sponer of Gt. Dunmow, yeoman	William Wright of Gt. Dunmow, yeoman	Mess. in "Tanners Lane" Oct. 18th, 1666
Bond	John Brett of Langford, yeoman	Robt. Mountford of Gt. Dunmow, yeoman, and Robt. Barker of the same, weaver	£200 Feb. 15th, 1672
Sale	Samuel Bordman of Denham, Suff., gent.	James Raymond of Gt. Dunmow, tanner	Two closes of pasture called " Jaikles Croft " cont. 4 acres at Shingle Cross abutting on highway to Chelmsford W., Dunmow Park N, meadow by the river E and a way leading to said meadow S 13th July 1672

Release of Legacy	Thos. Haselfoot	George Scullard	£200 under the will of Elizabeth Lund of Islington, widow, on property in Gt. Dunmow and High Easter 14th May, 1747
Lease (paper)	Hannable Constable of Gt. Dunmow, widow	Henry Baxter of Gt. Dunmow, glover	Parcel of ground used for a watering yard, part of the orchard of the said Hannable

CHAPTER XIX

Lionel Lukin and his inventions

Lionel Lukin of Long Acre, parish of St. Martin's-in-the-Fields, Co. of Middx, Coach Builder. An improvement in the construction of boats and small vessels for either sailing or rowing, which will neither overset in violent gales, nor sudden gusts of wind, nor sink if by any accident they be filled with water.

This patent has been included because Lionel Lukin was born at Dunmow on May 18, 1742, the youngest son of William Lukin and Ann Stokes of Clopton Hall, a member of an old Essex family. The family moved to Blatches, Little Dunmow, soon after Lionel was born, but they still kept a hold on the town and church and his wife was later buried in Dunmow churchyard in 1803. Besides being a renowned coach builder to the London elite, he invented many other things. In 1790 he published a description of his life-boats, illustrated and to scale. He built another life-boat and named it *Experiment* (this was confiscated as a smuggler in a foreign port) and another he called *The Witch*. He also invented a raft for rescuing people from under the ice, which he presented to the Royal Humane Society, and an adjustable reclining bed for patients, which he presented to various infirmaries. Lukin died at the age of 92 on February 16, 1834, at Hythe in Kent. Unfortunately he was blind for the last ten years of his life. See illustration.

Copy by David L. Lipson.

Lionel Lukin, who made the first life-boat and was the originator of that principle of safety by which many lives and much property have been saved from shipwreck. This is a family miniature. The back of the frame contains locks of his light brown hair and his familiar monogram, L.L.

CHAPTER XX

The Beaumonts of Clock House (or Goston Lodge)

Thomas Beaumont, the second son of Sir Thomas Beaumont, of Coleoton, Stoughton, Leicestershire, came to be vicar of Great Dunmow in 1678. His youngest brother, William, soon followed. I can find nothing regarding him except his burial entry in Dunmow register, but his grandson George Beaumont was born at Clock House in 1726 and afterwards succeeded to the estates in Leicestershire as well as Dunmow and was sixth baronet. He was married in 1751 to Rachel Howland, of Stone Hall, near Dunmow, but his married life was of short duration, for he died in 1762. Two of their sons—William and Charles—died in infancy, and only one—George Howland Beaumont—remained, becoming the seventh baronet at the age of eight. His mother remained at Clock House, evidently used as a dower house of Coleoton Hall, which had been uninhabited for a century and rebuilt. She died here at the great age of ninety-eight and was buried in the grave of her husband in the chancel of Dunmow church in 1814. Her son, Sir George Howland Beaumont, in 1778 married Margaret Willes, daughter of John Willes, of Astrop, and granddaughter of Lord Chief Justice Willes. This very gifted pair were associated with the great poets, men of letters and artists of their time. We can scarcely think of them without recalling Wordsworth, Coleridge, Southey, Scott, Reynolds, Haydon, Wilkie and others of brilliant genius. Scholar, artist and no mean judge of literature, Sir George was distinguished by many social qualities, by that delicate tact which never failed him, and by that sympathy and generosity which so often raised struggling genius to recognition and success. In an age when society was to a large extent gross in living and indifferent to religion, George and Margaret were conspicuous for their refinement and Christian example. Lady Beaumont was a discerning critic of her day, and a gentlewoman of great charm. Coleridge stayed with them in 1804. He waxed eloquent in praise of the beautiful scenery and quiet serenity of Dunmow. When Wordsworth came to Dunmow in 1809 he also was impressed by the solitude and uninterrupted quiet of the place. Perhaps if they could come back today they might change their minds! Sir George Howland Beaumont was instrumental in persuading the Government to present to the nation the Angerstein collection, and he also gave sixteen pictures of his own. This was largely responsible for the opening of the National Gallery.

Rachel, the mother of Sir George Howland Beaumont, was a widow for fifty-two years, and when at last she died in 1814 her son wrote this very lovely epitaph to her:

" *The dreadful hour is come, 'tis come, 'tis past;*
That gentle sigh, dear mother, was thy last,
And now, diffused among the blest above,
Glows the pure spirit of maternal love,
Tinged by whose beam my very failings shone,
Graced in thy eyes with something not their own.

Sir George Howland Beaumont, Bart., of Goston Lodge, now known as Clock House.

No more affection shall thy fancy cheat,
Or warp thy judgement when again we meet,
But every action, in its native hue,
Rise undisguised and open to thy view.
May every action then be duly weigh'd,
Each virtue cherish'd and each duty paid,
That when my trembling soul shall wing her flight
Through death's dark valley to the realms of light
I may expect, where no false views beguile,

The approving look of that accustomed smile;
Blest smile, becoming her sublime abode,
And harbinger of pardon from my God."

Sir George had a seizure and erysipelas set in, which proved fatal. This happened in February 1827. In less than two years his wife, Margaret, whose life had been so irradiated with spiritual light, died and the world-famous group of poets and artists lost two loyal friends. They are both buried in the family vault at Coleoton, Leicestershire.

Clock House

Clock House is the oldest brick house in Dunmow. For a long time it was called Brick House, there being no other large house built of Tudor brick. It was built about 1580, with a fine front of three stories. It has much original detail, especially windows and gables. The E front has a curvilinear gable at each end with moulded brick coping and ball finials, and there are similar gables on the north and south sides. There are moulded brick string courses between the stories and a moulded brick plinth at the base. Nearly all the windows are the original ones (some blocked) and have plastered or painted moulded brick heads and jambs, mullions and transomes. The E front has windows of three and four lights and the gable windows are surmounted by small brick pediments. Some windows have original glazing and fastenings. There is a central projecting brick porch on the front with moulded brick pilasters and entablature. There are original rainwater heads and pipes on east, north and south sides. On the centre of the tiled roof is a square timber turret with an old clock (a replica of the one on Dover castle) and an octagonal cupola containing a bell by Bryan Eldridge dated 1651. There are two original chimney-stacks with octagonal shafts, two priest-holes and other interior features.

On the right is Clock House and on the left is The Limes, the former well known as the home of the Beaumonts for about 250 years, built in 1586.

CHAPTER XXI

Resolutions and declarations

At a meeting of the inhabitants of the hundred of Dunmow and several adjoining Parishes, in the county of Essex, Holden at the Saracen's Head in Great Dunmow on Tuesday the first day of January 1793.

Whereas certain publications at once inconsistent with the fundamental principles of the English Government, subversive of civil subordination, destructive of social happiness, and by their fallacious plausibility strongly tending to excite sedition, have been dispersed among the people of this kingdom, and an opinion generally prevails that associations have been formed and correspondences entered into calculated to introduce confusion and anarchy.

We, inhabitants of the Hundred of Dunmow, and adjoining Parishes, think it our duty to declare our zealous attachment to the British Constitution, consisting of King, Lords and Commons, our full conviction of the advantages derived from it to persons of all ranks and all denominations, and our firm confidence that as it has attained its present degree of perfection by successive improvements through a long series of ages, so it is fully competent to make such further improvements, as from time to time may be found expedient.

And we do therefore RESOLVE that we will oppose to the utmost of our power all attempts to subvert injure or disparage it, and use our best endeavours to bring to justice all such persons as shall utter treasonable words, post up or distribute inflammatory hand bills, or adopt any other means to raise commotions, excite disloyalty to the King or disaffection the government.

And in order that the zeal of no person may carry him beyond proper bounds we declare that we will exert our utmost endeavours to prevent every insult or molestation to individuals which may at any time take place, to the terror or injury of His Majesty's loyal and peaceable subjects.

And it is recommended to the officers of the several parishes and hamlets within the Hundred of Dunmow to transcribe the said Resolutions and Declarations and to request a signature of approbation of them and all such principal inhabitants of their respective parishes that may not have attended this meeting that their such signatures now obtained be entered with those resolutions and declarations in the parish book in which the overseers accounts are usually kept and that they be brought for the inspection of the magistrates at the next meeting that thus the whole may remain a perpetual memorial of the attachment of the hundred of Dunmow to the principles of the British constitution and be satisfactory evidence and that it is not the language of party but the general voice of the people.

Resolved unanimously.

That the thanks of this meeting be given to the Rev. Nicholas Toke for advening this meeting.

Resolved unanimously.

That the thanks of this meeting be given to Sir Henry Maynard, not only for his readiness in taking the chair and his conduct on it, but also for his excellent speech, in defence of the British Constitution.

Resolved unanimously.

That the thanks of this meeting be given to the Rev. John Howlett for drawing up the above Resolutions and Declarations.

Resolved unanimously.

That the letter presented to this meeting by Mr. Wm. Johns from the Protestant Dissenters making the Hundred of Dunmow and signed by a vast number of respectable persons be inserted in the *Chelmsford Chronicle*, the *County Chronicle* and the *General Evening Post*.

John Parsons John Barnard	Churchwardens
James Scruby Wm. Portway John Scruby	Overseers

Extracted from Great Dunmow overseers' accounts, 1785.

CHAPTER XXII

Napoleonic wars

March 8, 1793. A list of those who are to carry the soldiers from Great Dunmow to the following:

Mr. Greenleaf a waggon to Braintree (baggage)
by Linsol Braintree
by Mr. John Barnard
2nd July by Mr. Woodley to Chelmsford
21st July by Mr. Woodley to Chelmsford
by Mr. James Scruby to Billericay
1774 March 5th by Mr. B. Foakes to Braintree
March 14th by Mr. John Scruby to Thaxted
May 10th by Mrs. Mills to carry the Militia to Chelmsford
September 5th by Mr. Clapton to Chelmsford
November 5th to carry the Cambridge Militia to Walden
Wm. Portway jun., Wm. Sweeting, Joseph Bright, Edward Day, Prudence Wyatt
November 8th to carry the baggage to Chelmsford
James Matthams, Mary Stone, Geo. Finch
John Barnard, James Scruby
To carrying baggage to Walden Geo. Greenleaf
April 20th 1795 Mrs. Mills to Walden
April 22nd 1795 Mrs. Hardy to Thaxted
April 23rd 1795 Mrs. Bush to Chelmsford
May 12th 1795 Mr. Woodley to Ongar

And so it goes on all through the Napoleonic wars. It would seem that we had troops stationed in the town. They could not have all been Dunmow men.

Dunmow was designated as a hospital centre, and hundreds of tons of hospital equipment were brought here against the time when " old Bonie " should arrive.

Draft List of Dunmow Volunteers 1800 (Mounted)

L. Maynard	Nich. Patmore	For the Horse:
S. Chamberlain	Ed. Harridge	A leath Halter each
G. Ward	J. Briggs	Russic Duc. nose bag,
W. Vintener. 1st	B. Foakes 8th	Corn Bag,
J. Jarvis	Thom. Barnard	Comb and brush,
[some crossed out]	J. Scruby	Main comb,
		Sponge Picker
A. Tabrum		
I. Tabrum		
S. Stubbings	J. Leader	
N. Lawrence	J. Clapton	

Nich. Potter. 2nd
John Speller

Fred Gibbon
N. Giblin
Jos. Giblin
Sam. Barnard. 3rd
James Haylock
T. Haylock

Mat. Davey
Chester Ginn
Nich. White
Clem. Cliftin
Wm. Gooth. 4th
Mr. Lance

Wm. Walford
J. Phillips
Chris. Phillips
W. Cheveney
Wm. Rogerd. 5th
Jas. Giblin

Saml. Norris
Chas. Davey
H. Seex
W. Seex
J. Woolly. 6th
J. Randall

M. Wilson
R. Barnard
Shelley Stock
J. Steward. 7th
G. Parris
[one crossed out]

Rich. Kidd. 9th
N. Baker
J. Raven
Wm. Kidd

N. Barnard
Chas. Barker
J. Barker
S. B. Chamberlayne
A. Chaplin. 10th
Genl. Henniker

Jas. Cornell
Wm. Clarke
J. Jewell. 11th
T. Mawood
James King
James Milborne

J. Johnstone
H. Joyce
J. Marshall
Thom. White. 12th
A. Poulter
[one missing]

To be taken with them:

Shaving apparatus
A good flannel
Cap with flaps.
A thick flannel jacket.
Everyone a great coat.
Haversack of canvas.
Knive, fork and spoon.
3 pair breeches.

Each Principal of the Troop to collect such money as is necessary to deploy the Common Expense of N. Vincomb for all his providing in equal shares.

Over hanging supica of

(yellow)
3 pairs shoes.
3 ,, socks.
3 Cloakes.
1 metal buttonary.

POOR RELIEF IN GREAT DUNMOW DURING THE NAPOLEONIC WARS

The problem of poor relief became more acute during the last decade of the eighteenth century than at any previous time. The duty of administrating and supervising the workhouse fell to the local authorities and the J.P. of the parish. At the vestry meetings the overseers were appointed to administer the poor relief for the year, and it is from their accounts that our knowledge of the conditions of the poor at that time is chiefly obtained. The overseers' accounts for the parish of Great Dunmow during this period show a great increase in the amount of poor relief given. As late as 1770 one could note in Dunmow a decline in the manufacture of bays and blankets, in which the poor were chiefly employed, but in 1793 only a few families still carried on the craft, owing to the rise in the Yorkshire woollen industry.

Furthermore, about this time the price of bread was rising, and by the end of the century the quartern loaf had reached 11d., while wages failed to rise accordingly. It was a time of great hardship for the agricultural labourer, and Dunmow had its quota of paupers. It is not surprising that some of the inhabitants became unruly, and in 1786 a riot occurred over the removal of the town pump. The turnpike Commissioners moved it to a slightly different place. The people's nerves were on edge, probably aggravated by empty stomachs. The townsmen proceeded to erect another pump where the other one had stood, whereupon the commissioners called a meeting to support them. A riot ensued, and the magistrates were driven into the Saracen's Head and the fire bell was rung. It was not till the justices read the Riot Act that the people dispersed. Various measures to improve the conditions of agricultural labourers and to prevent the increase of paupers were put forward by the vicar, the Rev. John Howlett, who published pamphlets on population, the poor, and other economic subjects. According to Howlett the position of the agricultural labourer had deteriorated absolutely during the eighteenth century, and since Parliament had legislated successfully against combinations of workmen it ought to prevent combinations of masters. In a survey of Dunmow based on a family of five he thought that on an average the condition of a wage-earning family in 1796 was no better than a pauper family in the workhouse sixty years previously. The toiling man who reaped our fields tore the clothes from his back, ground the flesh from his bones and had the food snatched from his mouth. So which was the better off, the toiler or the pauper? The remedy he proposed was compulsory provision for the support of the poor, legally regulated, not left to the discretion of local bodies. He was not to see this realized till 1834 by the passing of the Poor Law Amendment Act. From 1795 onwards the amount of relief paid rose alarmingly, and entries of the following kind began to appear: " Allowance to a child at Much Easton, 20 weeks £1. Money allowed 6d. a head for 4 weeks. In 1796 arrears of poor rate from land £6 5s. 0d. Eliz. Barnard unpayed." However, the main part of the book is made up of disbursements: " Paid to Thomas Joyce for beer for the burial of Wm. Hoy 3s. To Mr. Howlett and Clerk 15/3d." There were frequent entries of money to the poor in place of flour, which was becoming very dear. Another frequent disbursement was for spinning. In the workhouse the men were frequently set to work cutting up wood, while the women were given raw material with which to spin. " April 1795 Spinning £4 3s. 5½d." Other entries for 1798 show that breeches were bought at 5/6 a pair and shoes at 5/-, widow Bowtel's rent was paid, a doctor's bill was settled for £20/15/6, the governor of the workhouse was paid £10/9/10, and Mr. Draper was paid 16/9 for work on Burton's cottage. Likewise in 1801 £1/13/- was paid for the lying-in of Ann Achers, while Mr. Alliston's pest-house bill involved £2/16/3. The constable too received payment from the overseer, and in 1809 Constable Gibbons's bill came to £6/3/5. It was by his orders that the parish cage was repaired.

CHAPTER XXIII

Great Dunmow's vestry accounts

Held at the Town Hall
Extracts from vestry accounts, 1787-93

		£	s.	d.
May 9	John Linsell for farming the Workhouse for one month	13	8	0
July 22	It is agreed that Mr. John Burton be paid of the money for Easter dinner	2	2	0
Sept. 24	It was agreed that a meeting should be held at the Guildhall on Oct. 7th in order that every land-owner and house-holder shall be there to show their rents and sware to the same.			
Apl. 1788	Church House Rent to Lady Day	2	16	0
	Beer for Loader's wife's funeral		3	0
Oct. 1788	Beer for the burial of Wm. Hoy		3	0
Feb. 1789	For nursing John Starr in the pest house	1	7	6
Dr.	Dr. Raynor's bill	1	9	6
	Dr. James, left over from last year		19	7
Aug. 1789	John Taylor's Constable bill		19	6
	John Samuel's Constable bill	1	3	6
	Paid for the Marriage of Ann Eniver	3	3	3
	To the charge of marrying H. Williams		6	0
	For Jos. Pearmains and his wife a bill for nursing for 5 weeks in the pest house	2	10	0
	A month's payment to the man and his wife at the pest house	2	0	0
	Martin Willis, bill for wood	6	0	0
	Paid Mr. Ben Foakes bill for wood	14	0	0
	Edward Buttons Constable bill	1	2	11
	Abednego Vails ditto		8	0
June 1790	Paid to Jos. Pearmain for a month's nursing at the pest house	2	0	0
	Paid Widow Milbourne for carrying things to the pest house		4	0
	Dr. Raynor's bill for attending the poor for a year	16	16	0
	Paid Jos. Pearmain for nursing of the Small-pox up to this day	1	10	0
	Paid to Mary Ann Sampford for nursing of Small-pox 5 weeks in the pest house	1	5	0
May 1792	James Catchpole farming the Workhouse, 22 persons at 2/7½ each, for a week	10	15	0

		£	s.	d.
	Mr. Catchpole's bill for money laid out exclsuive from above	3	5	4
	Mr. Wm. Portway received of Samuel Taylor the sum of ..	24	0	0
	for and in consideration in discharge of a bastard child chargeable to the parish.			
	Allowance agreed by Parishioners to my journey to Rev. Toke and to attending the Marriage of Elizabeth Stammers ..		5	0
	Edward Reynolds's Constable bill ..	1	4	6
	Thos. Ford's ditto	4	2	1
	Dr. Raynor's bill ..	3	12	3
August	Quarteridge to the Chief Constable ..	4	4	6
	John Scruby's wood bill	11	11	0
	Minister and Clerk burial fees	1	6	0
Apl. 1793	Paid Wm. Mead for wood	6	12	0
	Jonathan Samuels expenses paid for binding of John Loader	2	2	4
	To a licence for Jonathan Samuels ..	3	3	0

Extracts from vestry meetings held at the Town Hall or White Lion

		£	s.	d.
1788	To the Constable of Harlow for John Barker ..	3	5	2
	Paid for the house in Rosemary Lane ..	2	15	0
	Mr. Burton for ground taken near the Star ..	1	1	0

1790 (Oct. 18) An agreement was made at the Vestry meeting between the parish of Great Dunmow and John Savill, bricklayer, that from and after this day he shall be allowed eight men to help to play the Fire Engines three times every year and the said eight men to receive one shilling and sixpence each for every day employed up to three days, and also John Samuel to be allowed ten shillings and six pence for the year, for taking care of the said Engines, and oyling them, and cleaning buckets etc., exclusive of oyl and repairs.

Names of the eight men who are to attend when called upon to work the engines:

John Samuel, engineer
William Owers
James Tyler
Thomas Joyce
James Samuel
John Phillips
Cavey Ackers
William Quilter
Samuel Samuels, spare

		£	s.	d.
1791	Paid J. Samuels for looking after the Fire Engines		18	9
1792	Paid for the tenement on the Causeway		3	6
	Paid for the house on the downs		2	0
	For looking after the Fire Engines		14	0
	To a Militia man and his wife	1	5	0

		£	s.	d.
1793	To a Militia man and his wife	2	5	6
1794	For the expense of Dame Parkin's funeral ..		15	0
	John Samuel for working the Fire Engines ..		13	6
	Mr. Greenleaf for Straw	2	14	0
	John Hitchcock (Militia)	1	16	0
1797	Half the expense of the Saillers [this occurs every six months during the war]	23	12	6
	[There are many instances of money instead of flower (flour) owing to the terrific prices of flour.]			
	Paid Dr. Brook for attending the Workhouse 1 year	25	12	6
	Paid to a soldier's wife, Ann Micle, by order Mr. Rainsford	6	0	0
	Paid Henry Clayton for wood laid into the Pest House	1	4	0
	Paid for removing John Perry from London to Dunmow	2	9	10½
	Mr. Bennett's bill for repairing the Cage ..	2	7	6
1798	John Samuels is ill. The parish is keeping the family.			
	Paid engineers and carpenters for repairing and exercising fire engines		16	0

The Account of Moneys Received by Rates, etc., and Disbursed by the Overseers of Great Dunmow Parish for the Necessary relief of the Poor for their purposes relating to the said Parish. 1797.

	£	s.	d.
Paid G. Thorogood for young Sanders from Sept. 7th, 1797, to July 11th, 1798, at 6d. a week	2	8	0
Paid Justice Toke order for 7/6d. for Wm. Taylor till an order can be got from his Capt. as promised to be procured by Mr. Toke.			
Paid Robert Laver for Fordham's wife's coffin		8	0
Paid Relief to Ben Clark's son ..		3	0
Paid bill for Fordham's burial ..		5	0
Paid to soldiers' wives	6	11	0
Mr. Alliston's bill for the poor house	10	14	7
Quarterage	6	5	9
Paid to Mr. Allcock's female child	1	1	10
Constable Smith's Bill	1	0	2
Mr. J. Barnward's Wood Bill ..	7	7	2
Widow Colies's Bill		15	0
Paid soldiers' wives	3	2	6
Easter dinner	2	2	0
Constable Nye's bill		19	4
Paid for beer for E. Wood's funeral		2	6
Yearly salary Drs. Pearson & Raynor, surgeons	25	0	0
Overseers' clerk	5	11	10½
Paid J. Samuels for Perrys boy ..		6	0
Mrs. Low's Christmas box ..		2	6
W. Bowyer 5/- horse and cart ..	1	10	9
To Mr. Wade for Quit rent ..		11	3
The widow Lindsell's rent		6	6
Henry Prior's rent		10	0
Workhouse straw		6	0
Hannah Gunn's rent till 29th Sept.		6	0
Wm. Prior's shoe bill		15	2
Burial of Twins	1	14	10
Dame Hockley's month's lodging		1	0
Parish meeting (Saracen's Head)		10	8
Paid Doctor's bill for Letch ..	1	1	0
Mr. Wm. Prior's Constable's bill	7	8	0
Extra allowance to Paupers at 6d. each		11	9

The sum of £26 0s. 0d. was paid to Mr. B. Foakes as compensation by the reputed Father for a bastard child born of the body of Sarah Hoy—Easter 1804.

March 13th, 1809. Receive £25 being the freedom of John Taylor sworn to be the father of a male child of the body of Lettuce Lazell.

July 1st, 1811. Vestry Meeting, Town Hall, Dunmow.

Present

Minister

Tabrum Clarence John Barnard	Churchwardens
John Taylor Abraham Barnard John Scruby	Overseers
George Wade William Cheveley Steel Lambert Jas. Suckling John Fuller John Clapton	Inhabitants

This day Mr. G. Wade paid Mr. J. Taylor, the present Overseer, the sum of £8 14s. 3d., being the balance Rates of last year due by Sir G. H. Beaumont, after deducting £213 6s. 5¼d. paid on account when Mr. Wade produced a list of the Great Tithe remaining unsold. And which appear to be estimated in the valuation of the annual sum of £367 1s. 0d., three fourths of which sum Sir G. Beaumont will be content to be charged in future Rates for Tithes.

The Vestry Clerk was ordered to make a list of such omitted persons in the Poors Rate upon the Great Tithe, to be presented to Sir G. Beaumont for his payment of such omitted Tithe same from Easter 1809, to Easter 1811.

Copied in 1811 from an old Vestry Book

A copy from an old Parish Book of the names of Farms and Houses to whom it belongs, to repair the fences of the Churchyard of the Parish of Great Dunmow on the south side beginning at the tenement of John Kembe down Eastward.

2 Perches to be made by Clapton Hall & Bumpstead Hill.

1 Perch Olives

½ ,, Minchin

½ ,, Martells

½ ,, Potters

½ ,, Birds House—the brick wall made from the gates down to the Malting, in or about 1808 by Thos. Bird, carpenter—

The North side fence.

1 Perch the Parsonage, beginning at the Vicarage pales.

1 ,, Newton Hall

½ ,, Hurlstocks

1 ,, Broadgroves

½ ,, Youngs Farm (late) now called Nether Hall or Lower Hall.

2 ,, Freestones (Alfriston) Hall, Otherwise Bigods Hall.

½ ,, Tooleyes

2 ,, Marks Hall.

All the fence from Marks down to Church Mead is commonly made by the Parish.

[It would be interesting to know the date of the old vestry book. I have not heard of the churchyard being fenced in. Only 13½ perches, but so many people to do it.]

Vestry Meeting Great Dunmow July 17th 1817

Memorandum

It is hereby agreed to build a brick wall not less than 6ft. high about the foundation of the Workhouse, and the Parish grants £40. Hollis Clayton agrees to pay £20 and has the liberty of making the wall higher if he thinks fit at his own expense, and it is hereby agreed the wall shall continue to belong to the Parish subject to this proviso, that should the Parish, or any other person to whom it should be sold, pull down the said wall within twenty years they should reimburse the said Hollis Clayton, or his heirs, the sum of £20.

James Suckling
Charles Barnard
Abraham Barnard } Overseers.

Vestry Meeting, Town Hall, September 20th, 1813

Resolved, that the Parishioners having been informed by Mr. Wade that they have committed an Error in having moved the stocks without consulting the Lord of the Manor on what spot they should be placed, are ready to make what reparation in their power by again removing them to any place he may think proper to appoint.

Signed.

Tabrim Clarance	Richard Samprell
John Scruby	Abraham Smith
Thomas Collis	Steel Lambert

Corporation Qtr. from March 6th Wm. Collis Overseer. 1815.

		£	s.	d.
	Paid Thom. Baker, soldier, by order of Magistrate	1	8	0
Aug. 3	Mr. Rich Lamprell engages to make the coffins at 14/- each			
Aug. 21	Paid A. Vails for 2 years cleaning the Town Hall	2	0	0
	Geo. Leeche's Bill for attending the Fire Engines		19	3
Feb. 1816	Paid surgeon Pearson for setting Cook's girl's arm	2	2	0
Apl. 1817	Ben Cheek (sexton) Burial fees		19	6
	Dr. Lynch's Bill ..	45	16	0
	Rec. of the reputed father of S. Barrick's child	25	0	0
	Ben Cheek's Burial fees	3	10	0
	Beer for Coal Carters		10	7
Jan. 1818	Making return to the Clerk of the Peace	2	2	6
	Parish Meeting at the " Lion " (this occurs once a month) ..	3	3	0
June 1818	Paid for Sparrows and eggs (2d. each and 1d. an egg)	2	1	2
Jan. 1819	Benjamin Cheek's bill for Wm. Clark's and Widow Watts's funerals		19	0
	Parish dinner at the " Saracen's Head "	5	0	0
	Expense of James Gray's trial	2	15	6
	Paid for sparrows and eggs	3	5	5¾
Dec. 1819	Coroner and Jury (J. Eniver's boy)	1	6	6
1820	Sarah Pevelin's allowance and burial expenses	1	11	6

Mr. Bennett's bill for repairing the " cage " was £2/7/6. Maybe some criminal had escaped again. The burial fee for three paupers cost 13/-. In 1810 eleven jackets were bought costing 1/9 each. Poor Milly Ackow was carted all the way to Bedlam (asylum), cost £7/6/11. In 1811 £11 was paid for firewood supplied to the Workhouse by Mr. Ben Foakes.

In 1803 the sum of £25 was paid into the hands of Clarence, one of the overseers of Great Dunmow, as a compensation from Mr. Livermore of Little Dunmow, and also as freedom from any further expense attending, or that might arise, from a male bastard born of the body of Ann Dennis, of Dunmow. Another entry reads " The parish of Rochford paid £15 for a bastard child born to the body of Ann Hammond of Dunmow." In December 1800 £108 was paid for the purchase of the windmill on Dunmow Downs, together with " the granneries and other appurtenances attached thereto."

Vestry accounts, 1818

Granted in Bishopswood Quarter April 22nd. James Cook to pay rates 3/7.

John Cook jun.'s wife 5 yards of flannel. Granted in Bigods Quarter March 30th, 1818.

There were on this date twenty-six applications for rent, cloth, shirts, shoes, petticoats, etc., and twenty-two were granted.

September 14, 1818.

On this date there were nineteen applications similar to the above and all were granted.

March 1, 1819.

Again we find thirty applications, which were all granted. Apparently Dunmow overseers found it difficult to refuse these requests from the poor.

A Vestry meeting held at the Town Hall October 30th, 1826. Mr. Clapton, Chairman. The following complaints were made:

Sophia Lynn's boy extra relief 10/-.
John Cootes rent to Rich. Lindsell.
What sum of money will be taken of John Chitwich of Foulness island for Eliza Milbarnes's child? £30.
Thom. Pitts and wife want more allowance.
Isaac Clarke wants breeches, shirt.
Natth. Hills wants 2 shirts and a pair of stockings.
Messrs. Harrison and Holmsted's bill 15/-
Wid. Harris (Woodham) pay to Mr. Tufnell 65/-.
Charles Mead (Mr. Cheveleys) clothing.
Thom. Mead sen. 30/- toward 45/- rent.
Marg. Allen wants 2/6d. a week relief.
The parish will pay £8 in part of Mr. Cox's bill of £12 8s. 0d. for attending etc. to Michael Bowyer's daughter.
John Clarke's son shirt and mending shoes.
William Harrington's wife needs midwife.
John Meads part of rent till Mich. 47/-.

		£	s.	d.
	Beer etc. to Pest House (Chas. Pigram) ..	1	13	4½
	Geo. Leech's bill for goods to the Pest House	3	4	1½
	Geo. Leech for working and repairing Fire Engines	3	0	0
1822	Paid for Port Wine for the Workhouse ..	3	11	0
	Paid James Mumford bill for buckets ..	12	0	0
	Thomas Monk's bill for Well at the Workhouse	3	8	9
	Mr. Clapton's bill for straw at the Pest House	6	0	0
1823	Ben Cheek for Thatching the Pest House	5	5	2¼

Jan. 4, 1819 £11 2s. 0d. was paid into the hands of Mr. James Mumford, one of the Overseers of Great Dunmow, being the remainder of £24 from John Pitt for a female bastard child born of the body of Susanna Atkins of Great Dunmow.

April 13, 1819 £40 was paid into the hands of Edward Knight, an overseer of Great Dunmow, being the compensation from George Francis for a female bastard child born of the body of Sophia Vail of Great Dunmow.

On September 6th, 1823, William Luck paid into the hands of Wm. Sweeting, one of the overseers of Great Dunmow, the sum of £12, and on the 10th day of April 1824 he paid into the hands of Wm. Sayer, deputy Overseer, a further sum of £10, and on the 5th day of June, to Mr. Wm. Sayer, a further sum of £3, making the sum of £25 as a full discharge to the said Wm. Luck on account of a female bastard child born of the body of Elizabeth Sweeting of Great Dunmow.

On 11th June, 1827, the sum of £40 was paid into the hands of Mr. Wm. Collis, one of the Overseers of Dunmow, by Mr. Edward Bird in Compensation for a female bastard child born of the body of Mary Archer.

The allowance to be reduced 3d. per head to the paupers in the workhouse "Seconds" flour, now 2/- peck. Number in workhouse 32.

John Gunn, Vestry Clerk.

This book runs from October 1826 to 1832. Meetings were roughly two a month, This might become boring to my readers, so I will just mention the more unusual incidents that occurred in these last years of the parish workhouse.

Nov. 27th, 1826. Poor Rate granted at 2/- in the pound. Should the numbers of paupers in the workhouse amount to 25, best flour at 10/- per bushel, the Governor to be paid 3/9 per head, if the number is less, and the flour as above to be paid 4/- per head. The above agreement to be subject to a month's notice of alteration on either side.

Edward Patmore's granary Value to be rated 30/-.

Nicholas Toke's coach house, stable, etc., 30/-.

Dec. 26th, 1826. George Mead's smock coat mended 1 yd.

Thom. Stock's boy fustian jacket, trousers and shirt.

Governor wants 3d. per head more, flour having risen 2d. per peck.

Jan. 23rd, 1827. Wm. Hockley's daughter to Mr. G. Leecher—Gown, flannel petticoat, pair shoes, pair stockings (wool) and apron.

Thom. Sewell's daughter Millicent to Widford Mills, gown, 2 shifts, 2 pairs stockings, 2 aprons hat and coat.

Feb. 19th. Eliza Milborne wants to leave the workhouse and take her child with her and 2/- a week.

Mar. 19th, 1827. Engine house wants repairing.

Rhoda Wright's child—druggett jacket, net, and calico.

Ordered that an account be taken of the numbers of paupers, belonging to, and residing in this Parish, distinguishing the number of children in each family, also of such poor as are relieved and not resident in this parish.

Agreed that the Folly Farm shall in future be charged to the rates in Bigods Quarter.

March 20, 1826

At the annual parish dinner at the Saracen's Head on Easter Monday it was decided to keep it on that day in the future. Persons present: John Clapton in the chair, Mr. N. Toke, Dr. Grice, Mr. B. M. Foakes, Mr. James, Mr. Hudson, Mr. Chas. Worrin, Mr. Charles Barnard, Mr. Thos. Barnard, Mr. S. Phillbrick, Mr. J. Franklin, Mr. Ed. Patmore, Mr. Chas. Portway, Mr. J. Sewell, Mr. Ed. Knight, Mr. Fuller, Mr. Briggs, Dr. Pearson, Mr. J. Scruby, Mr. W. Collis, Mr. Wm. Lamprell, Mr. Rich. Lamprell, and Mr. Robt. Taylor.

HUNDRED OF DUNMOW—CHARGES

Allowed to the Petty Constables of the said hundred on the Execution of a Magistrate's Warrant:

	s.	d.
Constable per day	5	0
Constable per night	2	6
For Subsistence of Prisoner per day	1	0
For Lodging of Prisoner ..		6
Constable's assistant per day ..	2	6
Constable's assistant per night ..	1	3

Essex.—We, his Majesty's Justices of the Peace acting in and for the Hundred of Dunmow, do thereby approve of the above charges and direct the same to be taken by the Petty Constables for every Parish within the said Hundred. Given under our hands the seventh day of April 1819.

These are the sums now allowed by the County to Constables, and they include the Subsistance of the Constable and assistant.	Thomas Jee W. Toke John N. Chesshyre John Pepper John Deedes J. Leapingwell

April 16th, 1827. The paupers from Mrs. Smiths, near Mr. Tokes, and at the Ford continuing towards Braintree, to be from this day to belong to Bishopswood Quarter. Margaret Allen's pay to be discontinued, or go to the workhouse.

Mr. Collier's cottage, late C. Byatt's, hired for the latter by the Parish at 18d. per week.

Soldier Mead's wife to go to the workhouse.

Jonathan Enifer to leave the workhouse.

Mary Archer to swear her child.

Ann Warner to swear her child after the Quarter Sessions.

It is the opinion of this meeting that the appointment of a standing Overseer would be beneficial to the parish at large, and until such an appointment is made a Select Vestry be nominated who pledge themselves to attend to pay meetings of the parish. The meeting then nominated such persons as they thought proper, which lists to be laid before the Acting Magistrates of this district for inspection—20 names including Rev. Dr. Richardson [the vicar].

I agree to make the parish coffins for the year ensuing with good sound 1in. Elm, oiled and browned, inside joints properly pitched and delivered to any part of the parish at 10/6 each.—Signed Abr. Holgate.

Amy Paremane (Marks) 1 gown, 1 shift, upper petticoat, 1 apron, pair of shoes. Left to Mr. Collis.

John Ginn wants one month's pay in advance. Says he can get admitted to St. Thomas's Hospital.

Thom. Goody's wife's funeral. Not to be paid by the parish.

Nov. 26th. Geo. Head Threader's Green smock frock.

James Dennis pair of boots 6/-.

Wm. Crow calico for family 10 yards.

A complaint being made to this meeting that James Furyedown has conducted himself improperly, Mr. C. Portway, Mr. J. Clapton, Mr. C. Barnard are deputised to investigate.

Persons without employment—John Savill Brook, John Pavelin, George Savill, John Wybrow.

Dec. 24th. John Smith's burial, etc., 32/-.

Is the widow of Wm. Joyce to be rated? No.

John Gunn in workhouse, to be taken before Magistrates.

Mr. Mumford's bill not passed. To be explained.

John Edwards to be rated 35/-.

A select vestry meeting held at the Town Hall, January 21, 1828

Eliza wants a bed. One lent.

Nursing Thos. Cornwall 18d. a week.

Elizabeth Rumble's shoes out of Parish Chest.

Feb. 18th. John Baynes Kersey, waistcoat.

Sarah Tuttleby expenses to London 25/-

March 17th. General Vestry Meeting, Charles Portway in the chair.

Robert Taylor wants a cottage, or to the workhouse.

Pattison Parker wants a parish girl at 1/- weekly. Left to Mr. Warner.

April 14th. New blankets, oven hoe, peel and gates, mended at the workhouse.

Charles Crow's wife's midwife's pay 6/-

Milicent Wybrow's boy's pay advanced for 2 months by Mr. E. Knight until June 9th, 12/-.

Thom. Mumford to work fire engines and find oil for £3 for the year ensuing.

Thom. Champress to make the parish coffins for the year ensuing at 9/- each.

May 12th. Joseph Swan a bed tick.

Jonas Perrin's boy pair of trousers.

Public notice to be given on the 1st June to take into consideration the repairs of the Barn at the workhouse on the 9th day of June.

James Lloyd wants £8 to learn the business of Hatter.

Left to Mr. Clayton.

The open part of the Cage to be plastered for lodging trampers and by permission of the Vicar, Rev. Dr. Richardson, and the Constable to be allowed to discharge them without taking them before a Magistrate (the doors not to be locked).

Peter Tyler and wife 5/- a week, granted.

July 17th. William Stokes's daughter Harriet to (Bowtells) Clothing shift, stockings and shoes.

James Lloyd's wife and family removal to London (apprenticed to Hatter there).

Widow Philpott to leave the workhouse, or be sent to prison.

Aug. 4th. John Hawkes at Mr. Cheveley's pair of shoes.

Thom. Downham to be rated 22/6.

Widow Gipson to be rated 10/-.

John Reid to be rated 15/-.

Sept. 1st. The Fire Engines to have a new leather pipe 35 feet long.

Gaol rate granted at 4s. in the pound.

John Wybrow rec. from the workhouse 1 sheet, 1 blanket, 1 straw bed, total value 8/-.

This meeting thinks it necessary to employ an assistant Surveyor of the Highways.

Oct. 27th. Surgeon's bill for Isaac Milborne 44/9d. granted.

Robert Tyler, sheet, and woman to wash linen, 6d. per week.

Samuel Prior sen. pair of shoes.

Unanimously agreed that the full earnings of the labouring poor to be taken into account with the Parish, and that every person employing such men be requested to send an account of their earnings instead of their being taken as 8/- per week, and no relief will be allowed unless such an account is produced. Also, children at and above 10 years of age be not allowed Parish relief.

Vestry Meeting held at the Town Hall, October 6th, 1826

Present

Charles Barnard Chairman, John Clapton Churchwarden.

Overseers: John Taylor, Charles Kirkham, Charles Portway.

The following bill examined, approved, and ordered to be paid:

Mary Savill's boy (Easton) frock, and pair of shoes.

Mrs. James wants a Parish girl.

James Cornwall's rent due Oct. 18th £1.

Wm. Crow's part of rent due Mich. 18/-.

Geo. Caton, 1 shirt.

Coals for Workhouse.

Wm. Sammons's two children to the Workhouse.

Sam. Briggs, waistcoat.

Isaac Milbourne £2 towards rent.

Thom. Clarke's son John one shirt and 18d. a week till Michelmas.

Geo. Doe (at Mrs. James) shirt, 2 pair socks, 1 pair shoes.

Marg. Savill, a shift.

Alice Savill, a shift.

Sam. Willis ½ year rent 39/-.

Eliza Savill's (Sutton's) child 1 shift, 1 petticoat.

Amy Savill, under petticoat.

Soldier Morgan, shirt and undercoat.

Soldier Morgan's boy, pair shoes.

John Archer, P. Downs, waistcoat.

Ann Savill, flannel.

Geo. Mead sen., shirt.

James Lloyd, 17/6d. rent, midwife & nurse.

Wm. Coote's wife, shift.

Jos. Eldrett, £4 rent.

Boy Bumble, 1 shirt.

Widow Joyce, 1 shift.

Edward Stock's girl, 1 frock and pair shoes.

Wm. Cook Broadway, 65/- rent.

Mary Doe's rent, 10/-.

Widow Franklin's rent, 26/-.

Widow Lilley's child, flannel and shift.

Late John Sewell's youngest daughter, clothing, left to Mr. Portway.

Widow Joyce, 1 sheet.

John Williams, 1 shirt.

Sophia Vail's boy, 2 pinafores.

Wm. Ketley's son Benjy, pair shoes.

Wm. Joyce, 50/- towards rent Pleshey.

Thomas Caton's rent, £4.

Widow Phillips, shift.

Mr. Clayton will continue to keep Judith Watts 1/- a week till Lady day and 6d. a week from then till Michelmas.

Wm. Rixon sen., rent £1.

Jacob Ginn's, workhouse clothing.

Jacob Pavelin, workhouse clothing.

Edward Pavelin, workhouse clothing.
Blankets wanted at Workhouse.
Sarah Brown, 2 shifts and pair of shoes.
Eliza Milbourne, 2 shifts and pair of shoes.
John Coote wants 13/6d. rent till Michelmas and 14/- previously left.
Widow Sweeting Bishops green nurse.
James Rixson, part of rent £1.
John Owers, part of rent £1.
If Mrs. Wade can get Michael Bowyer's daughter into hospital the Parish will pay the expense.
£1 sent to Mr. Butler, Surgeon of Romford, for Cornwall's rent.

Signed John Gunn, Vestry Clerk.

The overseers and churchwardens put the parish workhouse up for auction on December 8, 1840. The north end was sold, but I cannot trace any deeds for the other two portions. They were probably sold, but the deeds have not been handed into the Record Office. The north section, now Rumsey (furnishers), was bought by William Impey Clayton for £190, probably of Clayton House, now the International, and Andrews.

May 14th, 1827. Samuel Willis's window duty granted. What is John Samuels to be rated for a part of the Downs? 5/-.
What sum to be taken to exonerate the father of Mary Archer's child? £40.
Poor rate granted at 2/- in the pound.
Sarah Hasler wants a place [situation].
Mary Boatman relief 3/-. Brought from Takeley by order of removal. Mary Bird, brought from Staleford Abbots by order of removal.

July 27th, 1827. Wm. Rixon advanced 3/- towards making six pairs of women's shoes.
Aug. 7th. John Day's wife ill, wants relief. £1 granted.
Samuel Gunn's wife ill, wants Parish Doctor.
James Lloyd wants the Parish to pay for his instruction to make baskets.
No pay to paupers, except standing bill, or cases of illness, for 1 month.

Sept. 3rd. Widow Bambrook ill at Woodford. To write to Mr. Saddington, to allow the same as to one of their own paupers.
Mary Parker to swear her child.
Richard Turner's wife to come to the workhouse.
James Eldrett's wife and two children. No allowance granted.
John Wybrow to be summoned.
Mary Mead's son George at Mr. Cook, baker, Chelmsford, shirt, trousers, jacket, shoes, if his Master keeps him.
John Johnson to be rated 30/-.

Oct. 1st. Wm. Ketley wants £1 towards £3 10s. 0d. rent. 10/- granted.
Trampers to workhouse 1 meal brown bread and water.
The house in the churchyard wants whitewashing inside.
Constable not to be attending to order Vagrants away, or to public houses for lodging (left to Overseer).

Oct. 29th. What is Mr. Fuller's Mill House to be rated? £2.
What is each of Mr. Lamprell's cottages on the Downs to be rated? £1.
What is Mr. Randell's new Malting & Cottages to be rated? £6.
Will the parish take £5 from Mr. Thom. Raymond's debt of £8 12s. 0d.? Yes.

At a Select Vestry Meeting held at the Town Hall, November 10, 1829, Mr. James Weeks accepted the office of Assistant Surveyor of the Highways at a salary of £20 per year.

John Fuller, Chairman.

Jan. 29th, 1829. Church rate granted at 1/- in the pound.
John Coote, currier, pair of shoes.
James Leech, sawyer, wants a person paid to do for his family for the winter 2/- week.
Henry Barrick's son Wm. 5/- trousers, and shoes.

Feb. 16th. Poor rate to remain at 2/- in the pound.
Michael Bowyer's floor needs new bricks.
To enquire of Eliza Thompson in what manner she was treated at Bishop's Stortford.

All labourers without employ are to apply to John Gunn to have their names set down.

James Barthorp to allow 2/- per fortnight to reimburse the Parish, 36/6d. advanced, to redeem his household goods.

George Rawlings stopped 2/- towards shoes.

March 16th. Public Vestry Meeting, chairman Charles Portway.

April 13th. Coffins for paupers by Thom. Champness at 13/- each for the ensuing year.

Fire Engines, notice for tenders by May 11th.

Will this parish admit a pauper from Little Canfield for 1 month if paid at £1 a month? Granted.

John Warner rated 11/3d.

Geo. Saunders rated 11/3d.

John Coote's family straw bed.

What is the cottage, occupation of Joseph Dench to be rated? 11/3d.

What is the cottage, occupation of Simon Buck to be rated? 11/3d.

May 11th. Mrs. Jarvis not to be allowed any part of maintenance for Black girl at present.

Eliza Milborne's child 4/- fortnight, and pair of leg-irons with one pair of handcuffs with chains.

The Workhouse Barn to have the tiling taken off, and the timbers drawn to their right position, so as to secure the body and roof of the building, and to put in such girders, etc., as is necessary. The whole to be put into good substantial repair.

Thom. Champness for managing the Fire Engines, fined oil, and clean valves, at £3 per year.

June 8th. Mr. Gibson's Surgeon's bill for Mary Mead £2 13s. 6d.

July 6th. Will the parish admit a pauper (belonging to Good Easter) into the workhouse, on being paid? No.

5 chal. coals for workhouse to be carted by Skingle.

What is to be done with Catherine, the black girl, and her female child? Left to Mr. Clapton and Mr. Portway.

Elizabeth Button at Mr. Livermores, Little Dunmow, pair shoes, 1 gown, 3 yards calico, apron.

August 3rd. Is James Warner's family to be brought back to Dunmow? Yes.

Thom. Gibson, Bishop's Stortford, ordered to come to Mr. Franklin, Surveyor, for work on July 20th.

Sept. 28th. Mrs. Wright, "The Bell," wants a parish girl 1/- week.

Oct. 26th. Mr. Clapton (Marks) wants a parish girl 1/- week.

Nov. 23rd. Joseph Partner's daughter to Mr. Smith's, Great Waltham, woollen flannel apron, petti, 1 shift, 1 skirt, and pair of stockings.

Pump at Workhouse wants repairing, also floor of great hall. To be reviewed.

Wm. Starr's lodging 14 weeks 14/-.

Thom. Paveling's daughter wants a place.

Wm. Starr to the workhouse.

Dec. 21st. John Savill, Alms house, 1 shirt.

Geo Doe, smock-frock and trousers.

Jan. 18th, 1830. John Tuttleby's wife nurse 3/-.

Isaac Milborne no employment. £1 granted.

Poor rate granted at 3/- per pound.

Feb. 15th. Thom. Sewell, body flannel.

Charles Goody, £1 to purchase a box for cutting chaff, to be repaid at 1/- per week.

Thom. Bowtell wants a boy 1/- a week.

James Tyler can get admitted to Guy's Hospital, London, if the parish supports his family.

March 15th. James Rumble (Roffie) 1 shirt.

Wm. Archer's wife, midwife's pay 5/-.

Wm. Pigram, £1 rent to be repaid at 3/2d. fortnight.

Charles Cheek's widow and family (to consult the Council).

John Willis's son John apprenticed at 30/- wants clothing.

April 12th. Mr. Robt. Taylor will pay

Joseph Wybrow's pension but if in the event of his death the Parish will repay him the sum he has advanced previous to the next quarter after his decease.

The vicar making the following proposition, the Public vestry agrees thereto: To assign the upper floor of the Church House to the Vicar for the use of a girls' School.

It is proposed, seconded and unanimously agreed that the Law Business of this Parish be alternately between Messrs. Wade and Son and Mr. Nicholas Toke.

Ordered that each Churchwarden and Overseer is obliged to attend the Petty Sessions and shall be allowed the sum of 2/6 for his expenses.

May 10th. Rates on Bigods and Lower Hall. Council's opinion to be taken. It is unanimously agreed to pay the Vestry Clerk £40 per year. Not to include books, ink, and paper, etc.

Mary Trubshoe (Wades) wants expenses paid to go to St. George's Hospital, and tea, sugar, candles, soap, and washing paid, while there.

June 7th. James Tween, workhouse, wooden leg.

Charles Mead (Mr. Kirkham's) pair shoes.

Jane Enifer (Minchon) 2 pairs stockings, shift and pair of shoes.

June 21st, 1830. Will the Parish put the cottage of late in the occupation of Mr. Wm. Childs into tenantable repair, on having it free of rent up till Mich. 1831, and from and after that date pay for the use of Mr. Ben Baker of Bromley, Middx, the yearly rent being £6?

July 3rd. At this meeting it was agreed that Mr. John Polley should be appointed Governor of the Workhouse for a month, subject to a production of a satisfactory Character, his salary to be £30 per annum, and an extra allowance beyond the Bill of Fare for the Poor in the house of 6lbs. of meat, $\frac{1}{4}$ of Tea, and $1\frac{1}{2}$lbs. of Sugar, per week.

July 5th. Ordered that Arthur Barfield be summoned for his Poor and Gaol rates.

Bill of Fare for week at the Workhouse.

Sunday breakfast—for men $\frac{1}{2}$lb. of bread with milk pottage.

breakfast—for women 6oz. bread with milk pottage.

dinner—for men $\frac{1}{2}$lb. of meat, veg, & beer when at work.

,, for women 6oz. meat, veg, & beer when at work.

Supper—for men $\frac{1}{2}$lb. of Bread with cheese.

,, for women 6oz. of Bread with cheese.

Monday, breakfast same as Sunday.

Dinner—$\frac{1}{2}$lb. Bread with Pea soup—men.

6oz. Bread with Pea soup—women.

Tuesday, supper same as Sunday.

Wednesday ,, ,, Monday.

Thursday ,, ,, Sunday.

Friday ,, ,, Monday.

Saturday Dinner, 1lb. Pudding. Breakfast and supper same as other days.

July 19th. The following Gentlemen appointed as a committee to superintend the Government of the Workhouse, and to visit it at least once a week and to make such orders as they deem necessary: Rev. John Smith, vicar; Mr. John Clapton, Mr. Hollis Clayton, Mr. Charles Portway, Mr. Charles Barnard, Mr. Edward Knight. 3 to be able to act.

Aug. 2nd. Mary Mead, Springfield, rent and son's clothing. £1 granted.

Thomas Monk to be summoned to show cause why he does not pay towards the support of his wife.

Mr. I. Clapton to supply the workhouse with flour deducting 3/- per sack from the retail price.

John Young to pay 12/6 per cwt. for old lead from Cistern at the Workhouse.

Aug. 30th. Joseph Swann's daughter Ann at Merrets, 1 gown, 1 shift.

Joseph Swann's daughter Susan at Simpsons, upper petti, apron, shift.

Remainder of Dr. Miller's bill for Isaac Milbourne and to know if he is to attend him at this time.

John Collins's family, calico 12 yards.

Henry Leader's boy, pair of shoes.

Public Vestry Meeting held at the Church, September 22, 1830.

Gaol rate still 4d. in the pound.

To make the new Bell. Rates on £7 10s. 0d.

To be deducted from the old Bell £1 2s. 6d., leaving old Bell £6 7s. 6d. to deduct from Lower Hall:

	£	s.	d.
Green Lane Mead 1 acre 4 poles		15	0
Vicar tithes		3	4
Church Mead 1 acre, 2 rods, 4 poles	1	2	6
Vicar tithes ..		5	0
	2	5	10

2/- rate 4/7d.

Sept. 27th. Contract for building shed at Workhouse to Wm. Lamprell, if the parish desides to build, by Oct. 25th, £25 10s. 6d.

Dr. Miller's second bill for I. Milbourne till September 3rd, 22/-.

Wm. Crow at Mr. S. Mumford's Fustian trowsers, 2 shirts, 2 pair socks.

Thomas Cook's burial fee, 9/-.

Sarah Paremane at Mr. Clapton will keep her till Oct. 11th 1831 with 6d. a week.

Wm. Rixon's daughter Mary to be sent to school at the parish expense.

October 25th. Widow Sewell wants more allowance. 1/- week granted.

John Savill's son John, clothing. Left to Mr. Portway.

Wm. Aylett and wife want a cottage.

Ordered that Mr. J. Polley, Governor of the Workhouse, to enter into an agreement and Bond for the performance of Trust on Nov. 22nd.

November 22nd. There are still very long lists of bequests by the poor for clothes, and for help with their rent.

Rev. J. Smith and other Overseers to consult with Messrs. Wade to pursue the legitimate means of procuring from Mrs. Pepper the rates due on Bigods and Lower Hall farms prior to Lady-day last, with full authority to proceed thereon.

Dec. 20th. At this meeting it is agreed that one field belonging to the Parsonage farm shall be hired by the Parish, the rent per acre to be fixed by Mr. Robert Franklin.

It is likewise agreed that a field shall be applied for belonging at Merks Hill farm and to be hired on the terms as above, if agreeable to Mr. C. Barnard, also that Mr. Wm. Impey Clayton to be applied to for Sparrows Field to be hired on the above terms.

Jan. 17th, 1831. Mr. W. I. Clayton will continue to pay for one of Mr. Wm. Rixon's children's education.

February 14th. Mr. Livermore, Langleys, will take Charles Crow's son Charles.

Joseph Perry to be paid from his earnings, pair of high boots.

William Akers to be paid from his earnings, pair of high boots.

James Skinner to be paid from his earnings, pair of high boots.

5 loads of wood for parish order from Mr. Franklin.

Persons employed in spade Husbandry to be paid 4d. per rod.

March 14th. Churchwardens' rate at 6d. in the pound.

John Savill, Mill Lane, daughter to Mr. Wiltons.

Lydia Wright applies for medical attendance to Workhouse.

Mr. Joyce wants office of Constable.

March 28th, 1831. Will the parish continue 6d. a week for Widow Wybrow's rent? Yes.

Mary Mead, Springfield—left to Mr. Savill.

Wm. Collins's wife wants midwife.

April 11th. Parish coffins for the year ensuing to be made by Abraham Holgate at 12/- each.

Charles Crow's son left Mr. Livermore this day.

What is to be done with the Land that has been dug by the Parish Labourers? It is agreed by this meeting that each farmer shall take the Land, by paying to the parish 2d. per rod.

May 9th. Bed-ticking for the Workhouse.

Susan Dennis at " Priors " gown, 2 shifts, apron, and pair of stockings.

Thom. Perrin, smock frock.

June 6th. Ann Bakeman, 18d. a week allowed.

Samuel Bloomfield's wife midwife. Parish will not pay.

W. Wrights signs to keep Fire Engines in working order for the ensuing year.

July 4th. Ellen Watts " Newhouse," upper coat, shift, pair stockings, apron.

Charles Leader, 18d. a week and pair trowsers.

Geo. Prior's widow and child, 5/- week of 3 months.

August 1st. Thom. Monk agrees to pay towards his wife's keep, 4/- weekly.

John Archer's daughter at " Houltons," upper coat, 2 aprons, pair stockings, and bonnet.

James Franklin's wife midwife's pay 5/-. Granted.

Sept. 26th. Samuel Willis ½ year's rent. Granted.

Eliza Sammons to Ed. Hockley's with 1/- week, 2 aprons, 1 petti, shift, and stockings.

Samuel Prior's daughter Sarah to (Cambridge) with 1/- week and clothing.

Oct. 24th. Insurance on Workhouse.

Is Thom. Mumford to be rated? No.

Is Charles Joyce to be rated Yes. ?

Is Richard Griggs to be rated? Yes.

Henry Barrick's family to be allowed the same at High Easter as if he resided in Dunmow 3/- week from Mich. to Lady Day.

What part of the rate should be taken from " Three Tuns " laid on Widow Richard? £1.

What part of the rate should be taken from I. M. Hudson & laid on the garden sold to Wm. Cook? 15/-.

Nov. 21st. Canvey Akin's daughter Sarah to Smiths farm, undercoat, gown, 2 pairs stockings, 2 shifts, 2 pairs shoes, apron.

Dec. 19th. John Savill wants Pest House windows mended. Granted.

John Day's daughter to " Dunmow Farm."

Will the parish continue the allowance to Wm. Joyce's daughter to Lady Day? Yes.

Jan. 16th, 1832. Poor rate 3/- in the pound.

Widow Philpott, standing Bill 5/- fortnight.

Thom. Pigot, flannel for body 1½ yards.

Bateman's youngest son, clothing. Left to Mr. Suckling.

Paupers not having more than 3 children not to be allowed a coffin for a child by the parish.

James Rumble to be taken before a Magistrate for leaving the Workhouse without permission.

Feb. 13th, 1832. What's to be done with John Chapman jun.? Left over.

Widow Hinson wants more allowance. Left to overseers.

Wm. Franklin and Michael Bowyer have not paid their rent due last Mich. John Gunn applied to them as requested some months ago.

March 12th. John Perry, Workhouse clothing. Left to Mr. Suckling.

John Gunn, Workhouse clothing. Left to Mr. Suckling.

Will the parish pay for posting emigration papers? Yes.

Will the parish send men to dig one acre of land for Mr. Wade, at 2d. per rod? Yes.

John Gunn Bumpsted needs extra allowance. £1 granted.

March 26th. Drs. Grice and Salt want 40

gns. per annum to attend the paupers of this parish. £30, no more.

Wm. Rixon jun. promises to leave 4/- a week in Mr. Malsters hands towards the support of his children.

Wm. Stokes's daughter Elizabeth, 18d. week to John Thos. Brown of London by Watson, carrier, with 10/- for clothing.

Geo. Caton to be summoned.

April 16th. Northey Rowland considered a proper person to be Governor of the Workhouse, subject to 2 months trial, at a salary of 12/- a week and to carry on the trade for the Parish. A Committee of Churchwardens and Overseers to meet Northey Rowland on Wed. 2nd at 3 o'clock.

Persons who want to go to Canady: John Gunn Bumpsted and family, John Merret and family, Wm. Archer, Geo. Ray, Stephen Ray, Wm. Starr.

May 21st, John Tuttleby's wife, nurse 3/-.

Wm. Stokes's sheet from the workhouse.

Church rate 8d. in the pound.

Geo. Rixon's wife, midwife and nurse.

June 4th. Public meeting at the Town Hall. Edward Wright, chairman, Charles Barnard and Samuel Philbrick, Churchwardens. Wm. Cock, John Warner, Thos. Smith, Overseers.

In 1833 there were six dates when applications were made for clothing, bedding, etc., very much the same as previously and showing that there must have been a goodly number of houses in the Bigods Quarter amounting to forty-four grants. Also there were four items granted in Bishopswood Quarter.

Surgeons for the workhouse

1798 Drs. Raynor & Pearson at £25 per annum.
1799 Drs. Raynor & Pearson including Small-pox casualties but not fractures.
1800 Drs. Sims and James ditto
1801 Drs. Raynor and Pearson ditto
1802 Dr. R. E. Jones, but now including fractures and all other disorders.
1803 Drs. Raynor and Pearson.
1804 Dr. James.
1805 Dr. Pearson.
1806 Dr. Pearson.
1807 Dr. Pearson.
1808 Dr. Lynch.
1809 Dr. Richard Pearson.
1810 Dr. John Burke Lynch.
1811 Dr. R. Pearson at £30 per annum.
1812 Dr. J. B. Lynch.
1813 Dr. R. Pearson.
1814 Dr. J. B. Lynch.
1815 Dr. R. Pearson
alternate until
1821 Dr. Carrardine.
1822 Dr. Joseph Grice.
1823 Dr. R. Pearson.
1824 Dr. J. Grice.
1825 Dr. R. Pearson.
1826 Dr. J. Grice.
alternate until
1832 Dr. Thos. Salt. It was Dr. Salt who refused to do this for less than £40.

CHAPTER XXIV

Valuation of some Dunmow properties, 1803

		Total value			*Corn and wood tithes*			*Vicarial tithes*		
		£	s.	d.	£	s.	d.	£	s.	d.
Ann Barnard	Mudwall Farm	28	0	0	6	5	0	1	10	0
John Burton	Mill Farm	22	10	0	4	10	0	1	5	0
Lady Beaumont	Mansion House	73	5	0	5	0	0	6	10	0
Henry Clapton	Ford Farm	46	10	0	9	0	0	2	10	0
James Hallett, esq.	Marks Hill Farm	178	0	0	30	5	0	12	10	0
,, ,,	Mark Hall, rented to John Clapton	163	5	0	27	10	0	12	10	0
Mich. Pepper	Bigods Hall	279	0	0	55	0	0	17	0	0
Mrs. Payne	Hobland Farm, rented to Abe. Coleman	11	0	0	2	15	0		5	0
Lord Maynard	Stone Hall Farm, rented to Richard Cornell	37	15	0	9	0	0	1	5	0
,, ,,	Folly Farm, rented to Tabrum Clarence	331	8	4	56	0	0	22	12	0
John Wyatt	Old House Farm, rented to Robert Clark	41	0	0	9	10	0	2	0	0
Robt. Clark	Hulls Farm	24	5	0	5	0	0	1	10	0
James Hallett	Minchons, rented to Mary Day ..	133	5	0	26	5	0	7	0	0
Mary Day	Befords	31	5	0	7	10	0	1	5	0
Thomas Warner	Phillpot End, rented to Ben Ellis	26	0	0	6	0	0	1	5	0
Joseph Edwards	Broadgroves	65	10	0	5	15	0	8	10	0
Mr. Angur	Housegrounds, rented to Ben Eves	1	5	0		5	0		1	0
Sir John Henniker	Garnetts Farm, rented to Foakes jun.	18	10	0	4	0	0	1	5	0
Lord Henniker	Newton Hall	249	10	0	35	0	0	24	15	0
B. Foakes, Sen.	Gatehouse, Brands Farm ..	252	10	0	46	5	0	18	10	0
Sir George Beaumont	Parsonage Farm, rented to Mr. Frost	101	0	0	4	10	0	16	10	0
James Clark	Barnston House, rented to Rich. Freeman	9	0	0	2	10	0		10	0
Mr. Smith	Bishops Wood Farm and Birds Farm, rented to Wm. French ..	12	5	0	2	15	0		15	0
Rob. Felsted	Chequers Inn and butcher's shop	16	0	0		10	0		1	0

		Total value			Corn and wood tithes			Vicarial tithes		
		£	s.	d.	£	s.	d.	£	s.	d.
James Johns	House Buildings, tanyard, Malt-house, etc., rented to James Fuller	105	10	0	10	10	0	10	0	0
Edward Harringe	Smiths Farm	48	10	0	6	0	0	5	10	0
Homestead, esq.	Trutons Farm	92	0	0	19	15	0	4	0	0
Gen. Henniker	Mansion House offices, garden, yard, etc.	5	5	0	2	0	0		10	0
John James	The Park	86	0	0	8	0	0	10	0	0
Wm. Lukin	With house	15	0	0		4	0		1	0
James Linsell	Cox's Farm	3	15	0	1	0	0		3	0
John Livermore	Langleys	56	15	0	10	0	0	4	5	0
Lord Henniker	Bps. Wood Green Farm, rented to James Matthams	98	15	0	21	10	0	5	0	0
Glebe Land	Chapel Wood, rented to Morrell	4	5	0					15	0
Isaac Malster	Saracen's Head	25	0	0				1	8	0
Eliz. Mills	Tooleys Farm	116	0	0	25	5	0	5	10	0
John James	Poplar Farm, rented to Thos. Mead	3	15	0	1	0	0		3	0
Mr. Saltmarsh	Crumps Farm, rented to Geo. Navel	4	10	0	1	0	0		5	0
Mic. Pepper	Bigods Farm, mansion house, etc.	95	0	0	5	5	0	6	10	0
,, ,,	Rakefars Farm, rented to Wm. Potter	90	5	0	20	5	0	5	0	0
Isaac Rayner	Sparlings Farm	22	10	0	4	0	0	1	8	0
Rev. Bingham	Housegrounds rented to Edward Reynolds	56	5	0	11	0	0	3	18	0
Thos. Rolfe	Hounslow Green Farm	39	10	0	6	10	0	3	3	0
Church Land	Rented to Henry & Eliza Sweeting	8	0	0	2	0	0		8	0
Lord Henniker	Tanners Farm, rented to Wm. Sweeting	33	10	0	7	0	0	2	0	0
Wm. Sweeting	Halfway House Farm	6	15	0	1	10	0		5	0
Mrs. Millbank	Puttocks (Henry Sweeting) ..	15	15	0	3	15	0		15	0
Henry Sweeting	Sheggs and Cadgers	11	15	0	2	10	0		10	0
Thos. Wilson	Coopers Farm rented to Elizabeth Sweeting	17	10	0	4	0	0		15	0
Joseph Sweeting	Tanners Farm	2	5	0		10	0		2	0
P. Sweeting and T. Stone	Lower Roffie	15	15	0	3	15	0		10	0
Draper's Company	Clopton Hall	240	10	0	39	5	0	18	15	0
Rev. I. Brock	Scruby Farm, John Scruby ..	165	5	0	36	10	0	7	0	0
I. Scruby sen.	Crouches Farm	74	10	0	13	15	0	4	15	0
Mr. Watford	Slutts Green (Wm. Seale) ..	5	15	0	1	5	0		5	0
Mr. Chamberlain	Martins and Padlocks Moors (Edward Smith)	128	5	0	20	15	0	11	0	0

		Total value £ s. d.	Corn and wood tithes £ s. d.	Vicarial tithes £ s. d.
Geo. Wade	The Royal Oak (Mrs. Nash) . .	4 10 0		
,, ,,	Matthias Davey, The Mill . .	5 10 0		
Mich. Pepper	Lower Hall Farm (John Turner) and osier ground	131 3 1	17 10 0	13 15 0
Simon Hutchins	Hours, orchard and cottage . .		6 0 0	2 6
Ann Newman	Rented to Ben Cheek a garden . .	2 0 0		1 0
Thos. Joyce	King's Head and Brickyard . .	8 10 0		1 0
John Goodey	The Bowling Green House, garden and orchard	4 10 0		
John Gunn	Insurance Office	6 0 0		
Hollis Clayton	His shop and house	16 0 0		
Wm. Lukin	Rented to Taylor & Co., Maltings	5 0 0		
Nicholas Toke	His house and buildings . .	10 0 0		
Quakers Meeting House and Cottage		2 0 0		
Dissenters Meeting House and Cottage		3 0 0		
Catherine Wickens rented to Jos. Edwards house and garden, etc.		13 0 0		2 6
Dan Philpot	House, and yard detached . .	6 10 0		
,, ,,	Rented to Thos. Henson cottage and stable opposite	3 0 0		
Dr. James	House, garden, cott. and stable opposite	13 0 0		2 6
Wm. Short	Cott. and wheelers shop and the workhouse barn	5 5 0		1 5 0
Dr. Sims	House and land 3 acres. The Bowling green	21 0 0		
Sarah Stagg	Boar's Head	6 10 0		
Robt. Felsted	White Horse (Jos. Pye)	6 0 0		
Ben Foakes	Rented to Helston and shop in back street	3 10 0		
Mrs. Segg	Rented to W. Giver as a school . .	1 0 0		
Sir Geo. Beaumont	Rented to Wm. Hoy	1 10 0		
,, ,, ,,	,, Ben Johnson	1 10 0		
,, ,, ,,	,, Thos. Archer	2 10 0		2 0
Joseph Edwards	Rev. Howlett cottage and garden (The parsonage, house grounds and vicarage)	10 0 0		
Parish House	John Starr	2 0 0		
Town Hall		5 0 0		

		Total value £ s. d.	Corn and wood tithes £ s. d.	Vicarial tithes £ s. d.
Mr. Burton	Rented to Robt. Hindle school yard and garden	10 0 0		
James Mumford	House and close	5 10 0		1 0
Simon Hutchins	rented to Thos. Alliston, Maltings	5 0 0		
Thos. Bird	rented to Widow Hayden and blacksmith's shop	2 10 0		
Thos. Collis	rented I. Alliston "The Harp" ..	10 0 0		5 0

CHAPTER XXV

Dunmow charities

There were many houses, tenements, etc., in Dunmow whose rents went to the Church or the poor. The owners had willed their property at various times down the centuries, but around 1800 there was quite a " stir up " with the parishioners. A lot of these properties were in such bad repair that the occupants refused to pay their rent. Many of the cottages were occupied by paupers. Some people thought that the paupers should be removed and the houses cleared and let to other families.

Sir Geo. Beaumont thought that many should be pulled down and rebuilt in more airy and healthy situations. The expenses incurred by removing the Almshouses on Parsonage Downs amounted to £229.

In the interval of the declaration respecting the exchange with Sir George Beaumont being handed round for the signatures of the inhabitants, great dissentions and disputes arose in the parish and the carrying out of the exchange was suspended, but on May 25, 1805, proper deeds were executed by the trustees of the charity estates, and the property agreed to be exchanged was conveyed as follows:

"All that Toft Piece of Ground whereon a tenement divided into several habitations that lately stood, with a garden adjoining in Great Dunmow, in Church End, between the Toft whereon a tenement sometimes of John Cock, and afterwards of James Norris, formerly stood on the one part, and the Toft whereon a tenement sometimes of William Radley formerly stood, on the other part. [The path opposite the Bell Inn.] Part of the same Toft and garden, described to be then laid open to the adjoining road, to better the approach to the Church, and intended to remain open for ever hereafter, and the residue of being then laid to and made part of the adjoining Field of Sir George Beaumont, and the said Toft and garden are therein mentioned to be divided by a pale fence, were conveyed to Sir George Beaumont absolutely.

" And all that parcel of ground contain in length from North to South 9½ acres and in depth 4 rods, as the same was then marked and staked out being part and parcel of the waste ground of the Manor of the Rectory of Great Dunmow and called by the name of the Parsonage and upon which a Messuage divided into several dwellings and habitation have been lately erected. Together with the said Messuage and all other buildings now standing and with or being thereon with the appurtances and with a way thereto from the King's Common Highway there is a direct Luie up to the front of the said Messuage. In exchange for the Toft or parcel of Land, Garden, and Premises, granted to the said Sir George Beaumont and conveyed by him to the Trustees upon the same Trusts as they held the rest of the Charity Estates."

DECLARATIONS OF THE INHABITANTS OF GREAT DUNMOW AND THEIR REQUESTS TO THE TRUSTEES.

To the Right Honorable Charles Viscount Maynard, the Right Honorable John Lord Henniker, Bart., Sir George Howland Beaumont, Bart., Michael Pepper, Esq., James Raymond, Esq., the Honorable Major-General Trecothich Henniker, Henry Maynard, Clerk, Sir Thomas Maryon Wilson, Bart., Stanes Chamberlayne, Esq., Stanes Broket Chamberlayne, Esq., James Hallett, Esq., John Brock, Clerk, and Alexander Richardson, D.D., Vicar. Trustees for Charitable purposes for the benefit of the parish of Great Dunmow.

A messuage farm and land in Thaxted containing 31 acres and 36 perches, in the occupation of William Gilder.

A messuage called Cranes and about 13 acres, 2 roods and 9 perches of land in Great Dunmow in the occupation of William Sweeting.

A messuage of 3 roods of ground in Great Dunmow late occupied by Gregory Tiler.

A close of Pasture ground containing 2 acres, 1 rood and 32 perches near the Downs in Great Dunmow, in the occupation of John Scruby on part of which a Mill is erected, and which was let on lease for 99 years which expired at Michaelmas 1800.

Once acre of Meadow called Brady Mead in Great Dunmow, let to Mrs. Day.

Several cottages were removed from Churchend by common consent to Parsonage Downs in Great Dunmow, occupied by Paupers.

A messuage on the Causeway in the occupation of William Whybrow.

We whose names are here declare direct the trust to take such steps as they deem advisable.

Witness our hands this 13th day of March, 1806.

John Fuller	Abrm.Thorne	Ed. Harridge
Jos. Edwards	Isaac Malster	Wm. Barnard
John Scruby	Rich. Randell	Wm. Cheveley
Wm. Lukin	Thos. Bird	John Turner
Sam Philbrick	Ed. Smith	Thom. Rolfe
Thos. Collis	Henry Daires	Benj. Foakes
Geo. Wade	Ed. R. Smith	The mark X of Mary Day
Mary Waskett	Steel Lambert	
Rbt. Barnard	John James	Ann Barnard
Eliz. Mills	Wm. Taylor	William Frost
John Gunn	John Fewell	

THE MANOR OF GREAT DUNMOW

November 5, 1804, at a General Court then held, the Homage presented that on Nov. 2nd, 1803, Geo. Wade out of Court surrendered:

All that Customary or Copyhold Tenements or cottage with the outhouses, yards, gardens, and appurtenances thereunto, belonging, situated, and being in Great Dunmow aforesaid near to a place called the Downs, late in the occupation of Cave Ackers, and then John Joyce.

And also all that Customary or Copyhold Tenement or cottage with the outhouses, yards, gardens, and appurtenances in Great Dunmow at or near the said place called the Downs, late in the occupation of James Wilson, and then of Richard Turner.

Also, that cottage or tenement with its outhouses, gardens, and appurts. being in Great Dunmow aforesaid near the place called the Downs and late in the occupation of James Wybrow and his assigns.

To the use of John Fuller of Great Dunmow, tanner, and John Clapton, farmer, and their heirs and assigns, absolutely. Whereupon came into court John Fuller in person and John Clapton, by the said John Fuller, his attorney and prayed to be, and were admitted tenants of the said premises.

To hold to them, their heirs, and assigns for ever according to the tenor and effect of the said surrender.

This is held by Mr. Fuller and Mr. Clapton in trust for the parishioners of Great Dunmow, and is to be disposed of as the parishioners in Vestry shall direct, and it is now let by them to tenents at " rack rents " which are carried to the credit of the overseers' accounts.

The above mentioned surrender was made by Mr. Wade as a Trustee for the late Sir George Beaumont to whom a copyhold Cottage held of the Manor of Newton Hall and formerly belonging to the Parishioners was surrendered by the late Thomas Beaumont, Esq., who was a Trustee for the Parishioners by way of Exchange.

On the 27th May, 1805, all the rest of the Charity Estates were conveyed to the following Trustees, viz.:

Charles Vicount Maynard	Sir Thos. Maryon Wilson
Sir Geo. Howland Beaumont	Stanes Chamberlayne
John Lord Henniker	Stanes Brocker Chamberlayne
Michael Pepper	
James Raymond	James Hallot
Bridges T. Henniker	John Brock

Alexander Richardson

James Raymond, Stanes Chamberlayne and Stanes Brocket Chamberlayne are the only survivors about 1830.

May 24, 1808

At a meeting of the Trustees it was resolved that the house on the Causeway lately occupied by Wm. Wybrow shall be repaired immediately and used as a School Room and that a salary of £50 per annum shall be paid to such Schoolmaster as shall be recommended Do. Bell and approved of by the Trustees, and in addition to this Salary the Master shall be at liberty to teach Male children in the evenings, after the ordinary school hours. That proper desks and forms shall be provided for the use of the scholars.

That the Parish officers of Dunmow be directed to clear the houses on the Downs as soon as possible, to the intent that proper persons may be placed therein by the Trustees. That Mr. Wade shall write to the officers with a copy of this Order and request them to call a Town Meeting immediately, to consider the most convenient means of removing the present occupiers from the Houses on the Downs and at all events to get them cleared before 12th June next.

May 8, 1816

The will of the Rev. John Mangey in aid of the School in Dunmow.

When the Rev. J. Mangey died it was found he had left £200 to be applied to teaching poor children in Dunmow to read English, but both his executor and executrix died before him, his wife, Honoria, and a Mr. Topping of Colchester. This caused some delay and it had to be settled by the Master of the Rolls. This cost money, but eventually £117 was purchased in the name of the trustees, and it was further witnessed and declared by the said parties that having now settled the money in Consols the transfer would produce £191/2/2 to the said trustees, and from then until the present time this money has gone to the National School.

CHAPTER XXVI

Claytons of Dunmow

CREDIT LEDGER

1796	£	s.	d.	£	s.	d.
3rd Mar. In hand	20	6	3¾			
From shop	2	14	0			
,, ,, ...	8	10	0			
By cash paid for Duke stone				3	3	0
Of Thomas Day for horse valued to me	9	8	0			
Charles Hicks lent				20	0	0
From shop						
By expenses at Saracen's Head	9	7	6	4	4	9
From shop	8	3	6			
From shop	7	15	6			
By John Fry for stamps					13	6
From shop	20	9	6			
Received of Charles Hicks	120	0	0			
From shop	11	2	6			
From shop	14	18	0			
Received of Charles Hicks for clothes	4	1	0			
To Esdailes and Co., Bankers, of London............				120	13	0

This is a young man starting up in business. Hollis Clayton came to Dunmow with his cousin Sarah, a girl of 18. At first they had to stay at the Saracen's Head, until they could get a housekeeper no doubt, because he mentions expenses at the Saracen's £4/4/9.

Later he goes on to persons on the cash account. People certainly ran up big bills those days, such as Anne Clapton £20, Eliza Livermore £65/18/-, I. Malster £7/6/10 (postmaster and " mine host " at Saracen's), William Taylor £14, etc. Now we come to disbursements to all the firms with which they dealt for their varied stock.

From North and Frith of Gracechurch Street, 71lb. Horsehair £2/8/4; coats, print and russian from Clark, Phillips and Atkinson; from Fenn and Wickenden, muslin, handkerchiefs and calico; two dozen knives at 3/6 per dozen from Charles Hodgson, of Pond Well Hill, Sheffield; to Wm. Phillips for almanacks for the year 1800; stores hoes, cinder-sifters, etc., from John Vardon of Gracechurch Street; butter, cheese and bacon from Joseph Cuff and Co. of Whitechapel; from Nicholas Cheesman of Aldermanbury 5½ yards of Kersey £1/10/3, blue linen, crimped muslin and dimity; from James Ferguson, Wood Street, ribbons, Sunday ribbons to dye, satin and edging; Bowdons, Matkin and Co. for candlewick £7/17/-; Wm. Allen, London, cups and saucers, dishes, soap, garden pots; from John Rutter, Lone Lane, Aldermanbury, candles, snuff and tobacco £47/7/10 for one delivery in 1797; William Ranson of Old Jewry charged £15/19/4 for 1cwt. of tobacco.

Tomson Warner of Cripplegate sold metal goods, Miller Christy supplied all the latest in hats in 1796, and I seem to remember them still going in recent years. Plenty of goods for Sarah's department came from Colman and Weldon of Watling Street, such as lace of all descriptions, muslins and crepe, which was very much worn in those days. Smith Kemble and Co. sold tea, cheese and sugar. The latter was bought in large quantities. Dunmow people must have retained their sweet tooth far along life's journey. One consignment came to £233/3/8. I do not suppose it cost more than a halfpenny a pound at that time. Dunmow people must also have eaten quantities of salt, and even Maldon salt was attainable at 14/6 a bushel.

Not all goods came from London. Day and Green from Saffron Walden were candle makers who sold eighty dozen candles for £33. In 1798 Thomas Thomason of Thaxted traded in tallow, gloves and butter, and also could oblige with a pall for hire at 2/6, or 5/- if one needed a better quality. James Abell was a Chelmsford cutler. James Gurson of Newport supplied worsted as well as cheese, butter and candles. Trade increased rapidly. The counter receipts went up to £320 a month and payment to Esdaile and Co., bankers, to £5,000 a year.

Hollis Clayton married in 1799 Miss Impey, of Saffron Walden. This family was much beloved in Dunmow and the neighbourhood, and being Quakers they treated all sections of the community alike, whether it was the old woman in her shawl or the lady in her carriage and pair, and when Sarah died in 1813, at the early age of 35, folk mourned her as a dear friend. She was laid to rest in the old Quaker burial ground in New Street.

Hollis's son was a young boy at this time, and as he grew up he entered into the whole life of the town. William Impey Clayton kept his diary from an early age right through to the day of his death. An entry for May 2, 1822, says " Father took possession of Buttles Farm," and on February 20 of the same year " Father took Staggs Farm of the Assignees."

On December 16 " Left London half past 7 by Chelmsford Coach, the place was reached at 11, and safe home by 1. All well and comfortable for which may I be thankfull." On January 11 this young man was 22, having been born in 1800. He appears very engrossed in the business. His father made frequent visits to London, and sometimes William accompanied him.

We do not know who managed the drapery department after the early death of Sarah—probably a manageress. Hollis died on November 26, 1830, aged fifty-four. He was at the vestry meeting at the Town Hall on the 22nd, so his illness must have been short.

We hope his thirty-four years in Dunmow were happy ones. They must have been, for he did so much good in the town. William Impey was of the same mould, not only carrying on his father's good works but adding to them. He married his cousin Maria Marriage on April 7, 1832. I have given you a few extracts from his diary; now here are some more when he was fifty years old.

January 14, 1852. Annual meeting of Dunmow Literary Society.

January 17. Edward Knight of the " Follie" assigns his affairs over to W. G. Gibson and William Randall for the benefit of his creditors. Ed. Knight is well known to us as Churchwarden and at the Vestry Meeting.

January 25. At Trustees Charity Estate Meeting.

January 28. Catherine Warner dies [a governess of the British School, daughter of Warner of the Academy in New Street].

January 30. Attended Brother Hollis's marriage Bond and later attended Peel meeting in London.

January 31. Majority in House of Lords for Free Trade 49.

February 4. Me and Mine attended Qtrly. Meeting.

February 5. Committee respect Elders at Colchester.

February 6. Parliament getting on with doing nothing.

February 7. Commenced stocktaking. Got it all down on paper by seventh afternoon.

February 8. Brother Hollis and his new wife reached home this evening.

February 22. Attended Meeting for Sufferings.

February 27. Roads quite dusty. Dibbing Beans.

May 13. Mangle send for J. Bull 2/6.

May 14. Gave 2 Irishmen 2/-.

May 15. Frederick Tyler left us after residing with us 10 years.

June 30. Sir Robt. Peel spoke early today in the House of Commons; he had a fall from his horse in the evening.

July 2. Sir Robt. Peel died at 11 o'clock this night.

July 5. Examination at the British School today.

July 8. Fire at High Roothing soon after breakfast, 2 cottages burnt out. Our Fire Engine's pipes defective.

July 11. Duke of Cambridge died in his 76th year.

Extracts from a letter written to his son William while he was at school read: " Yesterday we all went to dine with your Aunt and Uncle at Broomfield Mill (the Marriages). You ask about the Harvey upset—if he had been a teatotaller it would not have happened, the facts are—he went to Braintree station for some cheese from Ipswich, and got too much beer, and when he got back as far as the ' Flitch of Bacon ' he got more beer and the horse went on, Harry ran after him and pulled him up so sharp that he reared up, and backed into the ditch and broke both shafts. . . . Dr. Joseph Grice's remains were interred at 2 o'clock last fourth day week, and such was the respect shown for him, that during the time of the funeral every shop, I believe, in Dunmow was closed. I have not heard what his widow and daughters are likely to do. . . . The day before yesterday your mother laid the first brick of the new houses where E. Wood's shop used to be, Maria laid the second, Charlotte the third, Sophia the fourth and Ellen the fifth. I mean to lay one at the side when they get to the white bricks, with my name on it, and intend to leave one for you to lay when you come home. James Tweed is now living at Braintree for a few months in consequence of there being small-pox at his house here. Wm. Childs called in today to borrow £19 which I lent him—he has re-signed the Pledge, and has just taken on a contract to build a Greenhouse for John Barnard at Olives. Poor fellow, I do hope this time he will be wise and keep close to his promise."

It was not for William Impey to have a long earthly life—only one more year than his father. He had been such a kind neighbour to so many. One evening after he had been meditating, as was his habit, in the garden he came in and sat in his usual chair, where he was a little afterwards found to have passed to that life to which he almost seemed to belong. Here we have a striking instance of the uncertainty of life in the passing of our beloved friend. When only fifty-five and filling a highly responsible position in society, and surrounded by temporal blessings, he was suddenly called to surrender his stewardship on November 23, 1855.

The daughters were all active in good works, and we meet them at the British School almost daily, especially the eldest, Maria, who married Joseph Alfred Smith, whose draper's shop at Chelmsford is still carried on in the same name. Maria often came over to visit the school she had loved so much. She also worked for the British and Foreign Bible Society both here and at Chelmsford.

Charlotte stayed with her mother till her death on May 1, 1875.

Ellen lived at Chelmsford till her marriage in 1882 to James Whitehead.

Sophia married her cousin Henry Marriage. They lived at Parsonage Farm, Broomfield, but after the death of Henry (senior) they moved to Ayletts. For over sixty years she worked for the British and Foreign Bible Society.

William the younger was already in the

business, and on his father's death he took over all his associations, such as treasurer of the British School, a burgess of the corporation, and a trustee of the literary association, and, again like his father, was intimately connected with the Dunmow Saving Bank, and there must have been many other connections springing up which claimed his thoughtful attention. He married in 1871 Louisa Goff of Gorleston and had five children. But very different from the quiet life of his father he was very fond of hunting, and until recently the mounting block still stood in the yard behind the shop.

Unfortunately he must have caught a bad chill, and he died on March 9, 1881, of bronchitis and congestion of the lungs after two days illness. He was only forty-five. He was buried at the Friends' meeting house in New Street on Wednesday, March 12. All the shops were closed and few opened again that day. Every religious denomination in Dunmow was represented. In all about 700 people were present, including many poor folk bound by strong ties of love and gratitude. They realized they had lost a dear friend.

The vicar, the Rev. W. L. Scott, wrote in his parish magazine for April 1881: " I cannot conclude my paper this month without referring to the loss which the parish has suffered by the most unexpected death of Mr. Clayton. He bore a name and held a position in Dunmow which was inherited from other generals of his family. His sun has gone down when it is yet midday, but his memory will long hold its day in the minds and hearts of Dunmow people. It is impossible to say how much the well-being of this town had depended on the moral character and the business habits and the readiness for useful service and needful work of this young man."

Ellen, his youngest aunt, who married Mr. Whitehead of Chelmsford, could not bear the thought of the business going out of the family, so she and her husband bought it from William's executors and carried it on until 1897.

In 1706 the Quakers of Dunmow applied for a deed to build a meeting house. This was the only deed applied for, and when this present meeting house was built in 1833 it was built on the same foundations in New Street. At the back of the building is the " old burial ground " and in the front the " new burial ground."

CHAPTER XXVII

Dr. Robert Courthorpe Sims

Dr. Sims was held in great respect in Dunmow, where he laboured for over fifty years. He took the degree of Doctor of Physic at Edinburgh University in 1744. In 1746 he married Rebecca Tritton. The first few years of his life as a doctor were spent at Canterbury, whence he came to Dunmow. He lived at the house called The Bowling Green. He was devoid of ambition and fame. His one desire was to be useful as a surgeon and apothecary in the little town in which the greater part of his long life was spent. He was a Quaker, though perfectly free from the narrow-minded spirit of his day.

He was a keen and knowledgeable botanist, and spent most of his spare time trying to rear new and unusual plants. He had about an acre of garden, and he seems to have changed the entire layout every few years, for it is said that anyone not seeing it for several years would not recognize what they had seen and perhaps admired on a previous visit.

Rebecca predeceased her husband, dying on April 29, 1781. They had a son and a daughter, Sarah, who married in 1775 at the ancient meeting house at Stebbing (built 1674-5) John Smith, grocer and linen-draper, of Halstead. Sarah must have died before her father. He retained his faculties almost to the end, and at eighty-eight he wrote a book, *An Essay on the Nature and Constitution of Man*, comprehending an answer to the following question: "Are there any satisfactory proofs of the immortality of the soul?"

Dr. Sims died on January 28, 1812, in his ninety-second year. The late Maria Clayton said that the Sims family were each laid to rest in the old burial ground at New Street Friends' meeting house. No headstone marks the grave of this good man, who, with his wife and daughter, was buried under the shade of a sycamore tree on the left-hand front of the burial ground.

JOHN BURKE LYNCH, SURGEON

Dr. Lynch died after two days illness on February 19, 1821, aged forty. In so many books and papers I have examined his name has turned up, so much so that I set out to find his burial place. It is on the old part of the parish churchyard. The benevolent sympathy instantly expressed by the town and neighbourhood where he had practised, not only by those who had benefited by his professional skill and attention but those who had known him during a period of nearly fifteen years and known his upright benevolent and amiable character and his sincere, consistent and unobtrusive piety, and others who felt for the widow and ten children deprived so suddenly of a dear husband and father, occasioned an appeal to be made, which it was hoped would "receive the kind of consideration of those whose disposition is to do good." I cannot give the names on the list of subscribers for the widow and ten children, for it would take too long, but there were 319 subscribers and the amount collected was £1,679/14/6. What a wonderful amount. We would not be able to collect all that today, it could mean perhaps about £4,500 now. The donations ranged from £50 to £1.

Mrs. Lynch was Frances Toke before she married, and I remember an old local saying " Where's there's Tokes there's money." In the subscription list all the Tokes contributed. I am sure Nicholas Toke, who was an attorney so many years, must have collected a good hoard, and could have kept his daughter and educated all the children.

When I was going through some books of Mr. Hollis Clayton's I came across a little book which he had taken great pains to write by hand. It was about Dr. Lynch's funeral. The first page was beautifully arranged and the rest of the book was the complete funeral service, in a lovely copperplate handwriting. He could not have done this at the service. It included the prayers, the lesson, and the address given by the curate, the Rev. G. Millet. I became " lost " in it, and failed to remember that it was over 150 years ago. I would think that Mr. Clayton and the doctor had been great friends. There would not have been much difference in their ages or, if I am not mistaken, in their general outlook—each to do his very best in whatsoever came his way. Hollis Clayton contributed £20 to the subscription.

We remember his crippled son who became our local hymn writer—Thomas Toke Lynch.

DUNMOW'S HYMN WRITER

Thomas Toke Lynch, Dunmow's hymn writer, the third son, took his mother's maiden name. He was a delicate boy, suffering from some kind of spinal trouble. For the greater part of his life he had to lie on his back, and suffered great pain, but in spite of this he succeeded in retaining his natural good humour. At an early age he started writing poems and hymns. His first book of hymns and poetry was called *The Rivulet*. The popularity of his hymns is shown by the fact that a fourth edition containing 167 hymns was issued just before his death in 1871. In his later years his health improved somewhat and he was ordained to the Congregational Church and preached to a small but cultured congregation in Hampstead Road, near Mornington Crescent, but the effort proved fatal. When he was dying he said " This is good; now I am really going to begin to live." On the centenary of his birth Dunmow Congregational church remembered him at both services in the address and prayers, and only his hymns were sung. There are still many of his hymns in the Baptist and Congregational hymn books, but the great favourite is " Gracious Spirit, dwell with me." It has been translated into many languages, so we can let that be his epitaph. People singing this today may well mentally salute its brave writer, who in spite of pain and ill-health never lost his trust in the supremacy of spirit over weakness of the flesh.

The Lynch family lived at the Laurels in High Street (now Mr. and Mrs. Chiswell's private house). The left part of the building was the doctor's surgery.

CHAPTER XXVIII

Coronation Day at Dunmow
June 28, 1838

A SONNET TO VICTORIA

Hark! Hark! Halloo! Halloo! What sounds are those I hear?
Like double thunders bursting on my wakeful ear,
What is it wakes me from my easy couch thus soon?
The General's guns salute the twenty-eighth of June.
Lakes, rivers, hills and dales respond the Royal sound,
To wake, to rouse the slumbering peasantry around.
Through Maynards spacious Park it finds its echoing way,
Salute the Nobles Lodge, just at the opening day.
Sounding and still sounding; rebounding as it flies
To the next festive Town, before the echo dies.
Tidings still resounding to nations we've not seen:
Victoria is Crowned, and Britons own their Queen.

Ye Nymphs of Dunmow wake! Wake up your minstrel throng;
A Virgin Queen demands your earliest morning song.

GREAT DUNMOW.

CORONATION OF HER MAJESTY,

QUEEN VICTORIA.

DINNER TICKET.

Admit ____________ Wife and ____ Children

______ Pints Beer.

By order of the Committee.

Signed ____________

A dinner ticket at Queen Victoria's coronation, June 28, 1828.

Your rosy garlands bring, your flowery wreaths prepare,
And with your ringlets weave, while floating in the air.
Your silken aprons fold; come, fill your laps with flowers
To strew old Dunmow streets, or build triumphal bowers.
Though blithesome days of Bess and Ann are passed away,
Hail! Hail! sweet nymphs your Queen Victoria's crowning day.
Like her illustrious Sire, may her large soul expand,
Defend our faith, defend the Church, the bulwark of the Land.
May she promote the state, like all the Brunswick line,
Till she in glory stands complete, in robes of glory shine.

Hark! What a cheerful sound sweeps along the vale,
The joyful parish bells with music load the gale,
The band has just struck up, with bugles sounding loud.
The people parade the streets, become a densy crowd.
" God save the Queen " they cry, but (here comes out the tale)
Old England's roast beef, and Randall's good brown ale
The Rich and Poor partake, and not one soul mistaken,
Every face look pleased, as if they'd won the Bacon.
Here we close the scent and now we end the story,
Come sing " God save the Queen " and long live Victoria.

Price one penny.

Carter, Printer, Dunmow.

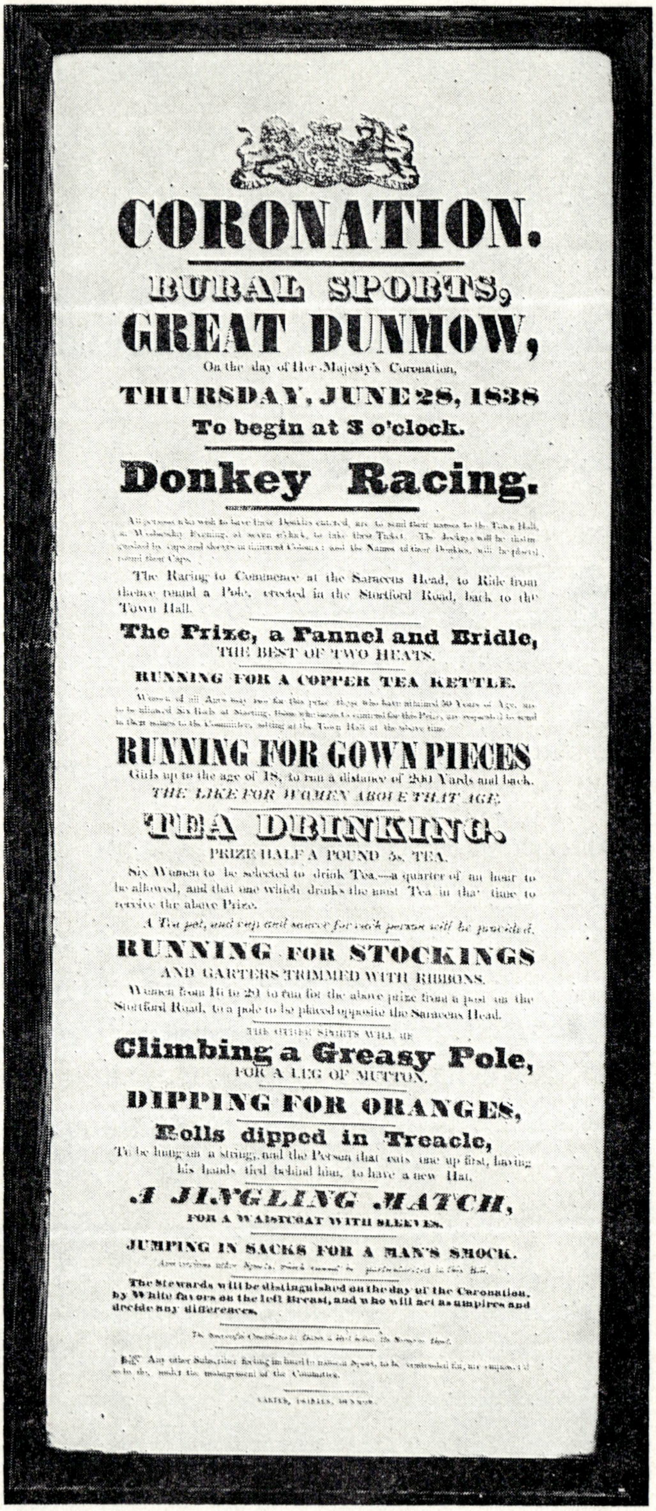

The bill advertising the coronation sports in 1838.

CHAPTER XXIX

Dunmow from old directories

1792

A bye post comes from Braintree hither, Sunday, Wednesday and Fridays. There is not a regular carrier to London, but Stubbings waggon from Great Easton calls every Friday at 11 o'clock to take up the butchers meat for the Saturday Market, to the Talbot Inn, Whitechapel, and returns on Monday afternoons.

A diligence which belongs to the Bishop's Stortford Stage Coach, sets out from the Saracen's Head to Harlow, where it meets the said Coach on Tuesdays, Thursdays and Saturday at 5 p.m.

This directory tells us very little, except to mention a few of the more important inhabitants: Sir John Bridges Henniker, Bart., Thom. Bridges, Esq., Sir George Beaumont, Bart., M.P., William Lukin (father of Lionel), Rev. John Howlett (vicar), John James (surgeon and apothecary), Rev. Aaron Wichens (dissenting minister), John Raynor (surgeon and apothecary), R. C. Sims (surgeon and apothecary), George Root (druggist).

1826

Postmaster: Isaac Malster.

Coaching inns: Saracen's Head, White Lion, Star.

Surgeons: Joseph Grice, Richard Pearson.

Academies: Wm. Bale, Rev. John Millet, Rev. Chas. Powlett.

Coaches: from the Star inn every Tuesday, Wednesday and Friday at 7 a.m., returning alternate days; from the Chequers every morning (except Sunday) at 6.30 except Monday, 5.30.

Millers: Steel Lambert, William Shed.

Tanners: John Fullar, Edward S. Phillbrick.

Attorneys: Henry Jackson, Nicholas Toke, Geo. and Wm. Wade.

Taverns and public-houses: Bell (Wm. Shed), Boar's Head (Wm. Wylton), Bowling Green (Geo. Franklyn), White Horse (James Archer), Three Tuns (John Weaver), King's Head (Wm. Cook), Harp (John Bush), Chequers (Wm. Smith).

Carriers: a wagon leaves the Star every Monday and Friday for London at 6.30 a.m.; John Yeulet from the Three Tuns every Monday and Friday to the Blue Boar, Aldgate; Wm. Watson from the Chequers to the Saracen's Head, Aldgate.

1839

Postmaster: John Perry Gunn.

Surgeons: Joseph Grice (registrar of births and deaths), Thomas Salt.

Watch and clock makers: Charles Knight and James Spurge.

Attorneys: Nicholas Toke (clerk to the magistrates), Wm. Johnson, W. Wade.

Chemists and Druggists: Thos. Franklim, Wm. Piper (and news).

Basket makers: James Grant, John Prior.

Blacksmiths: James Chiles, Benj. Cheek, James Drane, Guyver and Collis, James Young.

Carpenters and joiners: Samuel Franklin,

Abraham Holgate, Wm. Lamprell, Wm. Leech.

Miscellaneous: D. Carter, books and news, secretary to coal co, gas works secretary; Friendly Society, Town Hall; Thos. Hudson, veterinary surgeon ; Wm. Leapingwell, accountant; John Palmer, nurseryman; John Cock, gunsmith; Joseph Collis, ironmonger; Benjamin Cheek, parish clerk; Arthur Barfield, savings bank; Wm. Smith, cabinet maker, upholster and turner.

Coaches and carriers, 1839

A coach from the Saracen's Head Monday morning at 5 a.m., every other morning (Sundays excepted) at 6 a.m. The Times (from Clare) calls at the Star every forenoon at 11.30. Both go through the Roothings. To Clare—the Times calls at the Star every afternoon (Sunday excepted) at 2.30 p.m.

CARRIERS

To London—Garrett's wagons from the White Lion every Friday, Brands' every Wednesday, Theobald's van every Thursday, Yauletts wagon from Three Tuns Monday and Friday, Reynolds's wagons from the Star every Wednesday; to Haverhill—Brand's wagons from the White Lion every Friday.

1848

There is little change in coaches and carriers. By this time the wind is almost on the change, for the railway has reached Stortford.

Dunmow was by now a well lighted and paved town with a population of 2,792 at the 1841 census, and with a good supply of spring water.

Dunmow personalities, 1848

John Perry Gunn (postmaster), R. Anderson (police superintendent), John Bauser (inspector), Geo. Glencoe (excise officer), Rev. Rich. Frost (Independent), Rev. Sir A. B. Henniker (Newton Hall), Rev. Jeremy King (Baptist), Rev. Lewis Majendie, M.A. (vicar and rural dean), W. Wade (solicitor and clerk to the court), Joseph Grice (surgeon), Thos. Salt, (surgeon), Joseph Pearnain (sexton), Rev. T. Wallis (vet), Rich. and Wm. Randall, brewers, maltsters and corn merchants, Nicholas Toke, Attorney retd., John Rockhill (chemist), Robert Mizen (postman to Thaxted).

To Chelmsford, John Turner and mail cart (Thos. Olley) daily.

Academies and schools

*Miss Brown, the Misses King; *Henry Warner and Son; British School; Henry Ford and Cath. Warner; *Rev. Tweed, M.A.; Clock House Diocesan; Charles Nichols and Thos. Fox; National School Charles Marshall, Rebecca Cheek and Maria Barker.

Only twelve inns and taverns are given in 1848, which is a decrease on previous centuries, but this year gives us seventy-eight shops. I am sure we could not boast of so many today. Perhaps some did not require a shop to carry on businesses such as corn dealers and milliners.

There were five bakers, one of which was also a confectioner; four basket makers (osiers were still grown in damp ground); four blacksmiths (the horse was still man's best friend); seven boot and shoe makers (the vast majority had to " foot it "); five bricklayers and slaters; two butchers (with I expect, good English beef at about 3d. a pound); two cabinet makers and upholsterers; three corn millers; three corn dealers; two glass and china dealers; two glovers; two tanners; two watchmakers; nine milliners (what an assortment of hats to choose from!); three straw hat makers; seven tailors and drapers; four joiners and builders; two saddlers; three plumbers and painters; three wheelwrights; four shopkeepers undefined (I can be sure one of these was Samuel Thorn, who was reputed to have sold " anything from a flea to a sailing ship "; his shop was where Barclays Bank now is).

* Boarders taken

RECTORS

Geoffrey de Dunmow	1197
Master Reginald	1225
Simon Fitz Simon	1266
Hugh de Clare	1274
Bogo de Clare	1283
Roger de Clare	1294
Richard de Clare	1306
Richard de Ludlowe	1320
John Knyvet	1336
Thomas de Thunebry	1348
Robert Mauncer	1361
deprived on the institution of	
Sir John de Capel	August 7, 1368
John Lincoln	August 31, 1384
John Brandon	September 8, 1386
Thomas Overton	August 8, 1400
John Macworth	May 1401
Robert Tunstall	December 23, 1406
Thomas Banafter	
Richard Sherborne	
William Estby	July 15, 1440
Rad. Scroope, A.M.	December 23, 1480
John Turner	November 23, 1481

VICARS

Roger de Wyshoe	
Nic. de Hadeley	July 4, 1369
John Spicer	January, 1372
Thomas King	February, 1398
William Nash	November, 1434
John Lee	May 15, 1437
John Cowper	November 3, 1437
John Stowke	January 15, 1438
John Warde	Octcber 24, 1461
John Bernys, D.D.	March 3, 1478
Clem. Colynes, L.B.	April 13, 1491
Robert Sturton	June 17, 1492
Wm. Walton, c.a.p.	May 9, 1523
Galfr. Crispe, A.M.	December 12, 1540
John Bird, D.D.	November 6, 1554
Edward Stevens	April 15, 1559
Richard Rogers, A.M.	February 11, 1566
John Holland	September 26, 1564
Robert King, A.M.	November 15, 1578
Richard Vaughan, A.M.	February 19, 1591
John Gainsford	
Lod. Barfield, A.M.	February 2, 1593
Ralph Raven, A.T.D.	July 30, 1597
Jacob Colnett, A.M.	October 17, 1616
Thomas Weeks, S.T.B.	February 8, 1639
Joseph Crowther, S.T.B.	February 8, 1639
(A Royalist asked to resign)	
John Smith, M.A. (Presbyterian)	1642
William Parsons, D.D.	December 18, 1660
Thomas Leader, S.T.P.	August 6, 1671
Thomas Beaumont, A.M.	July 16, 1678
Robert Falconer, M.A.	1710
Samuel Burges, M.A.	1729
Thomas Knott	1744
John Mangey, M.A.	1754
John Howlett, B.D.	1782
Alexander Richardson, D.D.	1804
John Smith, B.D.	1829
H. Lewis Majendie, M.A.	1834
William Langston Scott, M.A.	1863
Arthur Courtney Roberts	1888
John Evans, M.A.	1905
Wm. J. House, D.D.	1915
Noel Mellish, V.C., M.C.	1928
David T. Callam, M.A.	1948
John Matthews, M.A.	1962

CHAPTER XXX

Dunmow inspires an " our town " homely poet of the past

The following poem was unearthed a few years ago by an old resident. It was written on tattered foolscap, and bore the watermark T. Parr, Beoley Mill, 1839.

" Our Village " has a niche in print,
  Why should not " Our Town"?
For in it dwell all sorts of folk,
  The fair, the dark, the brown,
Houses of plaster and of brick,
  The great as well as small,
And what our village could not boast,
  A very good Town Hall.

A " Lion " here, a " Bore's Head " there,
  A Saracen so bluff,
A " Star " to cheer the traveller,
  A " White Horse " rather rough.
And others too of smaller note,
  Where you may meet good cheer;
If you step in and draw your purse,
  Then they will draw the beer.

Two shops as good as Town could be
  Adorn the leading street,
Where most things that the House Wife
    wants
  She will be sure to meet.
Two butchers, one a Taylor [tailor] too,
  Who as the people say,
Were he to meet our Gracious Queen,
  He would not run away.

Two Doctors, both of famous skill,
  And be it here observed.
The very name of One, declares,
  His patients are preserved [Salt].
A Church, a Chapel, parsons two,
  And lawyers full of might,
In case of jars and quarrelling,
  To set the matter right.

An Office where you may despatch
  Your letters when they're done,
So many there have been of late
  They're sent off by a Gunn.
" Our Town " is an Old Corporate One,
  And of a Mayor can boast,
And Aldermen who play their parts
  Both at the boiled and roast.

Cordwainers, Factors, here we have,
  And Brewers of good Beer,
Wine Merchants that could Bacchus please
  Should ever he come here,
Dealers in pastry, and perfumes,
  Of Bakers, quantum suff.
Watchmakers, Grocers, Chemists too,
  Most folk think quite enough.

A market, rising in dispute
  As all do loudly cry,
Where pigs and other things you'll find
  And the best of Barley buy.
The new police have just arrived.
  To regulate " Our Town,"

But we're so peaceful, all their work
  Is walking up and down.

The printing press, if I forget
  'Tis clear I shall be wrong
And Carter very likely say
  He will not print the Song!
The song apart—'tis right to say
  A better can't be found,
Although you went from East to West,
  Or roam the country round.

But oh! the walks around " Our Town "
  Must not forgotten be,
For sure I am these walks are dear
  To many a He and She.
And well they may—for few can boast
  Of sweeter spots of Earth,
When lovers may repeat their vows
  And children sport in mirth.

And then the Fair of " Our Town "
  They do indeed excel,
That Beau must very silly be
  Who does not choose a Belle.
May every good attend " Our Town "
  To comfort and enrich,
The single every blessing find
  The married claim the " Flitch."

CHAPTER XXXI

From the first dissenters to the Congregational church

During the Commonwealth the mass of the people of Dunmow were glad to have John Smith, presbyter, and looked upon him as a godly preaching man, but no sooner was Charles II on the throne than John Smith and hundreds like him got their "marching orders." John Smith tarried here awhile preaching in the houses of his friends, but with the coming of Wm. Parsons from Birchangar to be vicar of St. Mary's he decided to go to Castle Hedingham, where we hear that he was "silenced" in 1662. Thomas Paine of Bishop's Stortford and Johnathan Payne of Saffron Walden found they could not sign the Act of Uniformity, so they, like 128 other Essex vicars, took to the road. Both are reputed to have preached to the dissenters in a small building near the White Lion.

It has for many generations been handed down by word of mouth that it was in the barn where now the present post office stands that many people gathered to hear the Word of God. Whether these men stayed for long we do not know, for a third Mr. Pain turned up, from where we cannot tell, for he was buried in the parish churchyard in December 1700. The first parson of whom any record survives is John Mason. He was succeeded by John Glascock, who was succeeded by Fereby Underhill, followed by Doughty. On January 12, 1715, Doughty requested a licence of the quarter sessions "that the house of Doughty of Great Dunmow in the County of Essex is humbly desired to be licensed as a place for Riligious Worship for Prodistant Disenters according to the Act of Parliament in that case made and provided."

Doubtless the early years of the dissenters were not easy, but for nearly 200 years "Christians" had been treating each other in the foulest manner. In 1664 Thomas Archer was cited before the court at Dunmow for "maintaining Conventicles tending to schism and making various and large sermons in his house and sometimes in his Barn, to which great numbers of people do resort from other parishes." However, by 1715 congregations were well over 400 and in 1728 the first chapel was built in New Street. Five years later the Rev. Wm. Teeton became the pastor and he stayed for twenty years. Next came the Rev. Samuel Beldam. He was held in such affection that when he died in 1769 many of his congregation made the long and tedious journey to the place of his interment at Royston.

Now followed a ministry of great influence, when large congregations gathered Sunday by Sunday to hear the Rev. Aaron Wickens. It is almost inconceivable what this man did, or how many hours his "day" consisted of. Besides his big "church" to succour he held a weekly evening meeting at High Roding and often preached at the old meeting house at Stebbing and held a meeting at Hatfield Heath on alternate Sundays. In addition he was secretary of the Associated Congregational Ministers of Essex and a founder of the Essex and Hertfordshire Benevolent Society, and in him the Essex Congregational

Union (which was actually founded at Dunnow in 1798) had an able and enlightened counsellor. In 1799 this great worker was called to his rest. His gravestone stating his many virtues is near the church he served so well.

He was succeeded by the Rev. Richard Frost, who ministered here from 1800-57, and during his time it was necessary to enlarge the chapel three times. A great deal was added to the existing buildings and to the minister's house. In 1844 the British School was built and opened, and the Congregational church contributed £1,500 to this.

Here I have overstepped the mark, and am running ahead too quickly, for up till 1875 the worshippers at New Street were still called " Protestant Dissenters." This sounds rather foolish, nearly eighty years after the Essex Congregational Union was founded here. To return to Mr. Frost. In his declining years he had a co-pastor to assist him. The Rev. Henry Gammidge came in 1854 and they were soon planning more improvements. A burial ground was purchased, a new vestry built and a Sunday school planned.

On November 12, 1867, the Rev. James Ervine was ordained to the pastorate and the next seven years saw great activity. The present church was built at a cost of £2,500, the erection of Olive View House for the residence of the minister cost £1,200 and a new organ was purchased for £300. In addition, contributions to outside causes totalled £4,500.

Had the pressure been too great? Had the time come to relax for a while? We hear of no new projects during the time of the next minister, the Rev. Geo. Jarvis, who served here for nine years. No doubt they were years of consolidation.

In 1883 the Rev. John Dadd commenced his seventeen years ministry here. Although a few years previously there had often been congregations of 700 the wave of indifference was on the way, and Mr. Dadd complained of " empty seats " and the irregularity on the part of members, which was influencing the godless and the undecided and blighting the prosperity of the church. Concern for the " godless " is revealed by the holding of open-air meetings and cottage meetings at Salletts Green, Bishopswood and Little Dunmow, and the introduction of quarterly youth services. On the death of Mr. Dadd in 1900 the Rev. Brychan Thomas (1901-13) was minister here. He founded a Bible class with a membership of three, which in the course of his ministry rose to eighty.

The Rev. W. H. Pace, B.D., succeeded him. Here was a young man ready to be the friend of all, and World War I breaking out the next year gave him an added opportunity. The fellowship helped to support fifty Belgian refugees, while the women of the church worked hard in staffing the Y.M.C.A., sewing for the Red Cross, and washing for the troops stationed in the town. Throughout the war years and after the Congregational and parish churches were drawn very close through the great friendship of their respective ministers. Their every effort was for unity, and they themselves lived it.

Unfortunately, Mr. Pace moved to Baddow Road, Chelmsford, in 1921 and Mr. G. J. Sparham, who had spent one year at Dunmow while Mr. Pace was a chaplain in the forces, came to be ordained here. He was a good preacher and very popular with the people. He was born in Shanghai, the grandson of the Rev. Griffith John, pioneer of the Inland China Mission. The vicar and Mr. Sparham still kept up their unity endeavours.

Next came the Rev. Norman Rowland, M.A., and seven years of inner harmony were enjoyed. There were no long ministries as in the past, and in 1934 the Rev. Macfadyen Scott came to Dunmow. Many remember his gracious ministry and his great devotion to duty. He passed away after a short illness.

The Rev. Gordon P. Breeze, B.A., B.D., was ordained here only three months before the outbreak of World War II. He was likened to Mr. Pace in build, youth and ways. In

1942 he felt it his duty to join the forces as a chaplain and after the war ended he took another church. From 1942 the Rev. G. C. Britton, a retired minister, gave invaluable leadership, his indomitable spirit rising to combat failing health.

After the war the Rev. John C. Carroll came. He had the reshaping and re-organization of Church life in all departments. Despite many discouragements a social centre was opened on two evenings a week and an intercessory prayer group established with the Anglicans. Under the able leadership of the Rev. George Dibden (1954-9) the church steadily strengthened its membership and took the bold step of changing the pattern of its youth education by introducing "family church." This able minister died suddenly, leaving a saddened congregation to mourn his passing.

The Rev. Norman J. Green came to Dunmow in 1959 and now serves the Stebbing church as well. In 1962 tercentenary celebrations were held from May 20-27 and a considerable amount of money was handed in for greater extensions to the church premises, particularly the Sunday school. A tercentenary bazaar alone produced £304—more than £1 for each year of this church's life. There was also a wonderful reunion of all who could be found to have belonged to the church at any time in their lives. This was indeed a great "get together," some not having met for fifty or sixty years.

Perhaps I ought to add here, under "dissentures," that on October 10, 1672, four houses were licensed at the quarter sessions to be Presbyterian meeting houses in Great Dunmow—Matthew Pinchback, John Pettitt, Thos. Burgess and Daniel Watts. I fail to find that a Presbyterian church was built in the town. These men had all taken office at the parish church during the Commonwealth and no doubt missed John Smith's form of service.

ROBERT HASLER

Robert Hasler was born at Trutons Farm on October 16, 1840, and passed suddenly to his rest in the early hours of June 14, 1920. He served the Congregational church at Dunmow through six ministries. He became a church member in 1861 and a deacon in 1874, and was for many years secretary and treasurer of his church. In September 1914 the members of the congregation presented Mr. Hasler with an illuminated address in book form, together with a framed portrait. He was the founder of Hasler and Company and lived to see the business advance at a surprising rate, but it was in the church that he was loved best of all. It was his dearest home.

CHAPTER XXXII

The bridge at Church End

At a special meeting at the Saracen's Head, Great Dunmow, on Saturday, January 7, 1828, Henry Joyce and Thomas Prior, constables of the above parish, with many of the influential people of the town, gathered to make a serious complaint concerning the condition of the footbridge at Church End. It appeared that the footbridge was not only broken, but lately it had been carried away by a storm, so that the king's subjects could not go, return or pass as they were wont to do. The river here crossed the king's highway and was on the estate of the Right Hon. Henry Maynard. A letter written and signed by the many persons present was sent to Viscount Maynard. It eventually came up before the quarter sessions at Chelmsford, but unsuccessfully. It was no new case for them. This bridge had been brought before them so many times since Elizabeth's time.

In her reign flood-water came in at three doors of the church. The footbridge may have been repaired from time to time by the landowners on either side. I quote here from the Rev. Langston Scott: "There was no power by which the quarter sessions were enable to throw a large portion of the cost upon the county funds, so we must not say too much about our forefathers in this matter. How a town like Dunmow should have suffered itself for long ages to endure such an inconvenient waterway, and narrow road leading to it, I do not know." At last, about fifty-two years after the meeting at the Saracen's Head, things began to stir. The quarter sessions at Chelmsford voted £300 toward a new bridge (the present one), the Dunmow Highway £500, Lady Brooke £100, the Rev. J. H. Hallet £25, and most of the inhabitants of Dunmow according to their means. Mr. H. Stock, the county surveyor, prepared the plans and the contract to build the bridge was taken over by Messrs. J. L. Glasscock, of Bishop's Stortford (the firm that is at this time restoring St. Mary's church), on September 27, 1881, for the sum of £790 and the work commenced the next month. Some ten feet of ground had to be purchased of Mr. Knight, watchmaker, of Dunmow, on the north side to accommodate the extra width, while the old ford on the south side still remains intact. More difficulty than was anticipated was experienced in securing a solid foundation for the bridge to rest upon, for after the removal of the subsoil to a depth of four feet it was discovered that there was a stratum of peat some eight feet thick. Some fifty or so piles had to be driven in, each twenty feet long and having 40lb. weight of iron at one end and a heavy ring on the other. This unexpected check brought the cost up to £1,300.

At last came the great day, Wednesday, June 7, 1882. It was a day to be long remembered. Again I quote Mr. Scott: "The weather was brilliant and the whole place presented a real gala appearance. Some 500 flags and streamers were displayed at every prominent position. Everyone was delighted to welcome Lord and Lady Brooke [afterwards the Earl and Countess of Warwick] on this their first appearance among us since their marriage a year ago."

The opening ceremony consisted of a

grand procession headed by the band of the 2nd Essex Rifle Volunteers and the presentation of an address by the bailiff of Dunmow, Mr. G. B. Clapham, who came forward and after reading the address (which was inscribed on vellum and handsomely illuminated) presented it to Lady Brooke. Lord Brooke, on behalf of himself and Lady Brooke, said how pleased they were to come to Dunmow and how much they appreciated the welcome they had received, and hoped the bridge would be the means of bringing prosperity to the town.

Then came the ceremony of laying the last stone by Lady Brooke, the formal opening of the bridge for traffic and a public luncheon. A crowd of about 3,000 gathered to watch the ceremony.

STREET LIGHTING IN DUNMOW

In 1839 it was decided to light the town now that the gasworks was operating.

A public meeting of ratepayers of such part of the parish as comprises the Town of Great Dunmow hereinafter mentioned and set forth, that is to say the street commencing and including the Public House known as the " Flitch of Bacon " (now the " Royal Oak") and to including the house of Steel Lambert at Park Corner—the Street leading from the Market Place down to and including the House occupied by Lady Henniker (Brook House). The Street called New Street, leading out of the Turnpike road towards the Independent Meeting (and the street known as Hemp Shop Lane), also Back Lane, or (Bullocks Lane).

February 19, 1839.

Charles Barnard, Edwd. S. Philbrick — Churchwardens.

Although it was passed by the Ratepayers concerned, it took 6 years to get the money (£85). In 1845 they considered they could put out tenders for Lighting the Town, from sunset till an hour before sunrise, but excluding 3 nights before full moon, and 3 nights after. This estimate was for 28 lamps at £3 per lamp. It was 1846 before anything was completed and the Lights were turned on in Dunmow.

W. Johnson, Jos. Grice, Jos. Sewell — Inspectors.

CHAPTER XXXIII

Poor Law Amendment Act 1834 down to Dunmow R.D.C. 1898

Although the Rev. John Howlett, in 1799-1800, wrote at length on poor law, and how the parishes could no longer continue to support the poor, it was more than thirty years before their burden was lifted. He was writing during one of our worst periods, when about half the population were paupers, and in this very room in which I am now writing were people perhaps weaving, straw-plaiting or groaning from the frailities of old age. But many of Howlett's books and pamphlets were knowledgeable and far-seeing. His books on husbandry, enclosures and the poor were being read many years after his death. Dying in 1804, he never knew the limits to which the poor had to come, and by the end of the Napoleonic wars the price of flour had risen to such a degree that only those whose means would allow it were able to get the necessities of life. The overseers were scarcely able to keep the poor alive. Just thirty years after this vicar's death Parliament passed, largely through the efforts of Edwin Chadwick, the Poor Law Amendment Act of 1834. Although Chadwick's Act did not contain all his ideas it did put an end to the parochial poor relief which had gone on since the Reformation, and even before then. The old vestry workhouses were closed as soon as a central one could be built. Most of the villages around had their own workhouses and the people from Thaxted, Broxted, the Eastons, etc., felt they were brought a long way from home, away from their relatives and friends. Mostly it meant walking all the way into Dunmow and back in order to visit them.

This new central workhouse was built in Dunmow. The building was designed by that well-known nineteenth-century architect Sir G. Gilbert Scott, cost £10,000 and held 500 inmates. The old workhouses at Nos. 43-61 High Street were put up for auction in December 1840 and were turned into cottages by their new owners.

A board of guardians was elected shortly after the Act was passed and first met at the Saracen's Head on April 7, 1835. This remained its meeting place for about two years, then the corporation let it meet in the Town Hall, charging it £15 per annum. When the new workhouse was completed, the board met there in its own board room. The Rev. E. F. Gepp, of High Easter, was the first chairman, and the clerk was Frederick Snell, a local solicitor.

For the next thirty years the board did its job unpaid and unloved. This was a period of hard, mingy Victorianism. The nineteenth century was one of " institutions, not of persons." That little something which previously had made life possible despite awful poverty had gone, and people became just numbers in an institution.

Now for a closer look at our board of guardians. When it had to appoint an inspector of nuisances it tried to get the superintendent to do the job for £75 per annum, although there was a spirited attempt to keep it down to £50. In a short, sharp reply

The brewery drays in the horse-and-cart parade about 1907-8.

the Local Government Board said " You can't do that there here! " The final choice was Mr. James Hamilton, as he had been a police sergeant. The more progressive members of the committee were always outvoted, and reading of the " remainder " today it is difficult to think of a more stubborn and illogical group of men.

Here are a few examples. When James Hamilton had been with them two years the Rev. E. F. Gepp moved that he be given an increase of £30 a year, so that he could have a horse and cart because he had such a large district to cover, reaching from Great Bardfield to White Roothing. It is difficult to imagine, but some of the " remainder " got on to the chairman and Mr. Hamilton never got his rise. After five years his salary was at least raised to £150, but not for long; at his next appointment the committee reduced it by £25, despite the strenuous opposition of Mr. Gepp and others. It was years before the inspector regained what he had lost.

After several years, when perhaps the " most progressive " had one or two more on their side, things went fairly calmly, but suddenly they committed a serious offence in the eyes of those who had seen too much of these supposed guardians in the past. The committee refused to continue the joint appointment of the medical officer of health with the other authorities and instead appointed its own official, a Dr. F. Williams, at £80 a year, saving of £54. This really brought the Local Government Board into action, and it not only refused to except the appointment but cut off its contribution to his salary and surcharged the chairman £40 for half a year's salary. This was a step in the wrong direction, as Mr. Gepp was strongly against it in the first place. Always a kindly man, and often likened to our Rev. Langston Scott, he had a very difficult task to manage this group of proved " flints."

The guardians had a crafty way of dealing with their bills. They did not pay them for at least a year. In 1878 the medical officer inquired when he might have his half-year's pay (£40) left over from 1876, but as they were likely to be surcharged if they paid him now, without government approval, the guardians quickly changed the subject by asking him for a detailed account of all his expenses. The Rev. John Howlett did not live to know, otherwise he would have written in even stronger terms than he did. There is no mention all through the years of the poor creatures who existed within the walls of this new nineteenth-century workhouse. Before 1834 everything was written down month by month by the clerk to the overseers of the poor. At the early part of the nineteenth century the annual estimate for coffins, perhaps, went to Mr. Lamprell or Mr. Holgate, at 14/- or 12/6 for best quality one-inch oak, etc., but even that last service went down and down through the century and into this one, for as far back as my memory takes me the coffins looked likely to lose their occupants before they reached the graveyard, where a certain part was allowed for paupers only. I think it was in 1912 or 1913 that Mr. Clark at Great Easton got the last estimate at 7/6 apiece.

Another thing that stands out in my mind is that it seemed quite usual at that time for a young man, or perhaps a middle-aged one, to say he would be going to the "spike" to "do out" his mother's or his wife's coffin that evening. This meant he was going to whitewash the inside, and perhaps put in a little cushion or pillow for the head. The "box" was whitewashed only on the outside by the undertakers.

In 1894 the chairman of the board of guardians, Mr. J. B. Frankham, of Little Canfield Hall, the clerk, Mr. F. J. Snell, and the inspector of nuisances, Mr. James Hamilton, had each had over twenty years' service with the Dunmow authority at the time of the foundation of the Dunmow Rural District Council. An election was held that year and the first meeting was held on December 29. One of the first things the council did was to appoint a surveyor about unsatisfactory water supply and the lack of proper sewage disposal, which made infectious diseases still prevalent. But slowly a change was in the wind.

The early years of the 20th century were a breaking up time of several of the "old faithfuls." Mr. F. J. Snell, the clerk, died in 1900 after a few days' illness. He lived opposite at The Gables, the offices of Mr. A. E. Floyd after, and now of Mr. W. Tanner, solicitor. That special old favourite of those days Mr. James Hamilton died the next year. In his twenty-eight years of service he must have tramped thousands of miles to spread the word of public health. He was a well-liked figure in all the villages and in the town of Dunmow and, as one might expect, his fatal illness happened while he was on duty at the court. As for the Rev. Edward F. Gepp, he died in 1903, aged eighty-three. Besides being such a devoted "father" of his flock in High Easter he must have spent an exasperating time trying to hold the heads of those hard-bitten guardians.

Mr. Hamilton was succeeded by a man named Carr, who was not here for long. Mr. Snell's chief clerk, Mr. A. Gifford, took on his work and Mr. J. Plumley the work of Mr. Hamilton. By 1906 Mr. A. C. Floyd had come to take over the solicitor's office of Mr. Snell and accepted the appointment of clerk to the guardians and the R.D.C. He became widely known and respected, and for a quarter of a century guided the affairs of the council with that quiet dignity for which he was renowned.

Jeremiah Plumley commenced his duties with the council, and for over twenty-seven years, first as inspector and then as surveyor, he carried out almost single-handed the council's first schemes of public sewerage and housing development in the 1920s and early 1930s.

There was one interesting result in the election of 1907—a young farmer of Little Easton, by name Humfrey Trembath, was decisively beaten, getting only nineteen votes. He was later elected and served for forty years.

In 1913 the isolation hospital in St.

High Street before the motor came, about 1905. Notice the lime trees.

Edmund's Lane was completed—rather late in the day, since the improvement in sanitation and pure water supplies was at last reducing infectious diseases to a minimum, so that it was not many years before it was turned into dwellings.

The war breaking out in 1914 put a halt to many schemes already proposed, such as council houses, which many local people were against as they thought it a waste of the public's money. Shortly after the war started those who were still inmates of the workhouse were moved to Braintree (St. Michael's) and the Army took over here. The Notts and Derbys, or Sherwood Foresters, had part of the workhouse but not the infirmary. Then a part was given over to Belgian refugees.

The name workhouse was out, and it became No. 1 Chelmsford Road, then a little later it became a P.O.W. camp.

It had been the custom of the guardians to send the boys on leaving school to Grimsby, where they were put on trawlers. In 1915, when the U-boat menace became worse, the Government commandeered the trawlers for mine-sweeping. It was in this dangerous occupation that many trawlers were blown up. Of our Dunmow boys Ernest Freshwater and Frank Sams lost their lives.

The master's assistant, Frank Willett, was killed in action and surveyor Mr. R. W. Burton's three sons were all killed. The large Victorian workhouse was sold in 1932 for conversion into flats. Something very different happened that year: Mr. J. B. Frankham died. For forty-seven years he had been a member, and for some of the time chairman, of the board of guardians and was a member of the R.D.C. from its formation in 1894. When a meeting was held to elect a chairman the voting resulted in deadlock between H. B. Turner of Barnston Hall and Col. T. Gibbons of Dunmow brewery. The colonel gave way to Mr. Turner, saying he was a " wild young fellow " and that he would support Mr. Turner.

Although the colonel served another twenty-four years he never became chairman. By 1925 the council had built 1,000 houses and modernized 100.

Another three old members died—Mr. D. H. Caton, Mr. Samuel Metson and Mr. W. H. Cox. Soon there was a lady on the council—Miss Blyth of Felsted—and in 1935 Mrs. Tench and Miss Gibbons were elected for Dunmow. Mr. Frank Stock beat Frances, Countess of Warwick 125-82.

A cinema was approved. A new school was built on the Downs. Then a few years later came World War II, the evacuees, the blackout, A.R.P. salvage drives, warship weeks, and the drone of enemy bombers with the resultant civilian casualties, only one in Dunmow, but eleven others in the Dunmow rural district.

In 1939, as in 1914, development came to a standstill. The council's main task was looking after the population, swollen by many women and children evacuated from London, and to find them shelter and homes, with a first duty to the children. The first swarm that descended on us on the Sunday that war was declared soon drifted home, but when the bombing of London started we soon got a much larger number of people. Some of these are still with us; their children grew up here and married here, and have no wish to move. During this war 700 houses were damaged in the rural district. In 1942 the council elected a new chairman, Mrs. M. L. Griffith, whose term of office lasted six years, and then Mr. J. M. Lukies took over.

The council has built 1,025 post-war houses and approved modernization for 1,031 private ones. It has also built 279 old people's bungalows, and two old people's homes are on the way.

CHAPTER XXXIV

From the parish registers

The parish registers do give us an interesting glimpse into the past, but one feels the swift passing of life's span from one generation to another. Many names with which they commence have come down almost to the present day, many families running for 400 years and we do not know how long before the registers started. Starting in 1538, when the Roman Catholic faith was the faith of this country, and continuing through the many changes the Church had to face—Protestantism and then back again to popish doctrine under Mary, and later on to the stark severity of the Commonwealth—the registers do help one to realize a little of what our forefathers went through.

The registers of baptisms, marriages and deaths were first introduced during Henry VIII's reign—in 1535—by Thomas Cromwell. At first the people did not take kindly to the idea, thinking that behind it might lie a scheme of Cromwell's to increase taxation for the benefit of the king. In 1538 Cromwell issued a decree commanding every vicar and curate to enter into a book or register, in the presence of one churchwarden or more, the names of all persons baptized, married or buried. For the safe keeping of this book the parish was bound to provide " one sure coffer with two locks and keys, whereof one key to remain with you [the priest] and one with the churchwardens." The penalty for disobeying this order was to be 3d. or 4d. for each offence, to be applied to the repair of the church.

The then vicar must have obeyed this order, but few did. Evidently this 1538 material was not of good quality, or not well kept, for Ralph Raven (1597-1616) copied the baptisms from 1538, as the book was " eaten out with tyme almost," to use his words. From 1557 the registers had to be made of parchment. If it had not been for this consciencious man 701 baptized persons would have been lost from the registers.

I would like to know how long some of these families had been going before 1538. The very first entry is Marjorie Long. The names that were in the first year and run through the centuries are Sweeting, Aylett, Phillpot, Fuller, Tyler, Scruby, Parker, Porter, Cooke, etc. From the manors there were the Jenoures of Bigods, the Melbornes of Merks, the Kenwelmarshes of Newton Hall and the Glasscocks of Minchons. Of all these families there must have been more than one line running in 1538, as the baptisms are so numerous. The 1558 register started with burials: January 3, Kathleen Smith, a nun. You will read in the quarter sessions of the son of a tailor in Dunmow who was hanged at Braintree on July 25 for murdering one Grey in his bed at Stebbing.

" Joan Sparrowhawk wife of Lewis, the which Joan refused her husband's persuasion to receive the Blessed Sacrament at the Altar at Easter, and at the time of death, whereupon the Vicar [the Rev. Ed. Stevens] forbade her burial in sacred ground, but her friends got a commandment of a Justice to bury her, unworthily in the hallowed ground with small reverence, with neither ringing nor singing, and very little saying, having neither bell nor cross, holy water nor sensing, but she was reburied April 20, 1559."

Here are three children from Greyfriars, London. There must have been a home in the country for these poor London children in those far-away days, for there are several instances of them dying, but three on this occasion sounds like an infection:

Thomas, having no surname, Alice, the daughter of no man Margaret Gardiner a child from Greyfriars 1553	Children of Greyfriars.

Joanne Martin a walking woman 1558

A dum wench 1580

Robert Case, the "prentis" of Thomas Virgin, was drowned in the new pond at Bigods in August 1587. Lyleana, a working child, 1592. William Long, tenant of "Martells," November 1593. A poor strange child April 1597. — Parker, wife of Henry the fletcher (arrow-maker). Margaret Jenoure, the first wife of Sir Andrew, who had sixteen children. In "Dunmow's 17th Doctor" he was preparing pills for his "little" son, but we find that nothing he did effected a cure, for "little" James, the son of William and Francis Swallow, was buried at the age of nine.

In December 1599, with the dying century Richard Kynwelmarsh of Newton Hall was dying too. He was a person whom I would have liked to know. He was, I feel sure, a "character" in his day. He was an outstanding figure in the revels, often playing the "Lord of Misrule." Once he and two working men just broke into the priory and were fined 5/- each—I suppose for mischief.

In all things connected with the Church he was there, and when he made his will he thought of the people of Dunmawe, providing a sum of money from his lands to be paid each year to the vicar and churchwardens of Donmow for the relief of the poor. This payment probably expired in 1603.

Five died of the "peste" in 1609. We do not know if this was the bubonic plague as in 1603, 1625 and 1665.

Joan Cornell, wife of John, was drowned in the town "waier" on October 29, 1630—(the watermill on the river fields in the direction of the church from Mill Lane).

Thomas Judd died at "John Ellis, his house," on February 25, 1630.

A stranger dying in the Cage, May 8, 1631.

John Austin, a traveller, October 8, 1637.

Ye year of ye Rebellion 1642 (see the local meeting that year).

I think at this time it would be as well to speak of the going of Joseph Crowther, vicar (Royalist), and the coming of John Smith, M.A., Presbyterian minister. Board of elders: Wm. Milborne, gent.; Robt. Calthorp, gent.; and Wm. Swallow, surgeon.

"Election of the Registrar under the Act of the Commonwealth.

"The names of the persons who did choose Samuel Gentrie to be Registrar:

John Smith, minister.

Robert Milborne	John Barnard.
William Swallow.	Henry Seex.
Leofrie Draper.	John Barker.
John Kylwelmarsh.	Matthew Pinchbeck.
John Houthchin.	James Raymond.
Newman Meade.	Thomas Perrie.

This had to be approved by a J.P.

"Whereas Samuel Gentrie of Much Dunmow was lately elected and chosen to be Registrar of the said parish, according to an Act of Parliament of the 24th August 1653.

"I have approved of the said choice, made by Parishioners aforesaid concerning his faithful performance of the same office, and have sworn him, the said Samuel Gentrie, this first day of April 1654.

T. Milton, J.P."

Murder of King Charles January 1649 (still 1648 by the old calendar).

Elizabeth Gentrie, wife of the Registrar, 1652.

William Browne, a stranger who died in the Swan in September 1653.

Burials beginning at Michaelmas under the Act of the Commonwealth:

John Hockley, proprietor of the White Hart, buried June 22 1655.

Samuel Gentrie, registrar and clerk, January 27, 1658.

Susan Babs, a young maid, May 7, 1661.

Alice and Ann Burr, young maids, August 12, 1662.

Thomas Smith, an ancient man, June 27, 1662.

Robert Cook, clerk and registrar until the Restoration, August 27, 1663.

Ann Baker, an old maid, 1664.

Thomas Johnson, buried in a sheet, December 6, 1668.

Thomas Baker, aged 95, March 29, 1669.

Samuel Page, a parish child, May 1680.

Matthew Pinchbeck, buried in linen, October 8, 1680.

Mrs. Pinchbeck, buried in linen, February 15, 1681.

(Hereby hangs a tale. The Woollen Act of 1678 was an Act which was the occasion for much controversy until it was repealed about 1800. The poor were let off, but those who had sufficient money had to comply with the law. The penalty of £5 was imposed in cases of non-compliance, half of which went to the parish and half to the " informer." Mr. and Mrs. Pinchbeck were against this Act, so we can suppose their executors had to pay the £10.)

Thomas Marshall, ostler at ye Saracen's Head, January 30, 1681.

Francis Laurence, innholder of ye Horse-shoes, May 5, 1682.

John Milborne of Merks, justice and major of the Trained Bands, May 20, 1691.

Mr. R. Wragg, apothocary, March 18, 1686.

Newman Meade, formerly a mercier in the town, November 1, 1688.

Robert Reynington, surgeon, January 21, 1689.

John Osborne, a Trained Band soldier, May 20, 1691.

Sir Andrew Jenour, January 8, 1691.

Robert Raymond, tanner, January 27, 1691

James Edwick, pump maker, February 2, 1691.

William Young, an ancient shoemaker, June 22, 1693.

Charles Moyn, an old barber, August 18, 1693.

Mr. Henry Beaumont, the beautiful and most learned and hopeful son of the vicar, Thomas Beaumont, October 17, 1693.

Henry Vinegar, an ancient scrivener, November 25, 1693.

Henry Sewell, an ancient, February 8, 1694.

Robt. Calthorpe, attorney at law, September 26, 1696.

Mr. Wheeler, attorney at law, September 3, 1696.

Sir Swinnerton Dyer, Bart., of Newton Hall, May 21, 1701.

Thom. Goodey, a poor old tinker, January 3, 1702.

Sir Maynard Jenour of Bigods, Bart., January 22, 1702.

William Vinegar, apothocary, April 30, 1703.

William Wakelin, basket maker, May 15, 1703.

John Leader of the Star inn, August 12, 1703.

William Mills, ancient farmer, one-time churchwarden, July 5, 1703.

Thomas White, shoemaker, a worthy parishioner, October 23, 1708.

Richard Phillipe Clerk of ye Mercat, December 6, 1708.

Hannah Wood, aged 90 (Lady Dyer's grandmother), January 5, 1709.

Eleanor Southey, aged 89, January 6, 1709.

Francis Langworthy, aged 96, January 7, 1709.

Elizabeth Young, aged 90, January 9, 1709.

(All the folk did not die young in the old days, despite the lack of medical science.)

Thomas Wheeler, a most serviceable attorney, to be lamented for his worth, October 24, 1709.

Josiah Taylor, a rich clothier	all victims of small-pox	Feb. 8, 1710.
Henry Sewell, age 66		Mar. 8, 1711.
Ann Sewell		Mar. 27, 1711
Percivall Pitts, an old parishioner		Apl. 11, 1712.
Francis Watts, maltster		Apl. 16, 1712.
Humfrey Quilter		Apl. 16, 1712.
Sarah Crabb		May 7, 1712.

Phillip Pavitt, died from the purples (a skin disease of the face), May 2, 1712.

William Potter, killed by the fall of a tree, aged 24, November 24, 1712.

Now follow more people who died of smallpox during a bad epidemic in 1713.

John Taylor, clothier, died unbaptized and was not buried after the manner of the church, August 24, 1713.

Margaret Monwich, widow of an ancient weaver, aged 88, June 29, 1714.

Another group of deaths from smallpox, three in one family, 1714 and 1715.

Lady Ann Dyer, widow of Sir Swinnerton of Newton Hall, August 28, 1714.

Henry Sweeting, yeoman, a former churchwarden, aged 94, May 9, 1716.

John Joyce, master of the workhouse, February 26, 1726.

William Beaumont, of Clock House, younger brother of the late Vicar Thomas Beaumont, January 23, 1729.

Robert Hazelfoot, surgeon, June 14, 1748.

William Grimstone, schoolmaster, August 16, 1748.

William Watts, master of the workhouse, December 15, 1748.

Fever was prevalent in the parish for many months in 1782.

Three boy Tylers died of measles and were buried in one grave in December 1786.

Daniel Phillpott, late farmer of "Wells Tye," aged 84, buried at the Quakers, December 7, 1788.

Pitt's window tax, another crazy idea, taxing daylight, 1790.

John Parish, bay weaver, aged 90, January 23, 1798.

Sarah Shuldham, wife of the surveyor of windows, August 1798.

John Hostage, schoolmaster and exciseman, January 24, 1793.

John Hays, aged 24, killed by a fall from a cart, July 12, 1794.

William Coker, aged 7, accidentally killed upon the mow as he was helping his father, by a pitchfork being thrust in his eye, September 1, 1801.

Samuel Taylor, aged 71, clerk and manager of Cloptons baize factory, May 14, 1801.

Elizabeth James, sister of Dr. John James, aged 33, January 7, 1803.

Anne Coleman, widow, of the White Lyon, aged 25, February 25, 1803.

Anne Lukin, wife of Lionel, aged 62, February 27, 1803.

Eleanor Nash, of the Royal Oak, aged 85, April 19, 1804.

Dr. John Raynor, aged 54, after whom the pond is named, December 8, 1804.

Dr. Richard James, aged 39, October 8, 1806.

Dr. John James, aged 50, November 19, 1806.

Dame Rachael Beaumont, aged 98, May 13, 1814.

Sir Bridges Henniker, aged 45, July 12, 1816.

Dr. John Burke Lynch, aged 41, February 24, 1821.

An unknown woman who died in the Flitch of Bacon, 1823.

Sir Frederick Henniker, Bart., aged 32, August 13, 1825.

Joseph Joyce, aged 53, under coroner's warrant, August 31, 1831.

Elizabeth Joyce, aged 52, October 2, 1831.

Peter Mackenzie, a Scotch drover found drowned in the Chelmer, aged 45 (by coroner's warrant), October 3, 1832.

On December 27, 1647, one Mustafha, born in Tunis in Barbary, was baptized. His father was a Turk and his mother a Moor, and he was then a servant of Mr. James Milbourne, of Merks. He was baptized in the name of Thomas, and was about thirty years of age.

About this time there was born to Jos. and Mary Eniver a son, but by reason of the smallpox then raging the child was baptized by Mr. Chiss Webb at Sawbridgeworth.

In the seventeenth century there were many people in Dunmow who had remained Catholic and they were not allowed to be buried in sacred ground—such as Robert Cranish, buried in the earth as unworthy of Christian burial because he died an obstinate popish recusant. The following are a few of them: Chamberlayn 1601, George Baker 1610, Margerie Cranish 1607, Roger Smith 1613, someone who died in Dr. Cranish's house 1600, Alicia Dennis 1615, — Smart 1618, Elizabeth Cranish 1624, Dr. Nicholas Cranish 1610, Joan Godfrie 1627.

The Jennyns of Olives were popish recusants, two generations of them. There is a child of the Glascocks refused Christian burial, as it died before it had been baptized. Poor little thing. What did happen in those days? Were these people buried under their favourite apple tree, or just outside the graveyard wall? There were until a few years ago two graves in a cottage garden along the Broadway. An old man who lived in the cottage used to tend the graves, and always kept flowers on them. They might have been popish recusants, or someone whom none of the churches knew of. It could not have happened within the last century or two, as it would not have been allowed.

Marriages

Richard Kynwelmarsh to Philippa Schotte, August 28, 1558.

William Glascock to Joane Turner, July 1563.

George Howchin to Joane Glascock, February 1564.

William Glascock to Philippa Wiseman, July 1563.

John Glascock to Margaret Puffin, November 14, 1568.

William Glascock to Philippa Longe, September 30, 1575.

Thomas Maynard to Dorothy Jennyns, December 19, 1619.

John Osborn to Marie Swallow, October 13, 1633.

William Wiseman to Elizabeth Leader, October 26, 1656.

John Phillpot to Philippa Gentrie, May 10, 1655 (married at Pleshey).

Samuel Gentrie to Sarah Eve, March 6, 1667.

William More to Widow Mortlock, "lawfully asked by me, Robert Cook, three times in the market place last on June 25, 1661."*

* I have given this as an example of the new "marriage by licence."

CHAPTER XXXV

Tombs and memorials in the parish church

In the chancel east window are the arms of Edward the Confessor; in the window of the south aisle those of the Bourchiers; in the south porch, baron and femme, the woman's lost, the man's quarterly, sable a fess between three cinquefoils; in the south aisle Maynard's coat, crest and quartering; on the south wall a leopard rampant impaling Jenour and quarterings.

Monuments in the church

Against the south wall of the chancel: " Near this place lies the body of Sir Swinnerton Dyer of Newton Hall, Bart. He married Elizabeth, daughter of Rowland Johnston, of Grays Inn. He departed this life ye 17th May, 1701, in the 44th year of his age."

On the floor of the chancel: " Under this stone lies deposited the body of Ann, late lady of Sir Swinnerton Dyer and 4th daughter of Edward Belitha of Kingston-on-Thames. As she always showed herself dutiful to her parents, so the duties of love and obedience, fidelity, modesty and chastity, comfort and help, friendly and kind society and conversation which she prudently paid to her husband. She died August 21st, 1714, age 33. leaving her disconsolate husband only one child, Ann."

Other epitaphs on the Dyers are to Dame Elizabeth Dyer, wife of Sir Swinnerton Dyer, who died on May 30, 1727, aged fifty-eight, and Elizabeth Dyer, eldest daughter of Sir Swinnerton Dyer, Bart., who departed this life on August 10, 1728, aged forty-two.

On the north wall of the chancel: " Sacred to the memory of William Beaumont, Esq., son of Sir Thomas Beaumont, Bart., of Stoughton, Leicestershire, who departed this life March 21st, 1718, age 76, leaving issue by his wife, Jane, 2 boys and three girls. Also of William Beaumont, Esq., junior son of the above William, who died January 17th, 1729, age 47. The names of both of them for their singular sweetness of behaviour, probity of life, constancy in religious duties, remain with all who knew them, honoured and dear, a pattern of piety to posterity and an honour and ornament to their ancient lineage, derived from noble ancestors. This monument was erected by the pious care of Elizabeth, now the sorrowful widow of William Beaumont, Jun., supported from this comfort alone that she did bear and has now educated his five children, seeming already to aspire to the imitation of their parents' virtues." But speaking too soon, she lost their daughter, Elizabeth, on July 19, 1735, aged eleven years.

In the chancel are deposited the remains of " Sir George Beaumont, Bart., of this parish, who died February 4th, 1762, age 36, and of Dame Rachel his wife, who died February 5th, 1814, aged 98. Erected to the memory of his parents by Sir George Howland Beaumont. Here lyeth the body of Thomas Beaumont, Vicar of ye parish, second son of Sir Thomas Beaumont of Stoughton Grange, Bart., of the county of Leicestershire. He [the vicar] married Susanah, daughter of William Oddys, D.D., vicar of Alderburg, Oxon, by whom he had four sons and two daughters. He died January 15th, 1710, age 71" (arms very much defaced).

(Susanah's brother, who was known to be a royalist, even to Dunmow people, as he often visited his sister, went to Oxford to take his son to the university in 1645. He was aware of the risk he was running, and on his return journey, fearing he might fall into the hands of the parliamentary soldiers, he ordered his servant to ride at some distance before him, and if he saw any of them to drop his handkerchief as a signal for him to go back to the garrison at Oxford or Banbury. The man dropped the handkerchief, which his master passed without seeing. As soon as he perceived the enemy he turned about, but his horse would not leave the road, so he was shot through the back.)

" In this chancel are interred the remains of George Howland, Esq., late of Haverill, who died February 6th, 1698, age 85. This tablet was erected to his memory by his grateful nephew, Sir George Howland Beaumont, of this place and of Coleoton Hall, Leicester."

" Rev. John Mangey, for 28 years vicar of this parish, departed this life Nov. 1st, 1782, age 55. Near this place lies the body of Dorothy Mangey, the mother of the vicar. It was her son John Mangey who erected this monument, from a principle of sincere and tender regard to a most kind and affectionate parent, whom he always loved and revered. She died July 5th, 1780, age 88."

" Dr. Robert Hasel Foot, surgeon of this parish, died July 5th, 1748."

" Near this place lieth the body of Mary, daughter of John Wiseman, by whom she had seven sons and one daughter, which four sons lie here also. Her husband was Thomas Cullum of Thornden, Suffolk. She died in childbed August 31st " (no year given).

In the nave:

" John Pepper, Esq., of this parish, who died June 1822. He was the last surviving descendant of the late Michael Pepper, Esq., and grandson of Sir Richard Fitzgerald."

" To the memory of Lord John Henniker of Newton Hall in the parish, who died 1803 and is interred with dame Henniker in Rochester Cathedral. This monument was erected by his son, the Hon. Major General Bridges T. Henniker."

The last ones have gone, but in the time of Salmon and Weever there was a brass to John Calthorpe, of the parsonage, the first of at least four generations of attorneys. He died in 1616.

" Here lieth the body of Elizabeth, the wife of Francis Vassel. She was the daughter of John Smith, minister, of this parish and Elizabeth his wife. She died May 12th, 1652 " (tablet on the north wall). " In memory of Thomas Waskett of Barnston Hall, yeoman, who died in 1738, age 92, and of his son Thomas Waskett, who died in 1750, age 62. Also of John Waskett, who died June 21st, 1758, age 60. Elizabeth, wife of the above John, August 5th, 1771, age 75. Also of John Wasket, son of John and Elizabeth, March 1st, 1776, age 46." This tablet is on the north wall.

Salmon says there were partial remains to one of the Bigod family, Walter, March 16, 1397. In the middle of the church was this inscription: " Of your charite prey for the sowl of John Jenoure, Esq, som tym of the common pleais at Westminster and Alys his wiff." The next inscription is " Here lys the body of Richard Deardes of Newton Hall, gent, who died April 28th, 1630, and of Thomas Deardes his son, who died May 2nd following." On another monument Gulielma and Philippa Glascock are remembered. He died on December 3, 1579, and his wife on December 19, 1608.

CHAPTER XXXVI

The post office in Dunmow

Dunmow was a post town in 1783, and had its own deputy (this was the name for a postmaster of that time). In that year Joseph Edwards was the deputy and he received £7 a year for his services. Of this sum £6 was salary and the remaining £1 was for by-posts, that is for the delivery of letters to the villages around. In 1785 the mail-coach service for Norwich started and by 1786 coaches were running on two routes to Norwich, one via Newmarket and one via Ipswich. From these postal coach routes by-posts were run. Such a post would seem to be Dunmow, but which of the main routes was used for our post is not known. In 1791 our by-post came from Braintree on Monday, Wednesday and Friday, returning the same day. In 1792 the deputy was a man named Hostage. In 1793 our letters were sent out from London daily to reach Dunmow at 10 a.m. the following day. Letters for London left us at 1 p.m. The cost of postage was 4d. In 1805 Isaac Malster, landlord of the Saracen's Head, became deputy. He married Mrs. Hostage, widow of the former deputy. We do not know if Mrs. Hostage became the deputy at the death of her husband, but it does seem to have flowed in some way from her to Malster. The amount of Malster's salary is not known, but the penalty in his bond against lack of fidelity was £200. We shall soon be losing sight of these postal coaches and they rather intrigue me. I would have liked to have seen them leaving the Saracen's Head. The coach was a very stoutly built four-wheeled closed carriage with seats for four inside and four on top, with an extra seat on the box with the driver. It was drawn by four well-matched, strong, active horses.

The postmen meet at Bowyer's bridge, Easton.

In winter when the roads were very bad another two horses were often used, then a postilion would ride the offside leader. The coachwork was superb, in brilliant colours and highly varnished, probably a golden brown body with perhaps canary-coloured wheels with spokes lined out in black, or a dark blue body with scarlet wheels and the spokes the same as before. All the metal fittings would be brightly polished brass. The royal arms were emblazoned on the door panels. The coachman and horses were hired, but the guard was a state servant and would

The post office staff in 1913. Back row (left to right): J. Caryer, Ernest Rippingale, Frank Tyler, Frank Ward, Peter Tyler. Middle row: Ben Matthews, Mr. Boyce, Herbert Burles, Ted Kerrage, Fred Goodey, William Pitts, Harry Parmenter. Front row: Mr. Dace, Mr. Hughes, Mr. Johnson (postmaster), Becky Beard, ——, Miss Tetley.

wear smart, serviceable clothes, a cockade in his hat, a scarlet coat frogged with gold lace, buckskin breeches and top boots. He sat on a dickey seat at the back of the coach and had a four-foot copper horn on which he performed incredible fanfares, and sometimes a popular melody. This horn was necessary in towns and villages of the approach, or to avoid any obstruction. I think the rule generally was to sound the horn three times in a mile and always on approaching a turnpike, for the coach went through without paying, also on seeing a stranger on the road. Under the seat facing the guard were a blunderbuss, two pistols and a cutlass. The pistols and cutlass were handed over to the passengers in an attack by "gentlemen of the road."

This armament was necessary sometimes, for on a morning in 1775 the Norwich coach was coming through Epping Forest when it was set upon by seven highwaymen. The guard killed four, but was also killed himself in the encounter.

Perhaps I have deserted our town too long, but I do feel these coaches were something we have missed. In 1817 George Tyler became postman; his only duty seemed the delivery of letters around the countryside. Was it in the execution of his duty that he was drowned in 1821? Records do not tell us. However, George was succeeded by his son John, who was a man with a great sense of the dignity of his calling, for, like his father, he always appeared for duty in a top hat, a modernized version of his father's. He delivered letters over an area of six miles. John was described officially as a "foot" postman, and must have walked amazing distances every day and kept it up until his death in 1867. His son Thomas took his place, and continued till 1886, when he either retired or died. His wife carried on for a time and was paid the handsome salary of 3/- per week. Isaac Tyler, brother of Thomas, became postman. In 1889 his son Peter became a regular postman. For many years he had been an unpaid auxiliary, making long journeys to help his ageing father. Peter retired after completing thirty-four official years of service, and died on February 2, 1937, aged 73. Peter Tyler's son Frank joined the postal service on

August 13, 1905, and later became a driver of the familiar little red motor van. He retired in April 1952 and died in 1967. So ended a long family line of Dunmow postmen. The Tylers played an important part in the history of Dunmow's postal services; generation after generation of them served the G.P.O. faithfully and well.

In 1845 our postmaster was Mr. Percy John Gunn. When postal duties were not needing his attention he filled in his spare time by hairdressing. In 1848 he was followed by John Percy Gunn, his son. Now we get a glimpse of the post office of our day, for money orders were now on sale, and it is doubtful if hairdressing was an "extra."

In 1863 Mr. C. J. Howland was postmaster, and the post office was at 17 High Street (now Mr. Perry's "do it yourself" shop). By 1868 the post office had gone across the road to No. 18 (Mary Jane, or, as it was a few years ago, Johnson's shop). Here Mrs. Johnson ran the post office. When in course of time she retired her son William became postmaster. During his term of office it again crossed the High Street, to much larger premises at No. 7 (now Messrs. Lea). Mr. William Johnson retired soon after World War I. In 1939 our post office took up the position it occupies today.

The five generations of Tylers who served as postmen in Dunmow.

CHAPTER XXXVII

The flitch comes to Great Dunmow

To write on the Dunmow flitch in a book of the history of Great Dunmow is not easy. This ancient custom belonged to Dunmow priory (Little Dunmow) from very early days. It is thought that it was first instituted by one of the Fitz Walter family, but there seems no proof. It might have been one cf the early priors who felt he should encourage married couples to live according to the vows made by them before the altar and accordingly never forget their obligations to each other. After the dissolution of the priory no doubt interest began to wane, although there were awards made in Little Dunmow in 1701 and 1751.

In the last century that popular historical novelist William Harrison Ainsworth was responsible for reviving the flitch, but at Great Dunmow. Ainsworth had already written on " The flitch of Bacon, or the custom of Dunmow," which had been widely read and served to attract people to the custom, and to the parish of Dunmow. Soon local people (in Great Dunmow) formed a committee to revive the flitch ceremony, shorn of any manorial associations. No expense was spared in advertising this event; newspapers and periodicals, local and national, and other means were used to attract public attention. No sooner had notice been given that a flitch trial was to be held than claims as numerous as flies around a honey jar came rolling in. The great day was fixed for Thursday (just fancy a Thursday for such an event!), July 19, 1855. The couples chosen from the many applicants were James and Hannah Barlow of Chipping Ongar, and M. Jean Baptiste Francois Ernest and Madame Clara de Chatelain of London (the latter couple had applied for the flitch in 1845, when the lord of the manor informed them that the custom had fallen into disuse). At last the great day dawned wet, but that did not prevent a large number of people travelling by special trains to Bishop's Stortford, where they were met by carts, wagons, horse-vans and every conceivable thing on wheels capable of carrying passengers to Dunmow. These conveyances were decorated with flowers and branches of trees. Men with trucks of strawberries and barrows of oysters were hurrying to the fair field. All shops in Dunmow were shut and bonnets were thrust out of every window, especially the Saracen's Head, so eager were their owners to watch the arrivals at the Town Hall. Men who were on the roofs got wet through, but nothing could deter the enthusiasm of the crowds. The flitch had never come to Dunmow town before. Many of the clergy were opposed to the revival of the custom, but whatever the gentry might have felt it was evident that this excuse to make merry was very popular with the Dunmow people.

After the trials were over the sun broke out in full force and the procession left the Town Hall for Windmill Field (on the Downs) in the following order: marshal, stud of horses, mounted by yeomen in appropriate dress carrying banners with the names of all the claimants since the thirteenth century inscribed on them, and names of persons associated with the custom; ladies with gar-

The first scene from the 1912 pageant—the Shakeshafts, weavers, of Wethersfield, represented by Lewis Coates and May Mills. The man with hat in hand is Mr. Alf Knight and the man with scroll is Harry Johnson.

lands; banners borne by rustics; maidens and bachelors of the jury in a carriage; the clerk and the crier of the court and counsel in a carriage; other officers of the court; gentlemen with wands; flitch of bacon, carried by four yeomen; Dunmow Town Band; Mr. and Mrs. Barlow carried in a chair on men's shoulders; gentlemen with wands; two minstrels playing pipe and tabor; flitch of bacon, carried by four yeomen; another band (we do not know whose); le Chevalier and Madame de Chatelain carried in a chair; Harrison Ainsworth in a carriage.

It is reckoned that 7,000 attended this, the first flitch at Great Dunmow. After this very boisterous and spectacular event another trial took place in 1857, with J. W. Savill, F.R.H.S., as president and Charles Pavey as organizer. Whether this one did not go so well we do not know. It was under the patronage of Harrison Ainsworth. I can find no account of the attendance, yet the weather was favourable. It was twelve years before another flitch trial is reported. In this year (1869) the attendance was between 10,000 and 20,000. There is nothing to tell us where it was held, except in a marquee, but very probably it was on Windmill Field, Dunmow Downs.

These attendance figures sound stupendous and bowl our carnival crowds out completely. J. W. Savill was the organizer.

Subsequent trials took place in 1874, 1876, 1877 and 1880 with varying results, the last being a complete flop. The *Chelmsford Chronicle* said "This trial was farcical." The unnamed judge was very deaf, and was wearing a high stove-pipe hat and a dingy white waistcoat and cravat. He quibbled about awarding the flitch to the claimants, a Joseph Thorne and his wife from Bethnal Green (Thorne was born at Dunmow but must have picked up the "e" in his travels, for no Dunmow Thorn had it).

Thorne became forceful in demanding his flitch, so a visitor from Woolwich offered to give him one. There were many entertainments, including Braintree brass band, but so many people were too drunk to appreciate them. One can imagine that this meant at least a temporary " death " to the custom of Dunmow. The organizers were Mr. Friend of the Alexander Palace and Mr. J. W. Savill of Dunmow. Mr. Savill was a very modest man and a strict Roman Catholic, and must have been most disturbed at the trend of things. We suppose that after this it was thought best to give the flitch a rest, and it was ten years before it was revived again, in 1890.

This time it had come to stay for seventeen years, with a good committee of well-known personalities on the council, especially Mr. T. Gibbons for the bacon—he would draw humour from a lamp-post and his quick wit would make the soundest claimant " trip up." During these seventeen years one date stands out a mile—that of 1912, when a historical pageant, arranged by Hugh Cranmer-Byng and including representations of numerous persons closely connected with Great and Little Dunmow in the past, was held. Three hundred persons were in this pageant of Dunmow's history. Morris dancing by the Dunmow Progressive Club and fireworks finished off a grand day.

The trial was held again the next year, but war breaking out in 1914 put an end to the flitch for some years.

Before leaving the 1913 session one's thought is " How did the judge and jury arrive at their decision with those two great wits [T. Gibbon for the bacon and J. V. Mackenzie for the claimants] as counsel? What a fight it must have been."

The *Essex Chronicle* described Mr. J. V. Mackenzie as having a bombastic style and employing a great deal of rhetoric and Mr. T. Gibbons as cross and foreboding, yet with a waggishness that Dunmow people appreciated.

It was 1930 before the flitch trial was held again, and then Ilford held a mock trial the same day. Said a local who worked at the bacon factory " Oi downt reckon oi know where this ole Ilford plice is; oi count that must be somewhere out furrin. Ilford? Never heerd tell on't."

The trials continued till 1933 and have been held intermittently since, and as I write another is brewing, we hope.

CHAPTER XXXVIII

The Bishop's Stortford to Braintree branch railway

In November 1860 plans for making a branch line from Bishop's Stortford to Braintree were statutory with the clerk of the peace for Essex, but it took over three years before the first sod of the new line was cut. Below New Street was considered to be halfway between Bishop's Stortford and Braintree, so crossing the pathway to Olives on February 24, 1864. Lady Henniker of Newton Hall turned the first sod with a silver spade and wheeled it away in a silver-mounted mahogany barrow, in the presence of about 6,000 people. This was a great day for Dunmow. Arches elaborately decked with flowers were erected at the entrance to the town from Bishop's Stortford, and at the junction of the Braintree and Chelmsford roads another erection, described as three noble Gothic arches, was placed triangularly from the Saracen's Head to Mr. Sewell's shop to the Town Hall on the opposite corner. A grand procession comprising navvies bearing flags, children from the British National and private schools, with more flags, banners, etc., the bailiff and corporation of Dunmow, the vicar (the Rev. Langston Scott) in his robes, the tradespeople of the town, the directors of the railway company and the bands of the Dunmow and Bishop's Stortford Cadets and the Hertfordshire Light Horse wended its way through the town to the selected field, and as the 600 children passed through the town they were regaled with buns and oranges.

No function of this kind could pass without a banquet, so the gentlemen, about 160, retired to the British School, where they were entertained by the contractors, Messrs. Brassey, Ogilvie and Harrison, in a most sumptuous and elegant manner, and after this came a concert at the Town Hall organized by the local choral society.There was then a break of about two hours, which enabled the well-fed gentlemen to prepare for a grand

James and Hannah Ward.

ball at the Saracen's Head. Thus ended the great day of the "coming of the railway," and for eighty-three years the "Dunmow Flyer," as it was called, faithfully served the locality.

The Countess of Warwick for some years wished to have a station nearer Easton Lodge, where she could meet her many distinguished guests instead of coming into Dunmow station, so after negotiations with the railway Easton Lodge station was built in 1892-3, whether at her expense or not I do not know. The first couple to occupy the station house were James and Hannah Ward. Mr. Ward was a platelayer on the line and his wife worked the gates. At one time when Mrs. Ward was not well a man was ordered from Dunmow to do that operation, but he overslept, and the train crashed through, leaving just the ends of the gates hanging on their hinges. In later years they retired to New Street, Dunmow, having seen, I am sure, much of England's royalty and nobility.

On March 1, 1952, the last passenger train made its memorable journey. Before leaving Braintree station an evergreen wreath was placed on the front of the tank engine No. 67211 (built in 1890), which made its progress to Bishop's Stortford, arriving five minutes late.

CHAPTER XXXIX

The church in the nineteenth century

Previous to 1809 the singing was accompanied by a barrel organ. In that year General (later Sir Bridges) Henniker of Newton Hall built a west gallery in which the singers sat and placed an organ of the same type. A letter of thanks to the donor by the vicar, Dr. Alexander Richardson, was profuse in its gratitude.

In 1821 the chimers of Dunmow church bells were Daniel Cheek, William Dawson, John Bass, James Joyce, Edward Ginn, Joseph Pearmain and Henry Sweeting.

In 1832 the Rev. John Smith placed in the west gallery another organ played, like its predecessor, by machinery. The next one was given by Captain Ray of Clock House, who was a great benefactor to the church. It was first played at the harvest thanksgiving in 1876 by Mr. Studolph, organist of St. Mary's, Chelmsford (now the cathedral).

The Rev. John Smith was the founder of the Dunmow Friendly Society. He thought of the labourer who might be ill, or too old to work. There was nothing but the workhouse for him. Today, although most friendly societies have gone to the wall, ours is still going, and running successfully.

In 1855 the plaster concealing the sedilia and piscina was removed and these beautiful medieval remains were once more exposed to view. Just before he died the Rev. H. L. Majendie had acquired of the lady of the manor, Miss Maynard, the grounds near the pond for a school, and with the coming of the Rev. W. L. Scott £1,800 was raised out of the pockets of the churchpeople, and on May 8, 1868, the new school was opened. In 1874 the infants' room was added at a cost of £400.

Mr. Scott next turned his attention to the church. He said " The state of Dunmow church is a reproach to us. . . . The old and ugly pews still hold their place in the main part of the church and are becoming every day meaner and shabbier; the coarse brick pavement more worn and uneven; the boarded floors more crumbling and wasted; and every winter the temperature more chilling from increasing draught and damp. Each family is shut up in a box by itself. Often in these enclosures it is impossible to kneel during prayers. . . . These high enclosures offer an encouragement to light and unseemly behaviour. The west gallery divides with its unsightly bulk the beautiful western arch, while the northern gallery completely destroys the effect of the arcade which separates the nave from the aisle."

The following is a description of the church after the restoration: " The church is now quite clear and all who have visited it are astonished at the noble appearance of it. Without doubt it is one of the finest churches in the county. The removal of the old pews and galleries has greatly increased the apparent size and the effect of the pillars and arches, now showing their full height and proportions, is very striking. But perhaps the best effect of all is seen looking westward from the chancel; the arch of the tower, now cleared of all obstructions, is a very beautiful feature, and may divide, with the great eastern window at the opposite extremity of the building, the chief architectural honours of the church."

Two people lost their jobs with the going of the old box pews—Mr. Jarvis and Mr. Holgate, the " dog-rappers." The church was reopened on June 19, 1873.

In 1877 Captain Herbert Ray of Clock House gave Mr. Scott a cheque for £1,346, which was invested in Great Western Railway four per cent debenture bonds, the income to be devoted by the vicar and church-wardens " for the relief of the sick and infirm, and other needy persons of the parish of Great Dunmow."

This generous benefactor also gave the money for building the mission hall at Philpot End in 1875.

For many years Mr. Scott's daughters and Miss Sophia Cock used to walk over to Philpot End to hold a Bible class there. From that day to this the mission has never lacked willing helpers. Of course, not so many people attend now. There are few children around that way. Mr. Scott says in one of his monthly magazines that they had forty in the Sunday school. The services and meetings are full of vigour. It is a pleasure to go there even now, the atmosphere is so " homely."

CHAPTER XL

Dunmow in the nineteenth century

The Rev. John Howlett, vicar of Dunmow 1782-1804, wrote many pamphlets and books. " Published this day, 2/6 " would be outside our local bookshop. I have not been able to find who sold books in Dunmow about 1800. It would be too early for Dansie Carter. The books for sale came out very often, and it seems by a local printer too. *Published this day*. Some note of urgency about this. " Some of the causes to which the increase of the poor and the poor rate have been commonly ascribed. The true statement 2/6. With an inquiry into the morality of country houses of industry and a slight general view of Mr. Acland's Plan for rendering the poor independent."

Also by the same author, " Inquiry into the Influence of Enclosure on the Population of the Kingdom "; " The influence of Enclosures on the Price of Butchers' Meat "; " Influence of Tithes upon Agriculture "; " Insufficiency of Causes Assigned on the Poor and of the Rates "; " Dispersions of Gloomy Apprehensions Respecting the Corn Trade "; " Examinations of Mr. Pitt's Speech on the Condition of the Poor "; " Sermons Preached at Dunmow before two Companies of Volunteers, Yeomanry and Cavalry "; " Thanksgiving Sermon after the Battle of the Nile and the Destruction of a French Fleet off Ireland 1798 "; " Monthly Reviewers Reviewed "; " Enclosures a Cause of Improved Agriculture."

But he never ceased to protest against the unnecessary suffering caused to the former freeholders and copyholders by the new system. One would have expected him to defend the other side, but it is good to know he was ready to stand by the poor and oppressed. He moved to Bath in 1804, but died the same year and was buried in the abbey, where he went to be dean. He was born an Essex lad, at Toppesfield, in 1735, and must have grown up from childhood seeing and knowing the hardships of the labouring classes.

Dunmow brewery, August 14, 1821

The proprietors of this concern, in consequence of the death of their late partner, Mr. Thomas Alliston, request that all persons who may have any claims against them will send in their accounts, in order that the same may be examined and paid.

Dunmow Savings Bank, 1821

We have the pleasure of reporting to the public that the gross receipts from the first institution, to the first of this month, amount to £3,823/16/7.

Thomas Skingle of Great Dunmow, common carrier and farmer by indenture of the 17th January, 1822, assigns all his estates and effects to Thomas Skingle of Mashbury, farmer, Samuel Skingle of Great Dunmow, gent, for the equable benefit of each.

Mr. Warner's academy, Dunmow, 1823

With grateful acknowledgments to his friends for their support they have favoured him with most respectfully announces to them and the public that at his establishment young gentlemen are boarded, and taught the English language, grammatically,

Church End in 1820. Many people were drowned here through the centuries: in 1848 Thomas Olley of the "Star" inn, aged forty-one, mail cart contractor, was drowned, and in 1880, only two years before the building of the new bridge, a party visiting the Scotts at the vicarage (having driven from Little Bardfield) were overturned in the river and all drowned.

penmanship, arithmetic, book-keeping, mathematics and geography.

The Dunmow branch of the Bible Society, president Sir Frederick Henniker. The eleventh anniversary will be held April 21, 1823.

The death of the vicar of Great Dunmow, Dr. Alexander Richardson, occurred [no date] 1829 after breaking a blood vessel. [It was during Dr. Richardson's ministry that Major-General Sir Bridges Henniker (who fought in the Napoleonic wars) presented the decorations to the Dunmow men who had taken part in the same campaigns. I have not found the date of the presentation].

The Lord Bishop of London has collated the Rev. John Smith, B.D., to the vicarage of Great Dunmow.

Queen Victoria's coronation

[Queen Victoria's coronation was well prepared for. Several meetings had been held].

Collection to be made in the quarters of the town Corporation Bigods and Bishopswood. The list was headed by Viscount Maynard, who contributed £10. The total recorded was £109/8/6.

At a later meeting it was resolved that the dinner tables be arranged on both sides of the street from the Saracen's Head to the Boar's Head. The Bible Society was requested to lend its deal boards for the occasion. Several bakers offered to provide bread. Those attending the dinner were asked to bring mug, knife, fork and plate. Mr. Robert Taylor and Mr. George Watson were asked to supply three bullocks at 4/- a stone. Mr. W. J. Clayton and Mr. Francis Sewell offered to lend 200 yards of sheeting each for tablecloths. All shops in the town were requested to close all day on June 28. Three hundred puddings of 3lb. each were provided and beer

The Market Place in the 1880s. What are they waiting for? Is it the Prince of Wales?

was laid on to the following specification: men above 15 1 quart, women 1 quart, children 1 pint. It was to be supplied by Messrs. Randall at the wholesale price of 36/- for a 36-gallon cask. Old people in the almshouses were to be supplied in their own rooms.

There were 1,700 tickets issued and bread was paid for at $3\frac{3}{4}$d. per half quartern.

One can almost feel blithe and gay as one sings that sonnet on that glorious summer morning when the streets were thronged just after dawn and the rising of bright Phœbus was marked by a salute from a dozen six-pounders. At five o'clock in the morning the town band struck up the National Anthem in the centre of the town. A press report dated July 6 records that in the memory of the oldest inhabitant there never was at Dunmow such a holiday and gala day like this. No wonder the multitude seemed loath to part, but after fireworks they separated and quietly went home, and it has been said a hundred times that not a drunken man was seen during the whole day and night.

Dunmow Agricultural Society

President, the Right Hon. Viscount Maynard; vice-presidents, Sir George H. W. Beaumont, John Maryon Wilson, Esq., Rev. Augustus B. Henniker, Bart., Rev. C. H. Hallet.

Annual ploughing match

Will be held on the Folly farm on Monday, September 28, 1840.

Ploughmen	1st Prize	a coat.
Ploughmen	2nd prize	Hat, jacket with sleeves, and neck handkerchief.
Ploughmen	3rd prize	Hat, jacket with sleeves.
Ploughmen	4th prize	Hat, waistcoat, and neck handkerchief

Ploughboys under 18

Best Ploughboy, £1 0 0

Second Best Ploughboy, 10 0

There were many other interesting prizes. These prizes were to encourage the industrial poor.

Whether the industrial poor did not feel so encouraged one does not know, but no more ploughing matches were held until the Countess of Warwick revived the event in 1905.

The Dunmow pew case

At the spring assizes 1842 (in an action Pepper v. Barnard and Philbrick)—(churchwardens of Great Dunmow). The total amount of money needed is £485 to place the churchwardens out of debt.

At a meeting of the friends of the churchwardens of Dunmow held in the reading room on March 27, 1845, W. Johnson in the chair, it was resolved unanimously that the following statement be circulated among the friends of the church, in the hope of obtaining their assistance to relieve the churchwardens from the heavy debt incurred by them in the execution of their duty.

The last two constables appointed in Dunmow were Nathan Prior and William Smith in 1841.

One of their duties was to search the inns and alehouses in the night for people playing unlawful games.

Two leather sealers were appointed annually till 1820. Benjamin Cheek and James Tyler were the last to hold this office. These were officials of the tanneries. Two ale tasters were appointed each year to examine and assay all the beer and ale sold in the town and to take care it was good and wholesome. Finally there were the bread weighers. The last of these were appointed in 1885, the last year of the corporation.

Queen Victoria's diamond jubilee, 1897

For Queen Victoria's diamond jubilee celebrations Dunmow looked gayer than anyone could remember having seen it on previous celebrations, even the golden jubilee. The decorations were profuse and artistic. If any house should be singled out for individual mention it would be that of Dr. Lyle. At midday the Market Place was thronged

Queen Victoria's diamond jubilee, 1897. The inhabitants were asked to gather in the square at midday, when the town band would lead them in singing the national anthem. Notice that the men are raising their hats.

Mr. Edwin Piper standing outside the little cottages about to be demolished in 1899. Now Brown and Lee's

with the inhabitants who had been asked to meet there to join in the singing of the National Anthem, led by the town band (see illustration). Sports took place in the afternoon. There were twenty-one events on the programme. The rejoicings concluded with a monster torchlight procession and bonfire. The procession was formed on Jubilee field at 9 p.m. and, preceded by the band, marched through the town to Beacon field, a high point on the Braintree road, where it was met by another procession from Stebbing and another from Little Dunmow. Here an enormous bonfire was lighted at exactly 10 p.m.

Mr. George Wade was a solicitor here before the end of the eighteenth century, but also partly through the nineteenth. He lived at Westbury House. He was a lineal descendant of Jacques de Vins Seignear de Villetti in Hever'nois, Huguenot, who left France on the Revocation. Many are the deeds, bonds, conveyances, etc., I have seen in his hand, but not so many as of Nicolas Toke. It seems a great profession. This Mr. G. Wade died on December 10, 1839, aged seventy-five. His son William Thomas was already in the family business and, like his father, was well known in Dunmow. He died on October 2, 1871, aged seventy-four. His son William de Vins left Dunmow on his retirement. His last residence here, I think, was Clock House. He took part in various things connected with the parish, and was churchwarden, and Dunmow's last recorder.

Dr. Campbell Mellis Douglas, M.D., V.C., of Mill House, Dunmow, Licentiate of Royal College of Surgeons, Edinburgh, 1861. Joined 24th Regiment 1863. Medical officer to the expedition to the Little Andaman Island, 1867. Medical officer in charge of field hospital, second expedition, 1885. Received the Victoria Cross for relieving seventeen officers and men from a position of danger on the coast of Little Andaman Island in the 1867 expedition.

War veterans

The late Walter Smith, who lived in New Street, had many little things he treasured from his war service in South Africa. One was an autographed silver leaf presented to him by Rudyard Kipling. Mr. Smith joined the 1st Essex Regiment on January 21, 1889. He

Members of the Dunmow Friendly Society when visiting Sir Walter Gilbey in 1898 at his home at Elsenham Paddocks.

was wounded at the battle of Paardeberg, where Kronje surrendered with 4,000 men. It was while he lay wounded in the Wynberg field hospital that they were visited by Kipling. The author signed eight silver leaves collected on Table Mountain, and presented them to Smith and his fellow patients. Our Boer War veteran had many souvenirs of South Africa, including a marked Testament and the Essex colours.

Private William Gibson, 1st Battalion Grenadier Guards, was the first soldier to be given a funeral with military honours in the town. He died at the age of forty-six in 1914, and was buried at the parish church. During his service he gained the Khartoum Medal, the South African Medal (1901), the Transvaal/Cape Colony Medal and the Sudan Medal. William Gibson served in the London expedition of 1898 under Major-General Lord Kitchener.

1897. The Countess of Warwick, foundress and president of the Dunmow District Nursing Association, said at the second annual general meeting how much there was to encourage them (the committee). The subscriptions and donations were increasing and the nurse's kind attention and devotion to her work had entirely removed any prejudice that might have existed when the association started. Our hospitals exemplify the principle that the poor are utterly unable to pay for skilled nursing in the towns and villages, where ignorance of the simplest treatment of sickness makes even a slight ailment a burden that cannot be borne without assistance.

July, 1898. By the kind invitation of Sir Walter Gilbey, Bart., the members of the Dunmow Friendly Society gathered at Elsenham paddocks, inspected the horses and had tea together, and later the 600 present had their photographs taken. The society was formed in 1832 by the vicar, the Rev. John Smith, and Lord Maynard was the first president, now succeeded by Lord and Lady Warwick.

The first balance sheet in 1833 was £174. It was now (1898) £38,000. The chief features of the society were sick pay, old age pensions, and funeral allowances for all its members.

The oldest "original" member of the Dunmow Friendly Society was George Saunders. He died in November 1898, aged sixty-five. He became entitled to a pension of 4/- a week and was at that time still able to follow his occupation. He had received £230 in pension money at the time of his death.

For nearly half a century he had worked for the late Thomas Welch at Folly Farm.

He was the father of George Saunders, assistant county court bailiff, and furniture dealer, of North Street, Dunmow.

1899. During this year the roads committee proposed to spend £150 on stone paving in Dunmow.

June, 1899. At a meeting of the parish council Mr. B. H. Warner, vice-chairman, referred sympathetically to the loss the council had sustained since its last meeting by the death of its chairman, Dr. R. C. Lyle. Ever since the parish council was formed Dr. Lyle had presided over its meetings with ability and courtesy. Mr. Warner moved that the council express its deep sympathy with Mrs. Lyle and the family. Dr. Lyle died after about two days' illness at the early age of forty-four years.

Ford bridge, Braintree road, before World War I.

CHAPTER XLI

The schools—National and British

GREAT DUNMOW NATIONAL SCHOOL (GIRLS)

Log book. Headmaster, Mr. Marlow

1863

March 4. Made flags and banners for the coming royal wedding.

March 9. Very large attendances in consequence of the coming treat.

March 10. Prince of Wales's wedding day [to Princess Alexandra of Denmark].

March 9. Do not allow the monitor to take a class after yesterday's conduct; shall be obliged to dismiss her. Miss Majendie and her cousins came to the school this afternoon to hear the children sing.

April 23. Two girls sent out during Bible lesson in the pupil teacher's class. One submitted but the other was saucy and is always causing trouble; sent her home to remain there till she can behave herself. Miss Sewell and Miss Barnard visited the school this afternoon.

May 1. Thin attendance today; cannot get any children to scrub the stairs and passage, therefore have sent for a Sunday school girl and paid her out of my own money.

May 4. Full school today; had to make another class. There are six classes to be taught with one pupil teacher and a paid monitor. Rather hard work.

June 6. Dunmow fair day.

June 11. Two girls played truant, and picked lilac in the Vicarage garden.

June 18. First day of the girls sweeping the school.

June 19. Made the same girl sweep as did it so badly yesterday.

June 20. One of the girls appointed to sweep the school went home after I had left according to her mother's instructions.

June 23. Monitor absent through illness, school orderly, Miss Wade visited.

June 29. The vicar visited the school. Half holiday given for Dunmow flower show.

July 27. Mr. Marlow complained that the church singers were absent on Sunday afternoon.

August 5. Sent two girls home for having dirty heads.

September 26. Dunmow ploughing match, half holiday. Caroline Mary Anne Reeve gained first prize for a man's shirt, Cheek third prize for shirt, F. Burton first prize for boy's shirt, Lucy Hockley first prize for chemise, E. Button third prize for chemise, Sarah Ann Cheek first prize for untrimmed nightdress, Sarah Pitts first prize for buttonholes, Mary Ann Reeve second and Emma Linings third for marking. This school gained most prizes, therefore the £1 was awarded to me [headmaster].

October 11. A parcel of work for the girl from Mrs. W. Randall.

October 23. Attendance.

November 1. Mrs. Baker, Mrs. Fitzgerald and Mrs. Scott visited the school.

1866

January 9. Very severe snow, only twenty-six present.

January 17. Kept the third standard in

late, they having been very inattentive. Rev. W. L. Scott attended in the afternoon.

January 25. Children very disorderly when I came in the afternoon; made them sit still for quarter of an hour after 4 o'clok. Not at all satisfied with the order kept by the pupil teacher when I leave the room.

Ash Wednesday. Took the first four classes to church. Half holiday in the afternoon.

March 24. Wild beast show in the town. Attendance very bad. Took first and second classes to church in the morning.

June 14. Rev. Gibson came to school and gave the scripture lesson.

July 4. Half-day holiday on account of the flower show.

July 10. Rev. W. L. Scott visited the school in the morning and took the reading lesson in the fourth class. Afterwards questioned them on the Catechism. Most have returned to school who have been away with whooping cough.

August 7. Mrs. Fitzgerald paid 5/- for Gunn's school money.

1878-91 National School (infants)

September 16, 1878. School reopened after harvest vacation. The infants are now separated from the girls' department and placed under the entire charge of myself, Ellen Sillett.

November 7. The children from a distance have been unable to come on account of bad weather.

December 5. Rev. Powell visited in the morning. Miss Scott gave a knitting lesson in the afternoon.

December 17. Half holiday given owing to a " missionary sale " being held in the schoolroom.

January 10, 1879. Owing to the very severe weather the attendance has been very small.

June 3. Commenced working from the " new timetable " today. No more 7 a.m. session.

June 14. William Rixon returned on the " examination schedule " as six years was found to be incorrect, therefore will be retained in this department for another year.

December 12. The extreme cold has prevented many from attending school this week. Several cases of illness and bad feet.

July 15, 1880. A holiday given for the annual school treat.

July 26. Half holiday given—a fete held in connection with the Dunmow flitch.

October 22. Readmitted Annie Portway on Wednesday. Minnie Letchfield and Elizabeth Tyler absent with whooping cough.

November 3, 1880. Annie and Ruth Ketley marked absent, coming in at twenty minutes past 2 o'clock.

GREAT DUNMOW NATIONAL SCHOOL

Boys' log book, 1863. Headmaster, Mr. Marlow

March 16. A. Leech absent from morning lessons. All the boys from Stebbing late. Geo. Prior degraded from second to third class. Fred Rogerson punished for insolence to Mr. Britton in schoolroom.

March 19. Third class began reading New Testament. At the request of Miss Majendie I took the singing boys into the girls' room, where we sang glees, rounds and school songs.

March 23. Tom Goodey, Geo. Goodey and Richard Parr admitted from the girls' school. The Misses E. and A. Majendie paid their farewell visit to the school [following their father's death, Rev. H. L. Majendie].

March 26. First class small in number, a fine day, helping their parents planting potatoes. Rev. G. W. Lowe visited the school, having no vicar.

April 13. George Smith, late of Mr. Warner's Academy, admitted. Mr. Meyrick, H.M. inspector, examined the school 2-4 o'clock and complained of the untidy hair of the boys. Lady Henniker, Mr. Cockayne and Rev. W. Lowe were present during the examination.

April 20. A. Leech absent from lessons before breakfast. I was at the Vicarage ½ hour

Mr. Bush and his boys of the National School about 1870.

in the morning settling the shoe club up with Rev. W. L. Scott [the new vicar].

April 27. Commencement of schools being swept gratuitously henceforth. No boys are allowed to attend without payment of a fee by committee's orders.

April 30. Punished Thomas Bird and James Hawkes for neglecting consecutive evenings to sweep the schoolrooms. Kept them in at dinner time to fulfil their work. Received a threatening letter from Mrs. Mead, copy " Mr. Marlow." " If you insist on my boys sweeping the school I shall take them away, for I think it a most inconsistent thing for a child to be obliged to do. I send them to learn their books." Mrs. Mead (of the Wheatsheaf), mother of " Shadow." It was next tried by setting two boys to do this job; many stayed away when their turn came. If the boys started their job their mother or eldest sister came and fetched them away. No amount of punishment made any difference and many left the National and went to the British School. [So the children, backed up by their parents went on " strike." The headmaster had a rough time, so the committee had to give in. I personally am surprised that this could have happened in mid-nineteenth-century days. The strike goes on, the master tries hard to resist, but parents and children override him.]

May 6. Only sixty-nine at school. Osier stripping season, also Dunmow fair on the morrow.

May 6. Fair day; no register taken in the afternoon.

May 14. Ascension Day. Took classes 1, 2, 3 and 4 to church at 10.30 and sent class 5 home. In the afternoon Mead attempted to go home instead of sweeping the school, but I forced him back and insisted on his doing it, but his father came and took him away before he had finished it. All the Mead boys were withdrawn from the school. No school in the afternoon to enable the children to attend Sanger's circus.

May 22. Measles, Osier stripping and disaffection about school sweeping.

June 1. Sweeping the school gratuitously abolished. The Meads return to school. Measles still bad in the parish.

June 3. Dismissed morning school at 11 a.m. because of an archdeacon and clergy meeting in the schoolroom. Robert Waller and Arthur Owers played truant.

Queen Victoria's golden jubilee, 1887. The children having their tea outside the National School.

June 8. Thomas Perkins died yesterday [schoolboy].

June 17. Going to church on weekday discontinued.

June 26. Measles and haymaking still enemies to good attendance.

June 29. Coronation Day kept [annual event]. Horticultural fete, so half holiday.

July 7. Several boys taken ill. Rev. W. L. Scott visited the school in the morning.

July 16. I was absent from the pupil teachers' morning lessons, a birth in my family. Left the afternoon school to Alfred Leach and went to Lindsell.

July 30. Commenced using National Society's ink powder today.

August 4. I punished the boys from the Eastons for playing truant yesterday.

August 5. Prepared tickets for the treat on Friday.

October 19. Several boys are away through fear of catching smallpox, which is prevalent in the Church End area. Mr. Burton, relieving Officer, called to order all children to be vaccinated.

National Girls' log book, 1890-2

October 6, 1890. Admitted six new scholars from the workhouse. The Vicar and Mr. Sewell visited.

October 13. Half holiday given today as there is a circus in the town.

December 18. Mr. Clapham visited and heard the singing of the first Dis of girls.

February 12, 1891. Sent a Lodge for school money.

March 25. Received from Mr. Carter two dozen inkwells for the desks.

June 1. Sarah Legerton sent home for her school money (four weeks).

July 1. Mrs. Roberts and Mrs. Bartley visited and inspected the needlework.

August 5. It being the cottage garden show at Easton Lodge, the school was closed this afternoon. The girls sent twenty exhibits and gained fourteen prizes.

August 6. A holiday was given this afternoon for their annual treat at the Vicarage.

August 7. Report of diocesan inspector: " The girls throughout the school seem to be carefully taught, and may be regarded as excellent."

August 21. The school broke up today for five weeks. Rev. and Mrs. Roberts and Lady Fitzgerald distributed the prizes and certificates to the successful candidates. Her ladyship's prize for general and good conduct was awarded to Amy Marshall. In an address to the children by the Vicar he declared that from September 1 all school will be free. [Oh, what a joy! No more being sent back home for " school money," no more struggle for the mothers to find the necessary 4d. or 6d. a week or, with big families, perhaps 3d. per child, the average man's earnings at this time being 10/- a week, or 12/- for a stockman or horseman. What a great day it must have been when " free education " for all was announced.]

November 28, 1891. Rose Wilder was sent home for insolence and insubordination. [The latter is a fine word. I had almost forgotten we still had it in our dictionaries. Perhaps so much the worse, to a degree.]

December 23. At 3.45 this afternoon all the scholars assembled in the girls' schoolroom to present Mrs. Grout with a present on the occasion of her leaving the infants' school.

January 12, 1892. School opened with a very poor attendance, owing to influenza, bronchitis and whooping cough.

January 18. School closed for a week or more, as illness has very much increased.

June 27. Punished Annie and Alice Lodge for their unpunctuality.

October 31. The children from Church End unable to come owing to the excessive rainfall during the night. One group of cottages is completely surrounded by water.

Dunmow British Boys' School log book 1863-8

May 22, 1863. Resigned the mastership of this school [no name given].

May 25. Here the writing is very different.

The choir of the parish church about 1893 with the Rev. C. C. Naters, curate in charge.

Attendance very low owing to Whitsuntide being kept here as a bank holiday.

May 27. Mr. Robert Taylor visited the school and heard the first class read, afterwards giving them some good advice.

June 1. The Misses Clayton and friends from Liverpool visited the school today.

June 3. Weather close and sultry, and the children's attention somewhat flagging. Read an extract from *Band of Hope Review*.

June 11. Had five boys from High Roding come 1 hour and 10 minutes late. Kept them in $1\frac{1}{2}$ hours after time. Thought it would be a good plan to have some interesting exercise at the commencement of school to induce the boys to arrive punctually.

June 22. Rev. H. Gammidge visited the school and inspected the work of several classes.

June 23. Holiday in consequence of holding a bazaar to raise funds for the purpose of flooring the schoolroom.

July 6. Sold *Band of Hope* and *British Workmen* to the children.

July 20. H. Clayton, Esq., of Brighton, formerly one of the committee, visited today.

October 15. A report was brought to me that relatives of three of the boys were ill of the smallpox. To ascertain the correctness of it, and for the safety of the school requested the boys to go home and remain there until communicated with.

October 19. School visited by Rev. Gammidge, also by Mrs. Taylor and Miss Barnard. One parent called about her boy playing truant and requested me to correct him for it.

October 22. School visited by the Misses Clayton and Mr. and Mrs. Marriage of Chelmsford.

November 9. Today being Dunmow's autumn fair, the attendance was very low. Mr. Barnard, a member of the committee, visited the school. The weather having changed cold, a fire was lighted in the stove for the first time. Permitted the boys from Takeley and Stebbing during the darkest months.

November 13. Miss C. Clayton presented A. Robson, J. Warren, A. T. Wilton and J. and H. Gafney with a neat atlas each, in the name of Mr. Saunders, for good reading at the late examination.

January 19, 1864. School closed for a week, the room being hired by the railway for their dinner on Wednesday on the occasion of turning the first sod of the Bishop's Stortford —Dunmow—Braintree Railway.

January 26. George Bass, Mr. Barnard and Mr. R. Hasler called this morning.

May 6. Dunmow spring fair considerably affected afternoon attendances.

May 12. Today was especially remarkable for the number of visitors. Mr. Cullingford in the morning, and in the afternoon Miss Harvey and Mr. R. Taylor, who gave the children a very excellent address on duty to their parents.

May 20. Mr. Foster, one of the former masters, paid a visit to the school today.

May 27. Henry Gay, certificated teacher of the first class. Signed by Matthew Arnold.

July 3. Miss Clayton called to bid the children farewell previous to her marriage and removal to Chelmsford. Both girls and boys were assembled in the girls' room and Miss Clayton having spoken afterwards to the children a nicely bound family Bible was presented to her on their behalf as a present from the children. Miss Clayton was very pleased and gratified with it.

August 10. This being Miss Clayton's wedding day, the children had a half holiday in the afternoon. The children marched through the town with a band of music at their head to Mr. Clayton's field, where they were regaled with tea and cake, provided by Miss Clayton, who also, through her sister, presented each child with a little book in token of her regard. A pleasant evening was spent in games and amusements.

September 23. This afternoon had scramble for apples in the firlo of the schoolroom.

October 24. Spent some time this afternoon practising for the anniversary of the school. All classes sang their pieces.

November 1. Sold *Band of Hope* and *British Workmen* this afternoon (monthly occurrence).

November 8. Today twentieth anniversary of the school. Between the afternoon and morning meetings the scholars had their annual treat. Addresses were given in the morning and evening on the subject of education.

November 14. First day of 4 o'clock closing.

November 15. Took eighty-two up to the Town Hall to the annual juvenile meeting of the B. & F. Bible Society.

January 2, 1865. Rev. H. Gammidge paid a visit, and gave the children a new year's address.

January 12. Received a visit from Mr. J. W. Savill, book shop and antiquary.

May 26. Funeral of Lord Viscount Maynard. In consequence, several Easton scholars absent.

May 20. Sunday school treat of the Independent House, to which the majority of children belong, so half holiday.

August 2. Miss S. Clayton called this morning and wished the children farewell previous to her marriage and removal from Dunmow.

August 3. School closed after morning session for a month. In the afternoon a treat was provided for the children by Miss S. Clayton. After the tea in the school the boys and girls marched through the town to Mr. Clayton's field, where they amused themselves in various ways. Resigned mastership of D.B.S. today—Henry Gay.

October 9. Mr. Clayton and Rev. Gammidge visited.

October 16. Mrs. Smith (of Chelmsford) and Miss Clayton visited.

March 9, 1866. The order today was better than of late in all the classes in the morning. Attendance of country boys smaller owing to special services being held today in all the churches on account of the cattle plague.

March 26. Attendance very small in the afternoon as a menagerie is visiting the town.

April 13. Miss E. Clayton and her sister (Mrs. Marriage) visited the school in the morning.

July 4. Many boys absent on account of the flower show and fete in connection with the Literary Institute in the town.

September 28. Resigned mastership of D.B.S.—A. Prior.

October 1. Took charge of D.B.S.—W. Y. Thomas. Found the children in an extreme state of disorder and very backward.

October 15. Mr. Barnard called and expressed himself at the order of the school. Obliged to send Alfred Gunn from the school for bad conduct and answering me. His mother came up with him and I consented to give him another trial.

December 11. Entered Amos Bacon in the fifth class. Alfred Turner very stubborn. He has been very troublesome for some time and I was obliged to punish him very severely before he would do anything he was told.

January 11, 1867. Gave the children a holiday to attend an entertainment given by Isaac Esq. in the school.

January 15. Miss Clayton and Mrs. Marriage distributed prizes to Joseph Burton, W. Robson, L. Linguard and C. Wren.

January 28. Entered Charlie King and Arthur Scott, J. Barnard and Thomas Sewell again at school after being away over six months.

February 10. Ernest Mann again at school. He had been at home with a dangerous sickness. His mother wishes him only to come half day at first to see if it affected his health.

March 27. Wm. C. and Fred K. Cook from a private school. They are very backward.

April 1. A good number of children away on account of a company of horse soldiers passing through Dunmow. Frederick Dowsett again at school after being away more than six months.

May 6. First day of Dunmow fair; small attendance.

May 7. Entered Charles Sweeting. He had never been to school before, so let him sit with his brother for a time. He was extremely nervous.

May 8. Entered Arthur Crow, who is very timid. His brother James was back again after a month's illness. Entered Charles Fisher. Let him be with his brother for a time.

May 13. George and William Cock back again after having been in the Union for the winter months.

May 28. Punished James Stock for breaking a window.

May 29. Punished Burton for kicking the pupil teacher because he had not an oak leaf in his coat, although they had been told to do it.

July 5. New Independent minister [Rev. Irvine, called and expressed his pleasure at the order of the school.

July 17. Half holiday on account of the Independent Sunday school treat.

July 25. Several late, one of whom was Lewis Languard, who resisted the punishment, so as an example I punished him severely before the whole school. His mother, who had told him to resist, expressed herself sorry for what she had done.

August 14. Mrs. Stock came and complained of her son being struck on the head when entering the school by the pupil teacher, causing two wounds. She spoke seriously to the pupil teacher and cautioned him.

August 24. The father of Alfred King called to know why his son was punished. He had been kept in for inattention. He told his father that the master had caned him on the head.

November 4. Mrs. Paveling came to say her boy had spent his school money.

November 12. Small attendance owing to the ordination of Mr. Irvine, the Independent minister, and also to a show being held on the Downs.

February 12, 1868. Town boys away to attend Mr. Watson's funeral, Sunday school superintendent.

June 4. Usual school work. The three boys Rawlings came for the first time this week. Their father is a publican and two dinners were held at his house on Monday and Tuesday, at which the boys helped.

June 5. Spent the time usually devoted to drawing in questioning the school in tables, spelling, etc.

June 8. W. V. Thomas, C.T. of second degree; Alfred Robson, P.T. 4th year; Matthew Arnold. W. M. Clayton secretary.

British Boys' School, 1893-8

July 5, 1893. School closed for a week. A public holiday being given, with treat, to celebrate the royal wedding [Prince George and Princess Mary, later King George V and Queen Mary].

October 6. Edward East, a scholar of this school, was successful in obtaining a clerkship in the Civil Service, gaining the 137th place out of 200 vacancies.

June 1894. Chicken-pox, water-pox, measles and scarlet fever prevalent in the town.

July 22. Scarlet fever continues to spread. William Caton broke his leg in the playground. Mr. and Mrs. Whitehead visited (*née* Clayton).

July. Attendance very poor owing to the fever scare. Holiday on Wednesday, it being the temperance treat.

August 9. Miss Parrot left to be married.

September 28. Received a surprise. A. H. Sadd, H.M.I.A., Rev. J. B. Dadd and Mr. J. G. Mackenzie visited.

November 23. Measles becoming very prevalent; twenty-seven families affected at this school.

January 25, 1895. Owing to the bad weather there was no school on Tuesday or Wednesday.

February 1. The bad weather continued after the blizzard on Tuesday for the rest of the week.

February 8. No diminution in the severity of the weather; only twenty at school.

February 15. The cold weather continues with unabated severity. Attendance even lower than previous week.

March 26. P.T. third year Richard Roper absent from school owing to sudden death of his father from syncope.

April 15. Poor attendance, Wombwell's menagerie being in the town.

1898. Mixed school started.

September 16. Mr. E. Piper called.

1898. There was a sad accident in the playground this morning. A little lad Roy Lindsell, pulling on an iron gate which the workmen were repairing, fell upon himself, breaking his leg.

CHAPTER XLII

A Dunmow vicar

The Rev. Langston Scott in his magazine of the 1880s speaks of several instances of poor people of his time who lived hard, work-filled lives and then, worn out, sank to their rest. One, John Baines, died at seventy-two. He had worked for more than fifty years for one employer at Merks Hill. The Barnard family farmed there for two or three generations, so John Baines knew father and son. I expect he worked twelve to fourteen hours a day, with never a holiday .

Another this good vicar mentions is John Hinson, who lived in the workhouse some thirty years but died in 1882 at the age of fifty-four. Mr. Scott says that when he became chaplain of the workhouse and visited the infirmary he heard a cultured voice reading, so he paused and listened. Had someone forestalled him? But no, this man was reading in Braille. The board of guardians had bought him several books, including a complete Bible and a Prayer Book. He always read the lessons in the workhouse chapel, or played his concertina to cheer the folk, especially those in the infirmary. He was a friend to all. He must often have heard much in that place which " vexed his righteous soul " says the vicar, but he was always very happy. He had overcome his affliction by bringing happiness to those around him. He was buried at Great Canfield, so his home had evidently been there.

Mr. Scott also speaks of another poor man,

A picture from the Downs about 1900.

Thomas Bowyer, aged seventy-one. How many generations of Bowyers I have found in Dunmow, even before and since young Thomas, the weaver, was burnt at the stake at Stratford. " This quiet, retiring unobtrusive man, living an unmarked life in his lodging home for his last twenty-five years. He might have been seen any day working on the roads in one part of the parish or another. Only as he grew older was I able to draw him out. Twice on a Sunday he was at church, and poor as he was he never let the plate pass him. I was with him till near the end, and I never saw anyone so humble, less disposed to think of the harmlessness of his life, although all who knew him felt how blameless his life had been. There are some who have more knowledge, and can tell of more happy experiences, but I take him to have been one who silently and humbly walked in his Master's steps. Such deserve to be held in remembrance."

Mr. Scott again remembers those who try bravely to defeat their adversities, such as old Mrs. Aylett, who lived in New Street. The Ayletts must have lived in Dunmow for 500 years. They were having their children baptized in 1538 when the registers started—two or three families of them—and the line never broke till a few years ago. But I must return to Mr. Scott. This old lady of whom he speaks was very lame and stone deaf, but she came as often as she could to church, although it took her an hour each way and she could not hear a word. Says Mr. Scott: " She used to tell me she still enjoyed coming to church. I think I see her now with her large-print books, her eyes, her lips, her heart engaged all through the service. Through the sermon she would meditate, or read a chapter." So this dear soul who would not be defeated stood out as an example to others.

Mr. Scott thinks of old people, and in doing so uses the words of our hymn writer who wrote many things besides hymns. He says: " I was struck by a clause I found in a poem by the Rev. Toke Lynch, whose father was known and loved in Dunmow more than sixty years ago, and was a relative of my own. I may sound quaint and odd, but there's a great deal in it. It runs thus: ' Much Bible and rest upon his chair he loves.' "

It seems to me a delightful description of an old man's life. Their work is done. " Man goeth forth to his work and to his labour until the evening." We shall hardly find this evening time better described than in Mr. Lynch's words: " If it is your time to rest, God has appointed it for you. No man grudges you it. Yes, rest from your old and finished labours, rest by your fireside. Rest in the shade of your old tree—the only friend you have older than yourself. So your rest shall be sweet till it lose itself by and by in the rest that remains for the people of God."

These little stories show the man Mr. Scott was, and where his heart lay. After twenty-five years he passed away quietly and peacefully. He was a man who won over his people by love, and it must have come back to him in abundance. His flock thought of him as the good shepherd, so they collected round and bought a gravestone, depicting the Good Shepherd caring for the sheep. You can still see this stone today, bought to show his people's love for him.

CHAPTER XLIII

Return of the C.I.V.s

On June 17, 1901, a presentation dinner was held at the Saracen's Head hotel to welcome home the eight Dunmow men who volunteered to go to South Africa. Mr. Tom Gibbons, then a sergeant in the local company of Volunteers, full of humour from the cradle to the grave, made up a song which he sang himself to the tune of " Little Billie." It is probable that no one else *could* sing it, for more likely he made it up as he went along.

Eight Men of Dunmow City

There were eight men of Dunmow City,
Eight freemen all of Dunmow City,
They left their homes in Dunmow City,
And took a boat, and went to sea.

And should you wish to know their names, sirs,
They're written on the scroll of fame, sirs,
I'll tell you all respectivelee.
Now the first to go was George Willis,
A Yeoman bold was Georgy Willis,
So like a shot went Georgy Willis,
For a man of right good will is he.

And Harry Hales he went as well, sirs,
To face the hail of shot and shell, sirs,
They seemed to suit him very well, sirs,
He swallowed them quite cheerfulee.

Then up spake bold young Percy Worrin,
Said could you tell me on what foreign
Country is this blooming War in?
They said it's in South Africee.

There went also one Jimmy Easey,
He could shoot like lightning greasy,
Bull's-eyes to him they were quite easy,
He went out with the C.I.V.

Then went also a man named Tulip
(A very tender flower was Tulip)
Straight from his sawpit out jumped Tulip,
And joined the service companee.

And with him went his comrade Shadow
(He was the king of all the shadows),
And now he's back we find his shadow
Has not grown less, appreciablee.

Now the Boers they say are very fly, sirs,
But the Stebbing lads can wipe their eye, sirs,
You want a Webb to catch a flie, sirs,
So Arthur Webb, we sent out he.

And the youngest he was little Jack Brazier,
He was a plumber, and a glazier,
The Boers were slim, but he was Brazier,
He was so slim they couldn't hit he.

And now we've got them back in Dunmow,
We'll give three cheers for them in Dunmow,
And I'm sure there's not a man in Dunmow
Who will not give them three times three.

CHAPTER XLIV

Tradesmen of Dunmow

MESSRS. HASLER & CO. CENTENARY, 1963

In 1863 the firm of Hasler and Co. was founded, and civil war in America entered its second year, and in Lancashire there was a distress which has come down in history as the cotton famine. It was under these conditions that this firm commenced business.

Robert, the founding father of Throws, was a well-known farmer, a J.P., a C.C. and a deacon of Dunmow Congregational church. William his son joined him and the two traded as R. Hasler and Son, and things soon began to happen. An amalgamation with G. F. Clapham, the owner of another windmill, stores and stables in the town, took place at the turn of the century, when the business trading as Hasler and Clapham was based in Great Dunmow, continuing to use Throws mill.

A telephone, claimed to be the first in the district, connected the office at Dunmow with the mill at Throws, and afterwards with a store at Felsted, before even the Post Office telephone reached the town. A brickworks was started and for some years did a thriving business. At the time when farmers were using quantities of steam coal for ploughing and threshing another amalgamation, with Wafford, a coal merchant, brought Hasler into the coal trade through a separate company, Walford, Hasler and Co. Ltd.

With business growing rapidly it was decided to build a modern mill at Dunmow and close the two windmills. Sam Clarke from Throws mill moved into Dunmow, and carried on with the new machinery under Jim Hockley, who had succeeded Jim Lovat as foreman in 1912. In 1917 G. F. Clapham retired and Hasler and Co. Ltd. was formed. William Hasler was a man of enterprise and energy, with a keen brain and a lifelong interest in agriculture. At one time he farmed over 2,000 acres in Essex. It was William Hasler who pioneered the growing of sugar beet in the country and was largely responsible for the foundation of the Dunmow bacon factory as an aid to stock raisers. When he died in 1935 Francis J. Nickolls became chairman. He had an irresistible way with him that made him an unsurpassable salesman. He was for many years closely associated with William Hasler in building up the business, and his kindness and courtesy gained him many friends. Unfortunately he became crippled with arthritis and had to retire, and the many years of suffering he bore were a measure of his stature as a man. In 1941 David Hasler took over the chairmanship. His brother Leonard was to have shared it with him, but unfortunately he was killed in World War I. David was seriously wounded on two occasions. Both brothers were awarded the Military Cross. It was at first thought that the strain of business would be too much for him, but with only one foot he rose against his afflictions. Towards the end of World War II he had an attack of thrombosis, but recovered and in October

1946 was able to go on a fishing holiday in Scotland, but there he died suddenly from the same trouble.

He had such a likeable personality, and never gave orders. Both in the Army and in business he just expressed a wish and it was done. Being a natural leader, his authority was never questioned and he had the respect and affection of all who worked with him. On his death Mr. F. Baldry took over the chairmanship. He had been with the business for thirty years. When, at the height of his powers, a stroke deprived the company of his services his place was taken by John Roper, who had managed the branch at Ingatestone since 1920. John Roper was of the Dunmow family of that name, the late Richard Roper, chemist.

John Roper joined Hasler and Clapham in 1900, became a director in 1931 and was made chairman in 1951. After over fifty years' service he retired in 1954. On his retirement a board of directors was formed, with Allen Hasler, a younger son of William Hasler, as chairman and Henry Nicholls, son of Francis Nicholls, as managing director.

The senior member of the board in years of service was N. H. Floyd, who joined the company in 1912, served in World War I and came back in 1918 as secretary, remaining in this post until 1960, when he handed it over to Stanley Bryant. He was appointed a director in 1941 and managing director in 1953.

So firmly is the family tradition established in the company that several of the third generation have now been with the firm some years. The present chairman is the third generation of the Haslers, Alan Nicholls is a grandson of Francis, and Timothy Roper, the grandson of John, is in the firm at Ingatestone. The names of Webb, Sewell and Brazier are as much part of the tradition of the company as the Haslers. William Webb, the present foreman at Dunmow, and his brother James are grandsons of George Webb, who was Robert Hasler's foreman at Throws, and also grandsons of Jim Lovat, the miller at Throws and afterwards the foreman at Great Dunmow. Their father, Arthur Webb, who married Jim Lovat's daughter, began work in 1893 at Throws, and worked as a carpenter and wheelwright for Haslers until he retired in 1947. He served his apprenticeship under Elijah Sewell, a craftsman of the greatest integrity. Elijah's son, Charles Sewell, started work at Throws and after a spell in the Royal Navy took charge of the engine room at Great Dunmow mill until he retired. He died soon after his retirement.

George Barrick, who retired in 1956, had fifty-five years' service with the company, having been foreman of the seed store since 1909, during which time he became an absolute master of the art of dressing small seeds. Luke Brazier came to Dunmow in 1900 to work for Hasler and Clapham. He drove a two-horse team and wagon until 1919, when he was transferred to the Dunmow mill. He continued working until just before his death in 1946 at the age of seventy. His son Ralph has forty years' service in transport behind him, while his son Peter is the company's carpenter.

There are many more who have thirty to fifty years of service to their names, like Mr. F. Cox, who retired at the age of seventy-one after fifty years as clerk in the purchasing department. Arthur Sewell served the company many years in charge of the trefoil milling plant. Last, but not least, is Jim Hockley, foreman of Dunmow mill 1913-59, who lived to the grand old age of ninety, passing to his rest in 1966. His long and honourable record exemplifies that loyalty and reliability on which the company built up its very extensive business.

WHITE'S THE WHEELWRIGHTS

Coach and motor body builders

Until recently Harry White was a craftsman where he was the third generation of his firm, for his family had been coachbuilders and wheelwrights for nearly 200 years at the same workshops in Back Street, Bullocks Row, now unofficially called White Street. Ten skilled men apprentices were employed by grandfather White, who provided them daily with two pints of home-brewed beer. In those days an apprentice would pay £5 premium and receive a wage of 1/- a week, rising after five years to 5/-.

Harry started in his father's shop as a boy. He afterwards went as an improver to East Suffolk Carriage Works, Haleswork, where about 90 men worked. There he earned 3d. an hour. The hours were 6 a.m. to 6 p.m., but usually they were so busy that they worked until 9 p.m. When at the end of a year he asked for a rise he was given ¼d. an hour, but only after great deliberation.

In their heyday of coaching the former generations were often called in to repair the coaches of the Maynard family and for Captain Ray of Clock House, well remembered for his charity. Harry's father made the first horse-drawn snow plough for Dunmow and sharpened the picks used for the cutting of the railway line. Included in the art of wheelwright was the buying of growing trees, felling and transporting them, and converting them into usable timber. " Oak for spokes " was the wheelwright's motto. After preparing the rough spokes Mr. White used to put an average of 1,600 of them into the ford at the back of the gasworks, to stay there for four months, after which they were stacked for about five years before they were put in a wheel. If you wandered through the workshops you would be shown uncle Frank's school books, dated round about 1866 and written in exquisite copper-plate at Mr. H. B. Warner's academy in New Street. Old ledgers reveal that in 1867 a set of horseshoes was made and fitted for 2/- and a tumbril cart with ladders for £16. In 1873 the water cart was greased for 6d., a wooden washtub for the Dunmow union was supplied for £4, and 2cwt. of firewood cost 3/4.

Uncle Francis (commonly known as Frank) was quite a character. After Harry had been in the shop for about three years he was given some wagon raves to mortise, with the promise that his uncle would give him a new rule if he did the job well. Says Harry: " I was frightfully bucked and took great pains with the job. When uncle came back he carefully listed each mortise and said ' No too bad for a boy.' " But Harry said " What about my rule uncle? " " Ah, yes, boy, here it is. Always measure twice before you cut once." Says Harry: " I didn't think much of it at the time, but over the years it has proved a valuable rule.

When John White, Harry's grandfather, was running the business he was passing the old cattle pound which was opposite Folly Farm in Bishop's Stortford Road when he noticed two horses inside the pound and a wagon outside. Returning home, he told his men " We'll have some fun tonight." After dark he returned with his men and they dismantled the wagon, put it piece by piece over the walls of the pound, reassembled it and put the horses into the shafts. One can imagine the owner's amazement when he arrived next morning (of such stuff are legends made). He scratched his head, viewed with horror the narrow exit from the pound and decided there was nothing but to send for John White and get his men to dismantle the wagon and reassemble it outside.

There was obviously no limit to private enterprise in those days. In 1937 a stranger walked into the workshops and demanded that a wheelbarrow be put on the train to London. It was sent to the Paris trade exhibition and won a diploma in an international competition. Harry White made the

Dunmow Football Club 1932-3.

side of bacon which hangs outside the Flitch of Bacon inn at Little Dunmow. To see that so realistic, I almost wonder that someone has not taken a bite. There is no further need to ask " Is Harry White a craftsman? "

THE KNIGHTS OF DUNMOW

About 1830 Charles, a son of John and grandson of Thomas Knight, of Thaxted, clockmakers, came to Dunmow and started up business in the High Street. He was born in 1811 and died in 1870, aged fifty-nine. On his death he was succeeded by his son, John, who ran this business till 1820. His son Alfred then took over the business till he retired about 1964 and died in 1966.

WOODS, THE TAILORS

Mr. A. Wood, tailor and breeches maker, first had a shop on Star Hill about 1894. In 1901 he moved up to High Street. He was known all around for his good workmanship, and before World War I took his men his workroom was a hive of industry. See illustration. This business closed in 1958.

A. W. Wood, tailor, Dunmow.

THE ARCHERS OF DUNMOW

In the 1880s John Archer was gamekeeper at Merks Hill. His eldest son, Arthur, was apprenticed to Mr. Scrivener, the white-smith in North Street next to the "cage." Arthur's idea was engineering and this was not exactly the job, but there were often "side-lines" where a boy could gain ideas. Travellers called endeavouring to sell the best and latest models of penny-farthings, but Mrs. Scrivener put her husband off buying these dangerous things.

One day, looking across the road, Arthur saw that the Gibbonses had company, with children and a nurse. He saw the nurse again—and somehow she "took his eye," so, to cut a long story short, they got acquainted and it was not long before Miss Dodkin became Mrs. Archer and they set up home at Beaumont Hill.

At this time a whitesmith was one who made springs and wrought-iron work, but Arthur must push, so he took some premises in Pratt's yard (this was where Savills the greengrocers now stands). There were several little places up there besides Mr. Pratt's plumbing shop. The bicycle was fast gaining momentum, and the only hopes of getting them repaired were smiths and general repairers. Mr. Archer therefore added cycle repairs to his business.

Next he moved to a shed with a loft up Angel Lane. Again, before 1900, he moved across the road to a real shop right on the street—35 High Street. By this time his two older sons were Arthur and Sam, and they, with Florrie, were working in the business. Here let Sam take up the story. "I saw the first car come to Dunmow. It belonged to a Mr. Hodges, who married the elder Miss Gibbons. Then came Dr. Tench's steam car, followed by Dr. Hutchinson's 6h.p. De Dion Bouton and the Daimler of Mr. Spurgeon."

After 1900 motor-cars began to appear on the roads in small numbers. Petrol at this time could be obtained only from some chemists. Arthur II learned the combustion engine, Sam stuck to smith's work, Florrie ran the taxi anywhere and everywhere by day and night, or at least very late evenings; she almost lived on the road.

Over again to Uncle Sam. "Up to World War I the roads were very rough. It was nothing for the highway authorities to put down loads of flints and leave the traffic to roll them in. This used to break the axles. I used to be keen on cricket and football when I was a boy, but I never had a chance after I left school. Never a half-day off. It was all work. But our mother gave us a wonderful home." Mr. Archer married in 1883 and by 1914 all his seven children were grown up. Just prior to the war the Ford agency was obtained.

Another first scored at this time was the electric light plant in Dunmow. Mains electricity was not then available. If one wanted electric lighting it meant installing one's own plant.

Again the story was repeated and the early repairers became suppliers and maintainers of electric light plants. A plant consisted of a stationary engine running on gas or paraffin driving the generator, which in turn charged lead/acid batteries. Foothold was also established in gas and water fittings. World War I speeded up mechanization on the farms and the Ford Motor Company began sending its agents, Fordson Tractors, to help with the war effort. A fleet of some twenty-five to thirty tractors, both Fordson and International Titans, was maintained by the firm during the war.

The youngest son, Percy C. Archer, was killed in France at the age of nineteen. Jack suffered from effects of the war and Stanley injured his legs playing football and became a permanent cripple. To help him overcome this disability he was introduced to the then new hobby of wireless, constructing several sets himself. One of these early sets made by him in the 1920s still exists. Wireless was thus added to the firm's activities, with television

No. 4 Section, A Company, 1/5 Essex, who won the cup for firing. Back row (left to right): Sam Archer, Jim Ruffle, Jack Brazier, Sgt. Instructor Johnson, Ted Hoy, Jack Eagle. Middle row: Lt. Frank Bacon, Capt. Tom Gibbon, Lt. S. Lyle. Front row: George Gunn, Jim Taylor, John Blower, Harry Halls.

The Excelsior Band, 1923.

following it in 1936. The firm took its present title (A. Archer and Sons) in 1930, and the founder, Arthur Archer I, died in 1932. The property in High Street and White Street was purchased in 1919-20.

In 1934 a similar business of N. Spearman, of 77 High Street, was acquired. Arthur II took up residence there with his wife and family. Jack died in 1944. This left only Arthur and Sam. The business is now run by Arthur III, son of Arthur II. To save the overwhelming overheads it was thought necessary to do like so many firms were doing, more work in a confined space. Each line of the Archers has worked till near the midnight hour. All my life I have seen their lights or heard their generators running until they left this end of the street, and the present owner has inherited the same complaint—that of keeping his nose to the grindstone till the old town clock signals its longest strokes.

Uncle Sam talked a lot about the times when it had to be so, but all work and no play never made him a dull boy. He was in the Volunteers and then the Territorials, and one of the crack shots in the Dunmow company of the " famous fifth " Essex (according to local estimation). See illustration.

Sam had a large shed at No. 77, and many people came to have a " chinwag " with him, for he knew everyone and everything that had taken place not only in the firm but in the town, at least since 1890. After all the big family that had been and Arthur II having died in 1953, he used to say " Now there's only me and the boy Arthur." Now Sam has gone (he had such simple and beautiful thoughts of the after-life) and there is only " the boy Arthur III." He is now continuing only the car trade, with vintage as a speciality (repairs and renovations). The value of old cars having risen to fantastic prices, they are more or less collectors' pieces and are in themselves a business on their own.

CHAPTER XLV

Doctors of Dunmow

I have spoken of the doctors in passing (doctors of the workhouse) down to Dr. Salt in 1832, whose daughter was the mother of the late E. T. Foakes. I am not sure who came to the " Hazels " on the death of Dr. Salt. Dr. R. C. Lyle lived there, but as he died at the age of forty-four it would leave a gap. Dr. Blackmore Clapham might have been one of this group of doctors. I remember him quite well, though only as a J.P. and as a very elderly man, but I rather fancy he was one on his own and that his surgery was at the door next to Blowers. As his house is about to be pulled down my readers may not know of this big square Victorian house, with a garden reaching a long way back. Dr. Lyle's partner was Dr. Hutchinson, but in 1904 he left Dunmow and the practice was taken over by Dr. J. N. Gardiner. He had had a very varied life in the medical services before settling down in Dunmow, where he was extremely well known, especially for his work in the church. He died in November 1930, aged fifty-six. Dr. Allman Hall and Dr. Roberts were partners, Dr. Hall dying at fifty-seven. The practice was bought by Dr. Castleden.

Dr. H. S. Howell was here in the 1860s at the Stortford Road surgery, but whom he succeeded, whether it was Dr. Pearson or Dr. Grice, I do not know. He himself was succeeded by Dr. C. Hartley, from whom Dr. M. Tench bought the practice in 1892. He was the medical officer for Dunmow workhouse and of the High Easter division of the Dunmow union, the Post Office and the Great Eastern Railway. His one great hope was that his elder son, 2nd Lt. Montague Beaven Tench, would succeed him, but he was killed in France at the battle of the Somme in 1916. Dr. Tench died on Christmas Eve 1930, aged sixty-eight. It was a sad blow to the people of the town to lose both of the doctors who had attended them for so many years so near together, and at their funerals were a great number of people who held these doctors in the greatest respect. Dr. G. Barber took on the practice of Dr. Tench.

CHAPTER XLVI

Edward Thomas Foakes

Son of Mr. C. L. Foakes, farmer, of Broadgroves (top of Barnston Hill), Edward Thomas Foakes was born there in 1852. His mother was a daughter of Dr. Salt, who lived and had his surgery at the " Laurels," now the Dunmow Club. When their parents died he and his two sisters came to Westbury House. He probably bought it after the death of George Wade, first of the family of solicitors in Dunmow.

The elder Miss Foakes was a partial invalid, and died young; the younger was so quiet and reserved that except at church on a Sunday morning she was rarely seen in public. She seldom visited or entertained guests, beyond an occasional tennis party. Their medical adviser, Dr. Tench, was sometimes invited to make up a foursome. The late doctor had a great sense of humour and he told this little story to a friend. It had been a very hot summer day which persisted into the evening. Miss Foakes played with her racquet in her right hand and held an open parasol in her left, and a reference to her dress left one to conclude that it was a work of art not to fall over it—at this period the fashion was ankle length at least.

One wonders sometimes if Mr. Foakes was a misunderstood man. He was such a quiet, retiring character, and this was often taken to mean a complete lack of interest in the people around him. Certainly he was much against development, and appears to have wanted Dunmow always to remain the same quiet country town it had always been. He liked walking and was a familiar sight with his inseparable walking stick, a well-built man of over six feet striding along at a good pace and always alone. He also rode horseback (at walking pace) around the country lanes of the Dunmow area.

As a young man Mr. Foakes held a commission in the 12th Essex Rifle Volunteers. He qualified as a barrister-at-law, but never practised. He was appointed a magistrate for Essex in 1892 and in 1914 succeeded to the chair of the Dunmow bench, to which his fine physique and legal knowledge added dignity and confidence. He and his sister were very liberal to every request for help, especially to the poor, but always anonymously.

He passed away, after a short illness, in 1922 and was buried at Hildersham (Cambridgeshire), where his body rests between the graves of his two sisters and in which parish his uncle was vicar. Thus passed a loyal son of Dunmow, by whose generosity the town possesses its splendid Foakes Hall (the recreation ground together with the club in the High Street) without stipulations or restrictions save the modest request that the club should always give a welcome to ex-servicemen. The Foakes Hall was opened on September 12, 1934, by the chairman of the parish council, the late Mr. F. J. Nicholls.

CHAPTER XLVII

Dunmow in the twentieth century

On the death of Queen Victoria in 1901 (after reigning for 63½ years) Edward, Prince of Wales, was proclaimed king. So at long last a coronation was arranged.

On June 24, 1902, it was announced that the king had been taken ill and the celebrations could not take place. A service of intercession for the king was held in Dunmow parish church. The whole programme of events was indefinitely postponed. A lot of the decorations were not again restored. On August 9, the revised coronation day, the sports were carried out and the bonfire was lit at Throws, in Beacon Field. How was it first called by that name? True it is the highest spot around. Was it used for beacons when "Old Bonie" was expected? Each parish was supposed to have a beacon somewhere, and many had them on their church towers, such as at High Easter, Hatfield Broad Oak, etc., but not the size of our bonfire, of course.

The second annual competitions in agriculture promoted by the Dunmow and District Association, of which the Earl of Warwick was president, were held this year at Bigods Hall Farm. In the unavoidable absence of the earl the chair was taken by Mr. P. W. Carr, a vice-president, of Newton Hall. The prizes were distributed from a wagon in front of the Saracen's Head by Mrs. Carr. This lady said "I have been out most of the morning watching the ploughing, and found it a beautiful sight." She went on to deplore that many young men were leaving the countryside for the towns, where they got better money but where rents and living were more expensive. Money can never make up for the benefits of the healthy and glorious countryside. I would like you to read some verses which figure on an old mug I have at Newton Hall:

"Let the wealthy and great
Roll in splendour and state,
I envy them not, I declare it.

I eat my own lamb,
My own chicken and ham,
I shear my own fleece, and I wear it.

I have lawns, I have bowers,
I have fruits, I have flowers,
The lark is my morning alarmer.

So jolly boys now,
Here's 'God speed the plough,'
Long life, and success to the farmer."

1908. Messrs. Hasler and Clapham of Dunmow, who were the owners of a large piece of meadow land known as White Post Pasture, decided to develop it for building purposes.

Their decision to do this has given us The Avenue and Station Road.

In March 1905 the Rev. A. C. Roberts decided to leave Dunmow in a hurry. No one could persuade him. He said he knew what he must do for the sake of the Church.

King Edward VII's coronation celebrations, August 9, 1902, showing Dunmow Town Band.

One of his daughters was very ill at the time, but he ordered a sale at the vicarage, and very soon left the county where his family had lived for over 200 years. He came back to Essex in the evening of his days, at White Colne, where he died in 1919.

The chancellor presented the Rev. John Evans, curate at St. Mary-at-the-Wall, Colchester, to the vicarage of Great Dunmow. He came to us with very high recommendations, which were fully appreciated here. He was very popular with all classes. This is a bad word, but was not so at that time. He was an exceptionally interesting speaker, who looked ahead, and a lot of what he saw there he did not like, but too much of it has come true. He left Dunmow in November 1914 for St. John's, Southend.

In 1908 the Dunmow fire brigade was presented with uniforms, consisting of brass helmet, tunic and boots, provided by the parish council.

September 1905. Old customs revived. The Dunmow District Agriculture Competitions Association decided to revive the order of competitions last carried out in 1840. Ploughing matches divided into four classes were held in October. Hedging, stacking and thatching competitions also took place. In a large marquee in the sale yard was a display of roots, corn, poultry, butter and eggs, labourers being allowed free entries to a special poultry class. Home-made bread was provided for, Mr. E. T. Foakes having offered special prizes to facilitate this industry. The Countess of Warwick gave out the prizes from a wagon in front of the Saracen's Head. This was continued until the outbreak of World War I.

1905. Although I have no intention of bringing party politics into this book I can hardly pass over the days when the Rev. Maxted of Tilty and other Socialists used to raise hectic scenes in Dunmow. Socialism was then in its infancy and the Dunmow worthies were quite unable to cope with its radiant dreams. Mr. J. N. Kemp of the White Horse was a regular " quick wit," and he and many others gave the Socialists a rough time, but it was no one-sided affair. Again and again in the years preceding World War I there were many hectic evenings in the market place which helped in their way to liven up the town.

W. Johnson, post office. King Edward VII's coronation, 1902.

Joe Hoy releasing pigeons after successfully walking the greasy pole. He was reputed to be " blind drunk," so had no nervous tension. The Doctor's Pond about 1907 or 1908.

The pump and drinking trough at the Braintree road corner, where we used to play marbles and five stones.

One Whit-Monday afternoon the Socialists again endeavoured to hold a meeting. They might have known people would be watching the horse-and-cart parade or doing their best to walk the greasy pole at the doctor's pond (see illustration). However, they parked their car in the market place and Mrs. Bridges Adams, who mounted the front of Lady Warwick's car, was allowed to speak for ten minutes. When she got down Mr. Jack Jones attempted to speak, but the uproar prevented him. Then the Dunmow brass band struck up close to the car and the proceedings were brought to an ignominious end.

In 1906 the Dunmow Friendly Society was again invited to visit Sir Walter Gilbey at Elsenham Hall. The two hon. secretaries of the society, Messrs. E. T. Foakes, J.P., and Hasting Worrin, J.P., were present. Conveyances were provided by Sir Walter. All sat down to a good meat tea, served in the riding school. To each guest a clay pipe, bearing the donor's inscription, and a packet of tobacco were presented; cigars followed. Sir Walter said there were many lessons to be learned from the society and its effect upon the people. Those who formed the society were pioneers in times very different from the present. He wished there were some M.P.s present to see what Essex men had done for themselves. Out of 600 M.P.s in the Commons not ten knew how the people lived or what they lived on. Mr. J. V. Mackenzie said that the Dunmow society was built upon a rock by careful management. Let me take this opportunity to inform those " wisacres " who are always chattering about men being too old at forty when our pensioners are sixty-five and over and are in receipt of full wages. The pensioners, numbering 100, had their photographs taken separately. Afterwards more refreshments were provided, and later they left the Hall.

In the same year the parish council entered upon an agreement with the gas company to introduce fifty-five incandescent gas lamps (instead of the flare type) into the town and to keep them lighted from August to May for £125.

In those Edwardian days what did people do? They were the days when we made our own amusements, and by this they were what we wished for and brought out the greatest fun and happiness. No one worried about

Election day. Col. Lockwood's figures have just been announced. In what years were elections held in the 1900s? Perhaps someone can tell the date of the car and count how many people they remember.

The Rev. John Evans with the choir. Standing behind him is Stacey King, the choirmaster, who was killed in World War I.

" keeping up with the Joneses." No use tearing around to try to find who would give you the biggest penny. Most people were poor but happy. Music was the great enjoyment for winter evenings. Most played some instrument, be it accordion, concertina, flute, piano, violin or banjo. If you were not having a sing-song evening a friend or neighbour was. Friends were friends and neighbours were neighbours, and one had no " telly "

The Excelsior Band, 1906.

The town band leads the horse-and-cart parade on Whit-Monday 1904.

to glue one's nose to; people went to each other's houses to have a " good old rowdo." In the town there were concerts by a very good string orchestra or two brass bands. On Whit-Monday there was the horse-and-cart parade and afterwards sports, which always included the greasy pole over the doctor's pond. On August bank holiday there was the " flitch " again, with many more sideshows than in these days, and in the summer there were picnics in the hay fields, or folk went by train or brake for a day by the sea. That kind of summer seems to have left us of late.

Sir Julien Byng lived at Newton Hall in those days and with Lady Byng took a great interest in the town. Soon after Baden-Powell introduced the Scout movement General Byng founded a troop here, with Mr. C. Lucking as Scoutmaster. This troop, together with Rovers and Cubs, had greatly increased in numbers when in 1911 it took part in the coronation rally in Windsor Great Park. Many notable people visited Newton Hall in those days, among them the brothers of the late Queen Mary. Prince Francis of Teck, who was a single man, came frequently, and there were Prince and Princess Alexander of Teck and Field Marshal Lord Kitchener. The Byngs left us in 1912 to go to Egypt, where General Byng was governor till the outbreak of the war two years later. On August bank holiday 1914 a notice was displayed on the post office stating that war was declared, and at the end of a happy day came the end of our world as we had known it. People up to that time had not moved far away from home, but the war burst like a bombshell and scattered all to the ends of the earth. Little wonder that it was as if one world ended, with all its happy days of peace, and another began which was to bring wholesale murder and endless discontent.

We could often hear the roar of the guns in France. It was seldom that we did not know when a battle was on, especially in Flanders, by the continuous murmur in our ears. Plans were drawn up by the military authorities for the removal of our people to the west in case of invasion on the east coast. Our route was by Green Lane (Bigods Lane) to Stansted, avoiding main roads, and our final destination was Oxford. Farm carts were allotted for the women and children, the sick and infirm, while the able-bodied were to march on foot. I never did hear of anyone taking it seriously. Surely the authorities had forgotten we had a Navy. In this war there were no public amusements such as dancing and concerts. Everyone was working hard, especially the women, to keep the jobs open "till the boys come home." Besides, most felt they should not be enjoying themselves while the boys were laying down their lives. The faith of the people was not yet broken and the churches were full of those who were praying for God's mercy.

In August 1918 a Sunday morning united service was held in the parish church. The Rev. W. H. Pace, B.D., read the prayers and lessons and the vicar, the Rev. W. J. House, welcomed the Congregationalists and other nonconformists and said that it was the first time for 300 years that the people of Dunmow had all worshipped together within those walls. The Congregational church was closed that morning and the parish church in the evening, when a combined service was held at the Congregational church. The vicar offered prayers and read the lessons and Mr. Pace preached, emphasizing the necessity for the people at home to prepare to welcome the soldiers home when the war had been won.

On a Sunday in November 1918 the Rev. W. J. House, vicar of Dunmow, conducted a service of thanksgiving at the Congregational church as Mr. Pace was not well. The vicar, who wore his surplice and preached from the pulpit, said that this was the first time that a Church of England minister had taken a service in Dunmow Congregational church since it was founded by a minister who left the established Church after the Act of Uniformity.

In November 1919 a "welcome home" was given by the Dunmow Parish Council to 230 men who had returned from active service. A dinner was held at the National School and members of the council served as waiters. After a good hot meal of roast beef and plum pudding had been served there was good high-grade ale and every man received a packet of cigarettes and a cigar. The accommodation of the school was taxed to the utmost. The only invited guests were the vicar, the Rev. W. J. House; the Congregational minister, the Rev. H. W. Pace, B.D.; Col. J. M. Welch, who had commanded the 1/5th Essex Regiment when it landed in Gallipoli; Colonel Tom Gibbons, D.S.O., who succeeded Col. Welch and carried the 1/5th through four years of war; and Dr. N. Gardiner.

In September 1919 the Rev. John Evans, formerly vicar of Dunmow, unveiled a marble tablet at the Philpot End mission hall in memory of six men who fell in the war.

On Sunday afternoon, July 17, 1921, the public memorial in the High Street was unveiled by our old friend Sir Julien Byng, now Lord Byng of Vimy. Written on its columns are the names of eighty-four men who made the supreme sacrifice. The town band led the singing from Mr. Floyd's garden. General Byng paid tribute to those who had given their lives in a war in which victory was to save those at home from enemy domination. He knew many of these boys personally. He said: "Would not these boys expect that in the future those who had come through with their lives should do their best for their

Lord Byng of Vimy unveiling the town war memorial on Sunday afternoon, July 17, 1921.

country throughout their civilian life, and endeavour to do all they could to make this country happier and better? " They must not only pay their respects to the dead, they must make every effort to attain that for which these boys who had fallen gave up all the blessings of this life. The buglers sounded the Last Post and the Bishop of Chelmsford then dedicated the memorial and gave an address and the benediction, and finally the buglers sounded the Reveille.

In November 1921 Dunmow had something of an experience in a simultaneous mission at the parish and congregational churches. For a long time the parish has been noted for the fraternal co-operation of its churches. The curate, the Rev. B. E. F. Mitchell, spent three hours one evening on a tour of the public-houses. He asked all and sundry whom he found in " highways and hedges " to come to the church next day, and he had the satisfaction when the male congregation assembled of seeing every man who had promised to come, with only one exception. At the final Sunday evening service there was an overflowing congregation. During the last hymn the missioner asked those who had received personal help to stay behind and the others to file quietly out, and not a person left the Church. This was encouragement indeed.

In twenty-five years it was war again. This time it came over the radio instead of on a telegram form on the post office window. What would those boys have thought who died in the first war—to end wars? Everything was so different by now. No one thought in the same way as in the first world war. Nothing now was so sacred. People had been let down and deceived. After the first war no work and no " houses for heroes to live in." Nothing mattered as in the old days. However, this Hitler had to be reckoned with. Night after night was spent in shelters or in the cupboard under the stairs. This was a war in the air; incendiary bombs, land-mines, buzz-bombs and rockets were " all in a night's rest." Dunmow knew nothing compared with most places.

It took six years to settle Hitler, and although the loss of life was not so great in the forces the civilian casualties were very shocking in the cities and big towns. We lost twenty-eight compared with eighty-four in World War I.

I hope that the minds and senses so overstrained by the disturbing elements of war may come back to an even keel when the present generation has passed on and, if ever, when this whole world stands firm for Peace.

CHAPTER XLVIII

The church as we know it today

The exterior has altered very little since it was built in 1350-1500. In 1907 the vicar, the Rev. John Evans, had the walls stripped and the flints repointed. It was hoped that the lay rector would have the chancel done the same, but that did not materialize. We may enter by the west door and make straight for the altar, the reredos and the great east window. The latter is a fine specimen of about 1350-75. In 1891 the stonework was restored. The Rev. A. C. Roberts notes that on Wednesday, July 22, at 12.15 p.m. to be precise, he himself keyed the last joint with a threepenny bit of that year's coinage. Sir Bridges Henniker put in the central light of the crucifixion. The four side lights were given by Dr. Blackmore Clapham, J.P., in memory of his wife, Frances Ellen. The altar is neat and the reredos also unpretentious, so that they blend neatly together. The latter is in memory of Joseph Napier Gardiner, M.D., and bears shields on oak—the Napier arms and those of his school, university, etc. Dr. Gardiner, who was a lay reader, did a great deal of work in the church.

For a quick look around the church we will start on the north side of the chancel. The second window is in memory of the Carter family, who traded in Dunmow for many years. Dansie the elder was church-warden for twelve years. The fourth window is in memory of Annie Crawley Thring, who died in India. A window in the south side of the chancel is in memory of the Rev. H. L. Majendie. In the north wall of the church is a window of modern glass which is inclined to catch the eye before aught else. It is of our Lord as the true vine, His hand raised in blessing, enshrining the text " I am the vine, ye are the branches." The brilliant colours of this window are inclined to detract from the rest of the church, especially when the sun is shining on it from the south. It is in memory of Charlotte Young.

There is another window in the north wall containing fourteenth-century glass in the figures of St. Mark and St. Luke, and the most north-westerly one contains fragments of ancient glass. Crossing to the south aisle next, east of the porch is a mix-up of fifteenth-, sixteenth- and seventeenth-century glass. The window nearest the south-west is in memory of Mr. and Mrs. William Johnson. The east window of the south aisle is modern glass and is in memory of Mr. and Mrs. Nicholls, of Dunmow Park.

The south porch was built in the fifteenth century in the Perpendicular style. It is of unusual height, battlemented and with panelled and crocketed pinnacles. It gives an impression of grandeur equalled only by a few porches in Essex. A nearer view presents windows, niches that once held saints, holy water stoups and consecration crosses, which speak of very early days when men pledged their lives to do a certain deed by the sign of the cross, come what may. The approach to the upper chamber is inside the church through an oak door studded and inset in a low arch, up a winding staircase, at the top of which is another low arch, which leads into the upper room. In pre-Reformation days this chamber was undoubtedly for the Virgin Mary (see accounts of the Reformation). This gallery rests on oak beams standing close to the second and third columns of the south arcade. These are of very ancient woodwork, which continues upwards and supports not only the gallery but the roof as well and is distinct from the aisle roof.

The oak pulpit is in memory of Charles Henry Scott (second son of the Rev. Langston Scott), curate of Saffron Walden, by the parishioners of that town as a memorial of their regard. This was in 1876. The pulpit, lectern and candlesticks were given by the Rev. F. Burnside, of Hertingfordbury, where the Rev. C. H. Scott was curate after leaving Saffron Walden. The lectern, a fine brass eagle, bears the following inscription: " To the glory of God and in loving memory of Dansie Carter, people's churchwarden of this parish 1876-1888, and of Elizabeth Ann his wife and their six sons and infant daughter, all of whom are interred in the adjoining churchyard. This lectern is given by their two surviving daughters. Whitsun Day 1902."

The handsome brass candelabrum with sockets for twelve candles which hangs in the chancel was given by John Henniker in 1766. The priests' desks and choir stalls are modern, the former carved by Mr. Marshall of Coggeshall in oak given by Mr. T. Goodey. That on the south side was given " in memory of a very dear friend and fellow choirman," James Edward Ellam, in 1921 by the choir and Sunday school teachers and scholars.

Mr. Ellam had been a member of the choir for many years, and superintendent of the Sunday school for the last ten years. He was the second member of this parish to be killed by a motor car, and, what is more, in the prime of a useful life. In 1922 Dr. and Mrs. Gardiner gave the desk on the south side in memory of their young son, Herbert Napier Gardiner. Mr. Marshall also carved the choir stalls. Those on the north side were dedicated on April 19, 1925, in memory of Joseph and Hannah House (parents of the vicar). The choir stalls on the north side were partly given by their children in loving memory of the Rev. J. C. and Lydia E. D. Thring in 1926.

In the chancel are three chairs. Two of these, of the early seventeenth century, have inlaid and carved backs and carved rails and legs. The third chair is a little younger and similar to the others but not inlaid. On October 10, 1888, the choir was vested in cassocks and surplices for the first time, and the vestry was built the next year. In November 1889 Mr. and Mrs. Wiggett presented the brass alms dish to the church, and on Christmas Day of the same year the carved oak credence table, the gift of Mr. Gibbons, was dedicated, together with the jewelled altar cross, given by Lady Brooke and Lady Dalton Fitzgerald. The engraved brass flower vases were the gift of Mr. F. Bartley. The white festal frontal was worked by Miss Frances Wade, and the orphreys were made by Miss Gibbons.

One of the finest features of the church is the tower. Built somewhere between 1400 and 1500 in three stages, it is 73ft. 10in. to the top of the battlements. There was within the south-west turret a winding stone staircase, which was filled in to strengthen the tower.

While Mr. Roberts was vicar the tracery and shields over the west door were restored, and the carved heads of Bishop Festing of St. Albans and Mr. Roberts were placed one on each side of the door.

The earliest dates of our present bells are 1613, 1671, 1673, 1674 (one with no inscription) and 1641, and in 1927 two more were added. This peal of eight is considered one of the finest peals in the county. Change ringers come frequently to have a good half-day's ringing. In 1925 the timbers of the bell frame were found to be in such a dangerous condition that it was necessary to take the bells down and replace them on a steel frame. On the bell No. 3, which had no inscription, was written the following:

J. W. House, D.D., Vicar.
F. Robus } Churchwardens.
J. N. Gardiner }

In 1893 fifteen handbells were purchased. They were sometimes used by the ringers for learning new combinations of change ringing, but they were also used on Christmas Eve, when the ringers took them round the parish to play carols wherever they thought they would be appreciated. It was so nice to hear them, and when World War I broke out and some of the team had to join up we never heard them again, and it did not seem like Christmas Eve. Handbell ringing is again becoming popular in some parishes. Let us hope it may be so in Dunmow.

Our present church clock is by John Fordham, 1706. He came to Dunmow as a clockmaker in 1700. It was a thirty-hour clock with one hand, but in 1892 it was converted to an eight-day with two hands.

In the south-west corner of the church are brasses of William and Philippa Glascock, of the manor of Minchon. There is another small brass which, translated from the Latin, reads " This stone was dedicated by Martha his widow in memory of her marriage and marks the grave of John Huthersoul, who died December 3, 1604, aged 33."

There are two chests, one of the early sixteenth century and one of the seventeenth century.

The War Memorial, 1914-8, was unveiled on Sunday morning, July 17, 1921.

There was a full congregation and the vicar, the Rev. W. J. House, conducted the service. The Rev. John Evans, former vicar, read the opening passages of the burial service. He had seen these boys grow up and knew their parents, and was conscious of the aching hearts that lay beneath their joy that the war was over. During the singing of " O valiant hearts " the Bishop of Chelmsford, the Very Rev. J. H. Watts Ditchfield, released the Union Jack covering the memorial. Col. Gibbons read the first lesson and the curate, the Rev. B. E. F. Mitchell, the second. The bishop, who preached the sermon, said " This service will live in your memories when others are forgotten, because it has touched your hearts and souls."

It was just over twenty-five years before another such service was to touch people's hearts again, but fortunately the toll was not so heavy. The memorial for the first war is in the south-west corner of the church, while that for the second is in the north-east, close to the book of remembrance. In the first war our losses were eighty-four.

CHAPTER XLIX

Colonel Thomas Gibbons, D.S.O.

Thomas Gibbons was the son of Thomas Gibbons of Down House. Born at Down House on April 7, 1873, and educated at Newport School, Essex, he was intended for the law and entered Clare College, Cambridge, in 1891, but owing to the sudden death of his parents he was obliged to give up a university career.

He became senior partner of Webb and Gibbons, Crown Brewery, Dunmow, a member of Dunmow Rural District Council, a guardian of Dunmow union, treasurer of Dunmow Parish Council, a trustee of Dunmow parochial charities, a manager of the Church of England school, captain of F Company the Essex Volunteer Regiment, having joined the company in 1893, and chairman of the committee of the annual horse-and-cart parade and of the corn and root show. He started Dunmow Miniature Rifle Club and was conductor of the Dunmow Musical Society. He was also an amateur entertainer and actor, and for twelve years acted as " counsel for the bacon " and seven years as judge at the historic flitch trials. He was married in 1898 to Annie,

Dunmow Cricket Club, with Jack Gibbons captain (centre), shortly before World War I.

Col. Tom Gibbons, D.S.O., who led the 1/5 Essex to victory in the Middle East 1914-8.

daughter of the late Joseph Sotham, of Holton, Oxfordshire, and of Braintree. When the Volunteers turned into the Territorials Mr. Gibbons became captain of F Company (Dunmow).

At the time war broke out in 1914 the 5th Essex Territorial Regiment was doing its annual training at St. Albans, and instead of a fortnight's camp the regiment went into intensive training for active service. The next April the regiment was ordered to Gallipoli, where it met with great opposition from the enemy, also sickness, of which many of the men died. After fighting a retreat, Gallipoli was abandoned, Colonel J. M. Welch retired through sickness and Major Gibbons took over the regiment. Colonel Gibbons received his first wounds here. After this the regiment went to Egypt and in the Nile valley recuperated and was reorganized. When Palestine became the centre of activities the 5th went up to Gaza and fought through the three battles at this important centre. Many men from this district lost their lives there, and Colonel T. Gibbons was twice wounded while in Palestine. He was twice mentioned in dispatches and was awarded the D.S.O. and the Order of the Nile.

After the war was over he quickly picked up the threads that had been temporarily broken. In addition to these he became president of the Dunmow branch of the British Legion from its inception. He was soon on the stage again, which was one of his greatest interests. It was mainly he and Miss Lottie Bacon who founded the Dunmow Players, and he was their president nearly to the end of his long, full life. He had impersonated many people, both male and female, always adding that extra little " pun " which would keep an audience in gales of laughter.

He and his elder son had been attending county cricket till one day, June 9, 1961, he had a heart attack from which he did not recover.

The funeral took place at Dunmow parish church, followed by cremation, and was attended by over 200 people. His ashes were scattered in a corner of the churchyard under a flowering cherry tree where his wife's ashes had been scattered at her death.

CHAPTER L

A look around the town for features of the past

Dunmow, like most towns, has not escaped the spoilers, and it is very difficult sometimes to know what lies behind the shop fronts. The chimneys and roof are often the features that tell a building's age. There was until a few years ago an old house in New Street (No. 56). It had a fine group of Tudor chimneys and was overhanging at the back. The house was very heavily timbered, with low ceilings, and had the appearance of having been a farmhouse. I spent most of my school-days there, taught by the Misses Wilton. Unfortunately the Dunmow Rural District Council got its hands upon it and destroyed it, for no known reason.

Coming down the High Street and turning towards the town centre we come to Angel Lane. The grocer's shop (No. 26) was the Angel inn. Running up on the left are the remains of the outhouses and appurtenances of the inn. The house itself does not contain a nail—the timbers are all wood-pegged. The attics are where the inn-holders kept their hay. The cellars are as they were in the Angel days. Farther on is the Baptist chapel, opened in 1823, near where once stood the smithy of the Drakes (see " Fragments from the seventeenth century"). This was also known as Shoppers Row. On the right side there is only the side of No. 28, which is older still but has been altered more. The next two shops were Barclays Bank before World War II. About 150 years ago it was E. Wood, the wheelwright.

The next group comprised two shops and houses (see chapter on the Clayton family). Next came Bradleys, another sixteenth-century house, but this needs to be seen from the back. Now we come to the Saracen's Head. This was a posting house in the post-coach days. Parts of this building are 400 years old, but it was largely restored about 200 years ago. In the early seventeenth century it was owned by the Deane family, whose son became Lord Mayor of London, in 1634. A landlord combined the calling of innkeeper

Barley Hall, 1370.

with that of smuggler and highwayman, frequently robbing his own guests after they left the house. The next two shops are again about 1630 or earlier.

The next group of houses are fifteenth to sixteenth centuries, and include the Chequers. They are among the oldest in the town. Note the projecting upper story of No. 15 with its moulded bressumer on brackets, also the chimneys—although largely rebuilt. No. 17 has a cellar of considerable interest. The Royal Oak is an attractive seventeenth-century house. Once in its history it was called the Flitch of Bacon.

Before the time of Queen Victoria one of the thatched houses on Threaders Green was an inn. Another which I cannot trace is the Cock. Now we retrace our steps, and on the north side of Stortford Road is Windmill Street of 1413; now the windmill has gone it is Rosemary Lane. Near here is, or was, the Three Tuns. The house is very old and before it was so much altered was another "nailless" house, very heavily beamed. At one time we read of the Green Man on the corner of Windmill Street and facing on to the highway from the market cross to Bishop's Stortford, so it would seem that at some time the latter was its name. It has a very attractive doorway, but is not now an inn. Still coming down Stortford Road, opposite the police station is a small building which was Mr. H. K. Cockayne's Academy, which was used for many years during the last century. Until recently it still had its bell which called the boys to their studies. Now down to the "Chestnuts," whose timbers outside are fairly modern but inside are late sixteenth century. Now we are at Rood End, as this side of the market place is called, facing the Town Hall. When this was being built there were meetings for several years, but at each the same subject always came up: "What shall we call it?"

Town House, Yeld Hall, Guildhall, but in none do we find the date that it was really opened. It must have been somewhere between 1560 and 1570. It was later enlarged and partly rebuilt. The market cross and the pump stood near to the town hall in the seventeenth century, but were there long before it. One hears of a great stone cross in the market place in 1413. It seems likely that it was replaced by the domed and columned building of 1578.

On this market cross was inscribed "William Stuard, Bayliff, 1578; William Swetinge; Smeeth Rayner, Bayliff, 1761; Thomas Swetinge, carpenter. Repaired and painted by Smeeth Raynor 1761." These later dates evidently refer to repairs.

The pump stood nearby, and in 1786 there was an action in the High Court. A new landlord who came to the Saracen's Head broke the ancient pump and filled up the well with stones. Why he wished to deprive the townspeople of water I do not know. He had his own pump in the Saracen's Head yard. However, the tumult was such that it became necessary for the Riot Act to be read.

An old saying so often used about something that has been in existence a long time is "since time out of mind," but on this occasion they went further—"since time of mortal man." This pump had never let them down in drought, pestilence or storm, and now . . .

I do not know how long the other pump has stood in the High Street. It did have a drinking trough with it, and it was usual to see the carriers' horses and others refreshing themselves while their masters did their shopping.

We come back on the east side of High Street to the White Horse. This house used to belong to Tiltey abbey in the fourteenth century, and until the end of the "ground rent" system the occupiers still paid their fee. It is probably not the original building. Like practically all these old buildings it has been spoilt in recent years. Some years ago there was an old building which is now Lloyds Bank. It had a fine frontage and was a toy and fancy goods shop, kept by the Misses Snow, but the house itself was of the old timbered type like many others in Dun-

Top left: the "huddle" of fifteenth-century cottages at Church End.

Top right: the Three Tuns, now closed, is seen on the right of the picture.

Centre left: 15 and 17 Stortford Road.

Centre right: the exceptional construction of the maltings, late Webb and Gibbons's brewery.

Left: Mr. Cockayne's academy.

Top left: Rosemary Lane (late Windmill Street). The thatched house on left is thought to have been the Bull.

Top right: Church Street, showing Angel and Harp, seventeenth-century.

Centre left: the Bell, which must have been built soon after the church.

Centre right: Brook House, fifteenth-century, near where the brook passed to reach the river.

Right: the King's Head, fifteenth and sixteenth centuries.

mow. Back Street or Bullocks Rowe ran as now parallel with the High Street, and had quite a number of shops and cottages in it. I remember the last two or three cottages being taken down as they became vacant (near the back of the White Horse and Ropers). Coming farther along the High Street is the Boar's Head, which actually joins Dove House. The latter is 1515, marked for all to see. It was a wonderful house to explore, especially the cellar. Now we come to the parish workhouse, of which there were three sections. At the sale in December 1840 only the most northern part was actually sold for £190 to Mr. W. I. Clayton, but I expect the other two sections were sold shortly after, though no conveyance of either can be traced. I know that Samuel Thorn owned this section 49-55 in 1870, but of the most southerly I have found out nothing. The first I mentioned, 43-47, was no doubt the home of a prosperous merchant. When I was a child I saw workmen wrenching out a beautiful carved doorway which had been covered up, and a circular pebble approach around this remained until this last rebuilding. There are gables at each end. I would think it was originally sixteenth century. This section of the old workhouse is much younger, 1636, and Nos. 57-61 have been so much altered that I have not a clue to their age. All are the same in one respect: each section is walled in. In the main street it is wonderful to have such privacy (see vestry accounts).

Now we have the modern White Hart, an old bakery of the seventeenth and eighteenth centuries, and then the Old White Hart. An early landlord was buried in 1655 (see registers). Now we cross the road to the White Lion, now a restaurant and dating from the sixteenth and seventeenth centuries, of two stories with attics. It contains some good timbers. This was once an important house, where brakes, traps and other horse-drawn vehicles could be hired. The next house to interest us is Saracen's Cottage. In the post-coach days the Saracen's Head could not accommodate the post-boys as they were called, so they had this house as a hostel for them. It is seventeenth century. Next to it is the "Laurels," no doubt of a similar age. We especially associate this house with Dr. J. B. Lynch, who died at forty-one, leaving his wife, *née* Frances Toke, with a young family, including our hymn writer Thomas Toke Lynch, who was a cripple.

Now where was the inn Katy-at-Mill? It was on the road leading to Chelmsford. I can only surmise that it was the old cottage that Mr. Fulcher enlarged, it being so near Mill Fields.

The Swan is very difficult to locate. When it was up for sale in 1620 the bill of sale said "abutting on the highway from the market of Dunmow towards Chelmsford, and on the other upon the crop of pasture of Richard Barnard." I do not know where Richard Barnard had a pasture. It could have been on the corner of Braintree Road facing High Street, or it might have been at the top of Barnston Hill. I am afraid I will have to give it up! After it ceased to be licensed it was called "Pollards."

Now we retrace our steps to the Town Hall. The west side of Market Street is all old, with one exception. It is difficult to give a date. The backs all tell of a long life; both sides of Market Street are similar. I would not think this street has changed very much (except the fronts) for several centuries. Webb and Gibbons is no longer a brewery. There are several cottages in the yard, also a kiln of the last century. Much farther back are another kiln and storehouse. This kiln is of exceptional construction and is really adjoining Boyes Croft. Next we come to the Star inn itself. This was the most frequented inn in the town for coaches and carriers to and from London. It has a fifteenth-century mural running the full length of the beam in the saloon. When the stables were made into garages a "Parliament" clock which hung above the stables was brought inside and is still keeping good time, although it has been at the Star since 1759. The inn is chiefly fifteenth century.

Tanners Farm, early fifteenth century.

Now we either go down the former Tanners Lane, now Star Lane, or down Star Hill, leaving the inn in the centre. We will take the latter and come to the doctor's pond (see Dr. Raynor) and Randell Gibbons's brewery on the right—now, unfortunately, closed. Next is the King's Head, lately very much altered inside. It was partly fifteenth and partly sixteenth century. It has a seat let into a chimney-stack which must have been there since the inn was built. It is a nice resting place, and while one sits one can imagine the many generations that have done the same thing. On the left is what was the National School and is now a youth club. Back again to the right side is, or was, the Wheatsheaf, now a private house. This inn made its own beer, and as far as I know still has its malting. Next to interest us is "Brook House." I do not know a definite date of construction, but it is one of those which I think will be much the same for centuries ahead. The beams seem to have almost grown in together in their companionship. From here it is quite a step to the end of the Causeway, where on the left we come to "The Limes" and the Clock House, Brick House, or Goston Lodge. "The Limes" is a little the older of the two, and is very early sixteenth century. The front rather belies its true age.

I have dealt with Clock House separately, so now we go on towards the church. On the right is a huddle of houses that are sixteenth century. They are of an unusual design inasmuch as they appear to be a group of old ladies with a secret to tell that no "foreigners" may hear. Next around the corner is the Angel and Harp. For a time it had no angel, and was just the Harp. This inn is chiefly seventeenth century. On the corner of Church Street was the Six Bells. I have a feeling that this was not an inn for long, perhaps the latter part of last century and the early part of this. The Bell, to which I find many references, was the four houses before one reaches the church (excluding "Windermere"). To view them from their backs is like a glimpse of the Middle Ages. There are very tall slender gables and each house has a cellar, opening outwards, where one rolled the barrels down. Until recent years the houses were panelled. They are very heavily beamed. You will say "Four houses for one pub?" but it is so, and it must have been the largest one in Dunmow, with the exception of the Saracen's Head and the Lion. The part nearest to the church is by far the largest. It has two staircases and must have been the main part of the inn. There were doors leading through from end to end. Maybe they took travellers in and supplied them with their needs for their journey. They certainly had a good pull in, and no doubt plenty of stabling.

The churchyard used to come out to the Bell, and on the opposite side at the extreme end was the Church House, or, as the people of Dunmow used to call it, the "Ancient House." I have no facts about the date when this alteration took place. When I was young the wall was lined with tombstones (on the right-hand side as one enters the churchyard). And I have always been given to understand that they were from the graves that were disturbed at the time the churchyard was shortened, and that the Church House was taken down at the same time to " even " the new entrance.

Another walk through Dunmow. This time we go down the left side of the Star. The road is now called Star Lane, but this is what people have given it; its real name was Tanners Lane, but since there are now no tanners Star Lane persists. At the bottom of the lane is the pond. If one stops to think, with three hills and the springs running down it was quite likely a natural pond. Alternatively it was dug out by man to save flooding, and this long before Dr. Raynor stocked it with fish. We had no North Street in the early days because of these springs coming from the Downs and across the fields near Brook House to the river. The Causeway had to be built up for the same reason. We still think it a long way to the church, but 300 or 400 years ago it must have been cut off from the town for a great part of the year. Little wonder there was enough water to drive a watermill on the Chelmer. The springs down to the pond are now being piped, so there will be no wet patches or ice in winter at the bottom of Talbards Ley. Up this hill we are in Rosemary Lane. In the days when it was called Windmill Street there was much talk about the Bull inn. It is quite likely that it was pulled down, yet I think the thatched house in the hollow looks as if it could have been an inn. There is no positive conviction about this. If you go straight across Rosemary Lane you are on the old " bowling green " of a century or two ago, while a part of the house you passed coming up was the Bowling Green (it was also the home of Dr. Sims) for over half a century. We can go from here to Parsonage Downs (if we know the way) or up Beaumont Hill. There are several old cottages going up the hill, but one on the right which used to be a lovely " old-world " cottage is so spoilt as to become an eyesore. At the top of the hill, behind the Cricketers pond, are two separate houses of over 400 years and across the green several real old cottages. A little way towards Easton is Barley Hall, of 1370. Whether they are the same buildings I am not sure, but they are very old and are church property. They are a very picturesque group

Behind is the modern parsonage. A few

Dunmow football team 1922-3.

years ago the long, slanting pasture which falls in a continuing decline to the church was ploughed up for the first time for centuries, and the foundations of the old parsonage were found, also one could trace the moat around it. A little way past the chase to the parsonage are three or four old cottages. One of these is said to have been an inn in about the sixteenth or seventeenth century. I have lost a few, not knowing where they were, but I cannot find out the name of this one.

LI

Finale

I hope you have followed Dunmow as it has been portrayed through the centuries. You may be disappointed, for you expected more. Perhaps I should have called it " The people of Dunmow through the ages." It is chiefly of the everyday people I have grown to know, generations of them. Another outstanding feature is the rectors, gentry and the mass of the people who were always on the side of liberty.

There were the trying times through which the Church passed, from one religion to another, burning on the one hand, hanging on the other; the many who would not conform, and were not allowed to be buried with those who did. And what with the Buried in Woollen Act and the Window Act, I am not sure that governments were not as crazy as they are today.

Because of the by-laws of Dunmow Corporation one could not do as one liked then. If they were held to Dunmow would

Photograph by David L. Lipson.

Queen of horticulture, Dunmow Park, August 2, 1948.

have been a very orderly place. We do not hear about witches in Dunmow except a yarn told me. I have heard of several in the district, but again only in the last century. People were still very superstitious even as late as that. The grandfather of an old lady I know was leading a pair of horses in a wagon by some cottages down the ford when a woman standing in her doorway stopped the horses. The man, Richard Stock from the Broadway, tried all means to make his horses go, but they were too terrified. Soon a mate of his came along and said " I have had this same thing happen. She [the woman at the door] is a witch. Strike the wheels with your whip, Dick." Immediately he did this the horses started and the woman went into the house screaming. The spell was broken. You may as well believe it as try to disprove it.

I have here something which was found recently when a fireplace was removed to open up an old inglenook. These bills were left inside when the more modern fireplace was put in. " December 19, 1785, Mr. Phillpot's Quitt Rent paid due at Michaelmas last to the Lord of the Manor of Barnston Hall by me M. Waskett £2 4s. 5d."

Now this is a sale of 9 lambs £5, one bullock 25 stone 3 pounds at 2/6 a stone £5/13/5, one bullock 61 stone 6 pounds at 2/6 a stone £7/13/4, two bullocks' hides 15/-. This farmer must have been preparing to leave Wells Tye. Prices had risen by Queen Victoria's coronation; beef cost 4/3 a stone.

People I would have liked to have known are the Claytons, Dr. Sims, Dr. Lynch and the Rev. Langston Scott and characters such as Richard Kynwelmarsh, Mr. Dossiter, Ben Mortier Foakes, and many others down to those I *have* known during my lifetime, even the poorer characters—" Daddy " Payne, Alley Wade, John Starr.

Again, who is there who could forget Mrs. House, the vicar's wife 1915 to 1928. If ever there was a woman divinely inspired it was this dear soul. She would go around lighting fires, getting breakfast for the old and infirm people, or taking little dainties to them for dinner.

At that time there was a " 4d. doss house " in Church End, kept by Italians who let out " hurdy-gurdys " (street organs) to gentlemen of the road, and a pretty rough lot they were. Mrs. House would visit them and gain their confidence. On Sunday evenings at 7 o'clock she would hold a service there, and these " roughs " looked up to and respected her. Most people would not have thought of going there, lest they got "crumby," but Mrs. House had no thought for herself, only for others. She had a grand sense of humour right to the end of her long life of ninety-one years.

The Rev. W. J. House and Frederick Robus, churchwarden, wrote a very nice little history of Dunmow which is still very much enjoyed as being most informative.

The Rev. Ed. Noel Mellish, V.C., M.C., succeeded Mr. House. He had led a very adventurous life both before entering the Church and after. He had been a mounted policeman (India) on the North-West Frontier. He went through the South African war and stayed, as he said, to do some clearing

The Sewell family were drapers, clothiers and boot and shoe retailers. Their shop ranged from the last shop in Stortford Road to what is now the Fruit Basket in Market Street. In Joseph's and Francis's time they were the competitors of the Claytons, except in grocery. When Francis died his daughter Fanny (back row, dark frock) ran the business. She was a splendid business woman. She retired during World War I and took in some soldiers of the Oxford and Bucks Light Infantry.

up. It was at this time that he started his examinations for the Church, passing the preliminary while still there. On the outbreak of war in 1914 he went to France as chaplain to the Rifle Brigade. He was the first chaplain to gain the V.C. in that war—for bringing in the wounded under heavy fire. This he did again and again, and it seemed to his men that he had a charmed life. For these errands of mercy he was later given the M.C. During World War II he so much wished to go with the boys again, but he had to be content with opening a " Naafi " for them in the town. He stayed with us twenty years, and while here kept the church lovely with flowers grown by himself in the vicarage garden.

He went to a little Somerset village for his last church. When he passed away his ashes were brought back to Dunmow and sprinkled in the churchyard.

I remember only one centenarian. She was Mrs. Spore, whose husband kept the shoe shop. Before her marriage she was a Miss Pitts. I am not sure if her sister died just before her 100th birthday, but I do remember Mrs. Spore dying at 102. On her 100th, of course, she had a letter from the king and friends came to congratulate her. She quickly told them she was not on show; she was not a figure in a waxworks!

On May 14, 1968, our market closed after 715 years. It seemed rather sad, but such is the march of time.

I hope you have found something in these pages to interest you. It is all history of our town; those who prefer fiction must look elsewhere.

CENSUS

At the time the first census was taken Dunmow was at a very low ebb and nearly half the inhabitants were paupers. The acreage was 6,775, but of course this does not alter much. Now for the census figures:

1801	1,828	1881	3,005
1811	2,015	1891	2,804
1821	2,409	1901	2,730
1831	2,062	1911	2,490
1841	2,792	1921	2,506
1851	3,285	1931	2,802
1861	2,976	1951	3,370
1871	2,983	1961	3,827

Taken from registration forms in 1967, 4,298.